THE MAORI PIONEER BATTALION IN THE FIRST WORLD WAR

CHRISTOPHER PUGSLEY

To the family

Published by Libro International, an imprint of Oratia Media Ltd, 783 West Coast Road, Oratia, Auckland 0604, New Zealand (www.librointernational.com).

Copyright © 1995, 2015 Christopher Pugsley
Copyright © 2015 Oratia Media (published work)

The copyright holders assert their moral rights in the work.

This book is copyright. Except for the purposes of fair reviewing, no part of this publication may be reproduced or transmitted in any form or by any means, whether electronic, digital or mechanical, including photocopying, recording, any digital or computerised format, or any information storage and retrieval system, including by any means via the Internet, without permission in writing from the publisher. Infringers of copyright render themselves liable to prosecution.

ISBN 978-1-877514-77-7
Ebook ISBN 978-1-877514-78-4

First published 1995 by Reed Publishing (NZ)
This edition 2015

Printed in China by Nordica

CONTENTS

Author's Note	7
Introduction	9
1 Te Ope Tuatahi: The First Maori Contingent	13
2 The War Party Sails	31
3 The Maori Contingent on Gallipoli	36
4 Forming the New Zealand Pioneer Battalion	45
5 The New Zealand Pioneer Battalion in France	50
6 The Diggers on the Somme	55
7 The Pioneers in 1917	61
8 The New Zealand (Maori) Pioneer Battalion	66
9 Digging to Victory	72
10 The Return	78
11 The King's Colour of the New Zealand (Maori) Pioneer Battalion	82
The Nominal Rolls of the Maori Contingents and Reinforcements 1914–18	85
Honours, Awards and Casualties of the New Zealand (Maori) Pioneer Battalion	131
Notes	143
Selected Bibliography	145
Index	146

Author's Note

This book grew out of an historic occasion at the Palmerston North Show Grounds in December 1993 when the colours of the New Zealand Pioneer (Maori) Battalion were paraded and honoured for the first time — 74 years after they were awarded by King George V. The discovery of the location of the lost colours is the achievement of Major Wally Fraser MBE, who continued his painstaking research long after everyone else had given up.

The story of the Pioneer Battalion is not an easy one to tell. All who served with it are now dead and the written record is sparse. The authority on the subject is James Cowan, who wrote much on the Maori in the early years of this century and whose book *The Maoris in the Great War* was published by the Maori Regimental Committee in 1926. Cowan's sources included the diaries of the first Commanding Officer, Lieutenant-Colonel George Augustus King, who was killed at Passchendaele on 12 October 1917, and I am grateful to his son, Group Captain E G King OBE, for allowing me access to his father's papers.

An equally important source are the letters and diaries of the battalion second-in-command and Medical Officer, Major Peter Buck (Te Rangi Hiroa), and I have quoted from J B Condliffe's biography *Te Rangi Hiroa* as well as from Cowan.

The history of the raising of the First Maori Contingent was compiled at the direction of the Hon. Apirana Ngata, and it has been included in this book as it was originally published in the *Kahiti*, or gazette, in 1915. I found it in the Cowan Papers in the Alexander Turnbull Library and its translation in the Maori Affairs files at the National Archives. Both the original and the translation are also in the Army Department files. Together with the published work of Wira Gardiner, Michael King and P S O'Connor, these are the principal written sources on the Pioneer Battalion. The Rarotongan experience in this unit has been recently told by Dick Scott in *The Years of Pooh Bah*.

National Archives hold the war diaries, but other files of the unit are scarce and appear to have been among those lost when the war archives were taken to the rubbish tip during the construction of the Dominion Museum in Wellington in the 1930s. Only some 10–20 percent of this collection was later salvaged. We have less than that small percentage of Pioneer Battalion files. The fortnightly magazine *Chronicles of the N.Z.E.F.* had a column on the happenings in the units in France and there is a regular entry on the Pioneer Battalion for 1918, but in terms of written material that is all there is.

The opportunity for recording oral histories — stories that the old men might have passed on — no longer exists, for the last of the Pioneers are now dead. Their story has to be looked for in other places, for example in the Memorial Church of the Ngati Porou, at Kahukura in the Waiapu Valley on the East Coast; in the graveyards at Tokaanu, and at all the other marae where memorial stones and faded, glass-fronted photographs recall the young men who fought and died overseas with the first Maori contingents.

Fortunately, however, most of the films in the collection of official New Zealand films of the First World War held by the New Zealand Film Archive feature the Pioneer Battalion and these images perhaps best capture the spirit of Te Hokowhitu a Tu.

This narrative also draws on my chapter in John Dunmore's *The French and the Maori* and in expanding that chapter I acknowledge the above sources as well as the National Archives of New Zealand; the New Zealand Film Archive; the manuscript, oral history and photographic archives of the Alexander Turnbull Library; the National Library; the Queen Elizabeth II Army Memorial Museum; and the New Zealand Defence Force Library in Wellington. The staff of these institutions have my grateful thanks.

Lieutenant-Colonel Eru Manuera, Group Captain Ted King, and Andrew Robb read the drafts and gave sound advice. It was also a family effort; Joanna compiled the list of the Second Maori Contingent, Susan prepared the maps and David did the index and some of the photo research. Mata Parakoti typed the roll of the Second Maori Contingent.

I was able to complete this work as one of my projects as Writer in Residence at Victoria University of Wellington in 1994, I am very grateful to the university for granting me the fellowship. The history department gave me a home and good company during the year, and the photographic facility produced many of the illustrations in this work.

I also acknowledge the support of Ian Watt and his team at Reed and my editor Linda Pears. In thanking them all, any omissions that remain are mine. This was a Defence Partners' initiative. Jim Rolfe and Lindsay Missen have my thanks and I am especially grateful to Lindsay for the design concept.

Christopher Pugsley

Note to the 2015 edition

I thank Peter Dowling and his team at Libro International for bringing this book back to life 20 years after it was first published. It gives me special pleasure that my daughter Susan has designed the marvellous cover.

Christopher Pugsley

INTRODUCTION

The New Zealand (Maori) Pioneer Battalion was formed as a Maori unit on 1 September 1917. Its forerunners were the Maori contingents, the first of which, Te Hokowhitu a Tu ('the seventy twice-told warriors of the war god', so named because 140 was the favoured size of the traditional war party or taua), sailed from New Zealand in February 1915; and the New Zealand Pioneer Battalion, which was formed as a unit of the New Zealand Division almost exactly one year later.

'Te Ope Tuatahi', the recruiting song of the First Maori Contingent tells of the travels of the unit and its successors to Egypt, Gallipoli, and then to France and Belgium.

The New Zealand Pioneer Battalion was a mix of Maori and Pakeha who as 'pioneers' provided the labour force of the New Zealand Division, laying railways and building bridges and trenches in the battle zone. The term 'pioneers' has sometimes been taken to mean second-class soldiers. This is not true. As the following pages show, the Pioneers were an essential part of the New Zealand Division's fighting effort — so essential that Major-General Sir Andrew Russell, the Divisional Commander, put his best man in charge of the battalion and gave it the same recognition as any of the infantry battalions. The Maori became pioneers because they could not provide the flow of reinforcements needed to sustain an infantry battalion. Maori wanted to fight as infantry and, as the photographs show, many did so. But it was the Pioneer Battalion that was always first onto the battlefield, that worked and died alongside the infantry, and was last out. This is the achievement of Te Hokowhitu a Tu.

The achievements of a military unit are traditionally embodied in their colours. This is usually a silk flag embroidered with the unit's title and sometimes the names of the battles in which it won fame. In 1919 the King's colour (or Union flag as it more properly should be called) of the New Zealand (Maori) Pioneer Battalion was returned to New Zealand along with its twelve companion colours for each of the three battalions of the Auckland, Wellington, Canterbury and Otago regiments of the New Zealand Expeditionary Force. These twelve colours were presented in the 1920s and now hang, faded, in cathedrals and museums throughout the country. The colour awarded to the Maori Pioneer Battalion, however, disappeared. It was only through the long efforts and patient research of Major Wally Fraser that it was finally found. Having been appropriately embroidered and consecrated, it is now being displayed on ceremonial occasions and on marae throughout the country, symbolising the achievement and the spirit of thousands of New Zealanders who served with the unit and who are now dead.

TE OPE TUATAHI!
THE FIRST MAORI CONTINGENT

E te ope tuatahi	We greet our first war band
No Aotearoa,	From Aotearoa,
No Te Wai-pounamu,	From the Island of Greenstone:
No nga tai e wha.	We sing of our warriors,
Ko koutou ena	Our gallant Five Hundred,
E nga rau e rima,	The chosen heroes
Ko te Hokowhitu toa	Of Tu-mata-uenga,
A Tu-mata-uenga:	The Angry-Eyed War God.
I hinga ki Ihipa,	Some fell in Egypt,
Ki Karipori ra ia;	Some on Gallipoli;
E ngau nei te aroha,	Now pangs of sharp sorrow
Me te mamae.	Our sad hearts are piercing.
E te ope tuarua,	From the Coast of the Sunrise,
No Mahaki rawa,	Came our Second Contingent,
Na Hauiti koe,	The men of Mahaki;
Na Porourangi:	Men of Tolaga Bay,
I haere ai Henare	Warriors of Ngati Porou.
Me to Wiwi,	Farewell, O Henare,*
I patu ki te pakanga,	Who led your company
Ki Paranihi ra ia.	And fell in war's thunder
Ko wai he morehu	Nobly fighting in France.
Hei kawe korero	And who will survive there
Ki te iwi nui e,	To take the last message
E taukuri nei?	To our own loved people
	In dark sorrow bowed?
E te ope tuaiwa	Our Ninth fighting Contingent
No Te Arawa,	Comes from Te Arawa,
No Te Tai-rawhiti,	From the Coast of the Sunrise
No Kahungunu.	From Kahungunu's land.
E haere ana 'hau	And now I am leaving
Ki runga o Wiwi	For France's red war fields.
Ki reira 'hau nei,	There I'll remember;
E tangi ai.	My heart will send greetings
Me mihi kau atu	O'er far land and ocean
I te nuku o te whenua,	To my own constant love.
Hei konei ra e,	
E te tau pumau.	*2nd-Lieut. Henare Mokena Kohere, died of wounds in France, 1916.

As originally printed in James Cowan, *The Maoris in the Great War*. Whitcombe & Tombs. 1926.

CHAPTER ONE

TE OPE TUATAHI: THE FIRST MAORI CONTINGENT

The Forgotten Maori Contingents. The Maori Contingent of 1915 was not the first to see service overseas. A Maori Contingent of 20 went to Queen Victoria's Diamond Jubilee Celebration in 1897. Further contingents went to the opening of the Commonwealth Parliament in Melbourne in 1901, King Edward VII's Coronation in 1902, and as members of the New Zealand Coronation Contingent to the coronation of King George V in 1911. This photo shows the Maori Contingent to King Edward VII's Coronation in 1902 proudly displaying their Coronation medals on their return to New Zealand. The Contingent was commanded by Captain K Te Au Taranaki and Lieutenant Hopere Wharewitu Uru, who are sitting in the second row. Both went as members to the 1897 Diamond Jubilee Celebrations, and also to Melbourne.

KO TE
KAHITI O NIU TIRENI.

[MOTUHAKE.]

HE MEA TA I RUNGA I TE MANA O TE KAWANATANGA.

PONEKE, TUREI, TIHEMA 14, 1915

He Korero mo nga Ope Maori o Aotearoa, o te Waipounamu i uru ki te Pakanga Nui.

HE MEA WHAKARAPOPOTO MAI E TE KOMITI O NGA MEMA MAORI O TE PAREMATA.—HE WHAKAMARAMA.

I RUNGA i to tono a nga Mema Maori o te Paremata, i tautokona e nga rangatira Maori i hui ki Poneke i nga ra timatanga o Hepetema, 1915, ka whakaae te Kawanatanga kia taia ki te *Kahiti* nga korero e rite ana mo te ope Maori kua uru nei ki te pakanga nui o te ao, nga korero hoki mo nga ope Maori e haere a muri ake nei ki taua pakanga. He take tika tenei kia maharatia i te timatanga ra ano o te pakanga. Engari ko wai i hua i tena wa tera e toro te ahi ki nga topito katoa o te ao? Na te mea kua heke te toto Maori, kua pa mai te mamae ki te iwi e tangi atu ra i ia marae, i ia marae, ka kimi te mahara i tetahi tohu whakamaharatanga ki nga toa kua hinga i roto i te riri. Koia i whakaarohia ai kia whakarapopototia nga korero o te whakatakanga ai i te ope Maori tuatahi, o to ratou wehenga atu i enei moutere, o to ratou nohoanga i Ihipa, i Merita, o to ratou taenga ki te marae o te riri, o nga aitua i pa ki a ratou.

Ko enei korero he mea kohi mai i roto i nga pukapuka o te Tari o te Minita mo te Whawhai, i nga korero Paremata, i nga waea tuku mai i te marae o te pakanga. Ka taia enei korero ki tetahi *Kahiti* motuhake a ia wa, a ia wa. Ka taia ki taua *Kahiti* te rarangi ingoa o nga tangata i pangia e te aitua, ahakoa he mate uruta, ahakoa he mate na te mata. Ko te tumanako a te Minita mo te Whawhai i a ratou ko te Komiti o nga Mema Maori, e awhina nei i nga whakahaere mo nga ope hoia Maori, ma enei korere e marama ai nga ngakau o nga iwi, o nga iwi kua tuku i a ratou tamariki, o nga iwi hoki e whakakeke ana: ma enei korero hoki e whakamama tetahi waahi o te pouri o nga whanaunga o te hunga kua aitua.

1. NGA TAKE I KARANGATIA AI HE OPE MAORI.

I te 28 o nga ra o Hune, 1914, ka kohurutia a Tiuka Paranihi, te iramutu o te Emepara o Auhitiria, ki Haratewho, he taone no Pohonia, e patata ana ki Hewia. Ko ia te tangata i waitohutia hei Emepara, ina mate te korokeke. I whakapaea na tetahi ropu e piri ana ki Hewia, engari na nga iwi ke ano i raro i te mana o Auhitiria, i kohuru a ia.

Kotahi te marama i whakakeke ai te ao i muri iho i taua kohuru. No te 27 o nga ra o Hurae, 1914, ka puta te kupu a te Kawanatanga o Auhitiria ka whawhai a ia ki te Hewia. No kona ka oho te Ruhia ki te awhina i te Hewia, ka piri hoki te Tiamana ki muri ki te Auhitiria. Tae rawa ake ki te 2 o Akuhata, 1914, kua toro te riri ki nga iwi nunui o te ao —ko te Tiamana raua ko te Auhitiria ki tetahi taha, ko te Ruhia, ko te Wiwi, ko te Hewia ki tetahi taha. No te 3 o nga ra o Akuhata ka takahia e te Tiamana te rohe o Peretia, o te whenua i kiia ai e te Ingarihi, e te Wiwi, e te Tiamana i roto i tetahi Tiriti i hangaia i te tau 1839, kia kaua ratou, tetahi ranei o ratou e tukino, e takahi ranei i Peretia, ina ara he pakanga. Ko te take tenei i uru ai te Ingarihi ki tenei pakanga. No te 4 o nga ra o Akuhata, 1914, ka puta te kupu a te Kawanatanga o Ingarangi, ka whawhai a ia ki te Tiamana, ka awhina ia i te Wiwi raua ko te Ruhia.

Koia ra i korikori ai te Kotahitanga o nga iwi katoa i raro i te mana o Kingi Hori, Tuarima o tera karangatanga, Kingi o Ingarangi, o Airana, o nga moutere maha puta noa i te ao, Emepara o Inia. Koia ra i oho ai nga mana, nga rangatiratanga, nga iwi kiritea, nga iwi kiri-tapouri, nga iwi kirimangu. Ko nga tamumu a nga iwi marino kau: ko nga riri tara-a-whare waihotia ake, he ngaki e hokia: ka heke iho nga rangatira i o ratou taumata kia tu tahi me te iwi. Te panga o te karanga o te riri ka kore e rangona te ngaeheehe o te whare, kei waho ke e whakamau ana nga kanohi ki te riri ka hangai ki te aroaro. Na, i te otinga o te hupu i te Runanga o nga Minita i Ranana i te 4 o nga ra o Akuhata, 1914, i te haringa a nga waea i taua kupu ki nga topito o te ao, ka oho mai a Kanata i Amerika, ka oho mai Awherika-ki-te-tonga, ka oho mai a Inia i tawhiti, ka oho mai a Ahitereria i tawahi tata ake nei, a ko taua i enei moutere kia moe? Kahore ra pea. No Niu Tireni te ope tautahi i rewa ki te moana, ara, ko te ope i haere ki Hamoa.

He rongo nui to te iwi Maori o Aotearoa, o te Waipounamu, he rongo toa i ana pakanga o nehe-ra, i nga pakanga hoki o te wa o te pakeha nei. Na reira i roto ano i nga ra tuatahi o te pakanga ka tatari nga motu e rua kia rangona he reo Maori, kia karanga ake "Tukua atu hoki te iwi Maori ki te tinei i te ahi e ka mai ra i tawhiti." Kahore rawa i roa e tatari ana. I te 6 o nga ra o Akuhata ka tae mai nga waea ki te Kawanatanga, ki nga Mema Maori hoki, na Te Arawa, na Ngati-Apa, na Ngati-Kahungunu ki te Wairoa, e whakaatu ana mai i o ratou hiahia kia haere he ope Maori ki te pakanga. I taua ra ano hoki ka puta i roto i nga nupepa te waea mai o Turanga, o whakaatu ana ki te tono a nga tangata o Te Raukahikatea kia tukua ratou ki te whawhai. Tera atu te maha o nga waea i tae mai ki te Kawanatanga, ki nga Mema Maori hoki, pera tonu te rangi o te korero. Haunga hoki ra nga waea tuku mai o whakahua ana i nga rau maha o tena iwi, o tena iwi—he hau era, he rekanga korero. Ko te mea nui, ia ko te rangona rawatia o te reo o tenei iwi iti, e takare ana kia tomo ki te pakanga a nga iwi nunui o te ao.

Tera nga Mema Maori tokowha kei te Paremata e noho ana, e whakarongo ana, ratou ko to ratou kaumatua ko Ta Timi Kara. Tera te whakarongo ra ki te hu o te tapuwae o te pakeha : tera te whakarongo ra kia pa mai he reo o nga iwi i muri i a ratou : kahore he kupu ma ratou i te mea e nohopuku ana nga iwi, notemea he take hou tenei kihai i moemoeatia e ratou, e nga iwi ranei. Mei rokohanga ratou ki nga marae o nga motu e rua, ki nga huihuinga e ata whakatakotoria ai he kupu, tera e hohoro ta ratou whaikupu ki te Kawanatanga, " Kei te penei na, kei te pera ra te whakaaro o te iwi Maori." Na, i te putanga o nga whakaatu kei te oho etahi o nga iwi, a kei te tono kia uru ratou ki te pakanga, ka whaikaha nga Mema Maori ki te tono ki te Kawanatanga kia whakatinanatia nga hiahia o nga iwi, kia whai waahi ratou i roto i nga mahi o te pakanga.

Ko te whakautu tenei a te Kawanatanga : ko te tikanga a te Kawanatanga o Ingarangi kaua he Maori e uru ki nga whawhai a te pakeha ki te pakeha. I muri i tena ka tae mai te rongo kua u he ope Maori o nga iwi Maori o Inia ki te whenua o te Wiwi e haere ana ki te awhina i te Ingarihi kua tae hoki he ope o nga iwi Maori o Aratiria (i Awherika) ki te awhina i te Wiwi, ara, kua wetekina te here kia kaua he Maori e uru ki nga whawhai a te pakeha ki te pakeha. Na nga Kingi, na nga Piriniha, na nga Rangatira o Inia i tapae atu nga ope Maori o tera whenua : na ratou ano i tono kia tukua ratou ki te whawhai. E hara i te Kawanatanga o Ingarangi i whakahau. No te taenga mai o enei rongo ka tuaruatia te tono ki te Kawanatanga. Ko te whakautu tenei a te Maahi (Pirimia) :—

" E nui ana toku mihi ki tenei kupu, kia whakaaetia te hiahia o enei o nga iwi o te Kingi kia haere ki te whawhai ra. Tera ia te tikanga e mea ana kia kaua he ope Maori e uru ki nga pakanga a nga iwi pakeha. Otiia i te mea kua tatu te ope hoia Maori o nga iwi o Inia ki Oropi, a mea ake nei uru ai ki te pakanga, ka whai huarahi mo te tono a te iwi Maori. Kaua hoki tatou e wareware kei te rite tahi o tatou hoa Maori ki a tatou i te aroaro o te ture. He aha hoki kia kaiponuhia i a ratou te mana whawhai te mana hapai i te Emepaea ina eketia e tetahi hoa-riri ? Noku ake toku whakaaro : otira tera e whakatakotoria atu e au tenei take ki te aroaro o te Kawana."

No te 1 o nga ra o Hepetema, 1914, tena whai-korero. No te 10 o nga o Hepetema ka uia ki te Pirimia, mehemea he kupu hou kei a ia mo te tono a te iwi Maori. Ka whakautua e te Pirimia, kua tae he patai mana, ara ma te Kawana ki te Kawanatanga o Ingarangi. Kua tae mai he kupu, engari e kore e taea e ia te whakaatu i tena wa. No te 16 o nga ra o Hepetema katahi ka whakaaturia e te Pirimia te kupu mai a te Kawanatanga o Ingarangi, ara, e whakaae ana tera Kawanatanga kia haere tetahi ope Maori, kia rua rau, ki Ihipa. No muri i tena ka tae mai te whakaaetanga a te Kawanatanga o Ingarangi, kia whakatakaia kia rua nga ope Maori, ko tetahi ope kia 250 e haere ki Ihipa, ko tetahi e 250 e haere ki Hamoa. Ko taua kupu i whakaaturia e te Minita mo te Whawhai ki nga Mema Maori, a i tukua o ia ki te Komiti o aua Mema ratou ko Ta Timi Kara nga mana whakahaere, a tae noa ki te wa e whaiti ai nga hoia Maori ki te waahi e whakaritea hei puni mo ratou.

Ka marama mai nga iwi ki nga take i karangatia ai he ope Maori, ara—

(1.) Na te karanga ka pa ki nga iwi katoa i raro i te Kotahitanga o Ingarangi, o nga Tominiona hoki i raro i te Kingi o Ingarangi ;
(2.) Na te rongo toa o te iwi Maori, ahakoa he iwi iti, ka hua te tumanako e kore te iwi Maori e whakaeke ;
(3.) Na te tono a etahi o nga iwi Maori kia whai awhi mo ratou i roto i te pakanga, ara, na to ratou ngakau mamae. Ka whakaarohia i kona kei te rato tena mamae ki nga waahi katoa o Aotearoa, o te Waipounamu ;
(4.) Na te rongo atu kua tae era iwi Maori, he iwi nunui ake i te Maori :
(5.) Na nga toto o nga tupuna toa, ko to ratou kakahu nei ko te pakanga, kei roto i a ratou uri e korikori ana, e kore e taea te peehi.

Mei kore te ohonga o nga reo o etahi o nga iwi Maori, e kore pea e rangaia he ope Maori motuhake, engari tera e uru takitahi nga tai-tamariki Maori ki nga ope pakeha o Niu Tireni : e kore hoki o ratou toto e taea te peehi.

2. Te Whakawhaititanga i te ope Maori Tuatahi.

Ka tae mai ra te whakaaetanga a te Kawanatanga o Ingarangi kia haere he ope Maori, a ka tukana ra e te Minita mo te Whawhai ki nga Mema Maori ratou ko Ta Timi Kara nga mana whakahaere, a whaiti noa te ope ki te puni kua rite mo ratou, ka hui nga Mema Maori me Ta Timi Kara ki te tari o Te Honore Takuta Pomare i te 18 o nga ra o Hepetema, 1914.

Ka whakaritea e to ratou Komiti ma ia Mema, ma ia Mema, e tuku te karanga ki roto ki tona takiwa, ki tona takiwa. Mana e whakarite he tangata, he Komiti o te iwi, he apiha ranei, hei kowhiri i nga tai-tamariki e hiahia ana kia uru ia ki te ope, hei whakahuihui i te hunga i kowhiria ki nga waahi e rite ana, hei arahi hoki i a ratou ki te puni kua whakaritea mo te ope.

Na, kia marama ai te whakahaere a ia Mema, a ia Mema i roto i tona rohe, i tona rohe, ka whakaritea te tokomaha o nga tangata ka kowhiringa i roto i ia takiwa, a i te rohe pooti o ia Mema, o ia Mema. Ko ia tenei te wehewehenga :—

Takiwa.	Mema.	Tokomaha.
Tai-Tokerau	P. H. Te Rangihiroa	100
Tai-Hauauru	Hon. Maui Pomare	180
Tai-Rawhiti	Hon. A. T. Ngata	180
Te Waipounamu	Taare Parata	40
		500

I whakaritea ano hoki, ina kore e eke te tokomaha o nga tangata o tetahi rohe, ma tetahi atu rohe e whakakapi.

Ko te reo karanga topu o nga Mema Maori ratou ko Ta Timi Kara ko tetahi panuitanga i taia ki te Kahiti, ki Poneke, i te 22 o nga ra o Hepetema, 1914. Ko te panuitanga tenei :—

" Poneke, Turei, Hepetema 22, 1914.

" He Panuitanga.

" He panuitanga tenei kia mohiotia ai kei te hiahiatia kia haere he ope hoia Maori ki Hamoa, ki Ihipa, ko te maha kia rima rau. Na, reira, he karanga tenei ki nga Maori me o ratou uri o Aoteroa o te Waipounamu kia awhinatia tenei tono. Tera e kowhiria i nga tangata i waenganui i te ruatekau-ma-tahi nga tau tae atu ki te wha tekau tau. Tera e kowhiria aua tangata, hei nga tinana ora, pakari, tu tika, a hei nga tangata e watea ana ki te haere. Ko te tumanako kia aranga te ingoa o te Iwi Maori, ahakoa iti, i roto i nga Iwi maha e hapai ana i te mana o Kingi Hori te Tuarima. Kia marama hoki te hunga ka haere nei ko te roa o to ratou hoiatanga ka tae ki te mutunga o te whawhai.

" E te Iwi, Whitiki !
" Whiti ! Whiti ! E !

" Timi Kara
" Apirana Ngata
" Taare Parata } Komiti Whakahaere."
" Te Rangihiroa
" Maui Pomare

Ko koutou e nga iwi kei te mau mahara ki te eanga o tenei karanga. Ko koutou hoki i kite i a koutou tamariki e whitiki ana i ia marae, i ia marae. Mai i te Rerenga-wairua ki Tamaki, i Tamaki ki Parininihi, ka rere i tera tahatika whiti noa i Raukawa ki te Waipounamu, ae ra ki Wharekauri ra ano : i Turakirae ki Matau-a-Maui, ka huri i Ahuriri, Mohaka, te Wairoa, te Mahia ki te riu o Turanga : i Toka-a-Taiau ki Tawhiti, Tawhiti ki Patangata, ka huri a tutuki noa ki Whakatane, Kohi ki Whakapaukorero, ma te Kaokaoroa, Maketu ki Nga Kuri a Wharei : Moehau ka tomo i Hauraki huri noa, ka rere i te taha moana, Whangarei, Kororareka, Whangaroa, Mangonui ki Parengarenga : tawhio noa nga moutere nei, tomo noa i nga moana, i nga awa, i nga ngahere o uta. Ko Whanganui tera, ko Taupo tera, ko Waipa tera, ko nga moana era o te Arawa. Kotahi ano te wa i rere ai te wero ki nga iwi Maori, " E te iwi, whitiki ! Whiti ! Whiti ! E ! "

Kotahi ano te marama i tukua mai e te Minita mo te Whawhai hei whakawhaititanga i te rima rau nei. A pa he marae nunui o te Maori o rokohanga mai ai e te karanga nei e noho topu ana tera e hohoro te kao. Otira i taea i te kaha ano o nga ropu, o nga tangata whakahaere i ia waahi, i ia waahi. Ahakoa nga taupatupatu ki nga tohunga pakeha i whakawahia hei titiro i a ratou, i te mate ranei o nga tinana o nga tai-tamariki, ahakoa te tawhiti o nga waahi i haere mai ai etahi o ratou, te pakeke o nga huarahi o etahi, te huhua o nga waka, kihai i hapa nga whakaritenga a te Minita. Ka tika hoki te Komiti o nga Mema Maori kia mihi atu i konei ki te hunga nana i whakawhaiti te ope Maori tuatahi : na ratou i mama ai nga mahi, na ratou i ea ai te karanga ki te iwi Maori.

E hara ta ratou i te mahi ngawari. Ko ratou i kite i te tohe a nga tamariki ra ki o ratou matua, i rongo i te tangi a tena wahine ki tana tane: ko ratou i eketia e nga kupu a nga tangata ngakau mamae, e pohehe ana na te tangata i tono a ratou tamariki kia haere.

E kore hoki e taea te tuhi ki konei nga korero o nga marae maha i poroporoakitia ai e ia iwi, e ia iwi, a ratou tamariki. Kei te mau mahara koutou ki ena, na koutou hoki i whakatau, i poroporoaki ratou.

Ano ra, no te Hatarei te 17 o nga ra o Oketopa ka u te ropu tuatahi ki te puni i Avondale, e tata ana ki te huarahi atu o te rerewe i Akarana ki Kaipara; ko tona ingoa Maori o tena waahi ko Waiatarua. Ko tera ropu no Mangonui etahi, no Akarana ano etahi. Tera kua maranga atu nga teneti ki te papa purei hoiho, a ko nga whare o te iwi nona taua papa kua tapaea mo nga mahi o te marae o nga hoia; he kainga ataahua, e tino tika ana hei marae whakaakoranga mo tenei hanga mo te hoia. Timata i taua ra i te 17 o Oketopa a tae noa ki te 22 o nga ra e whakaeke ana te hunga i kowhiria ki te marae mo ratou. I te Mane te 19 o nga ra ka u no te Waipounamu, tona rimatekau, no Hauraki, no Ngati-Maniapoto, tona toru tekau-ma-ono. Auina ake i te ata o te Turei ka u no te Tai-hauauru, no Whanganui, no Ngati-Apa, no Manawatu, no Ngati-Raukawa, no Ngati-Toa, tona iwa-tekau-ma-rua : huri rawa ake te ra ko mua o te Tai-rawhiti, ko Te Arawa puta noa ona rohe, ko Ngati-Awa, ko te Whakatohea, ko nga iwi o te rawhiti tae atu ki Tikirau, tena iwa-tekau hoki. No te ata o te Wenerei te 21 o nga ra ka eke ko te ope o Turanga tae atu ki Waiapu : ahiahi iho ko to Heretaunga me etahi o te Tai-tokerau. Ko te ope whakamutunga no te ata o te 22 o nga ra, no Wairarapa, no Ngati-Kahungunu ki te Wairoa. Haunga nga ope ririki i puta takitahi mai i muri, engari ko nga matua nunui enei i whakaeke, kua korerotia ake ra. Na, kotahi ano te wiki i whakawhaititia ai e nga waka huhua o te pakeha, ka mene te 500 ki te waahi kotahi.

Ko nga Mema Maori i kite topu i taua ope, i to ratou ahua i te wa i whakaeke ai ki te pa i Akarana, i waenganui mai i te mea kua matatau ratou ki nga mahi a te hoia, a i mua tata mai o te haerenga i wehe atu ai ki tawhiti. Ko te rite kei te pou totara a taraia ana e te tohunga whakairo. E takoto tuporo ana e kore e kitea iho e te kanohi kuware he aha te whakairo e whanau mai i roto. Ko te tohunga ia kei te titiro iho, kei te whakaahua i roto i tona mahara, hei konei te pane, hei ko nga ringa, hei ko ra nga waewae. Ka waenganuitia e heke ana te kapu, te purupuru, ka kite te kuware kua whaihanga te rakau ra. Muringa ra kia karohia, kia eke te whakapiko, te pakati, te whakatara, ka momotu te rakau ra. E hara te tahinga kia kore te kuka, kia kore te para, te whakapiringa i te paua, ka pukana mai te rakau ra, nana! tau hanga e te tohunga. Otira ko taua tuporo totara ra ano; e tu ana i te ngahere, e kore e kitea he taonga. Ka tu i te pakitara whare kei hea te taonga.

Whaihoki ko o koutou tamariki, e takataka ana i nga roro whare na e kore e kitea te tau o te tangata hei hapai patu. Ko te kaupapa ia kei te tika, he uri ratou no o ratou tupuna, no nga toa onamata. Ka tae ki te puni o Waiatarua ka tirohia e nga tohunga whakairo i tenei hanga i te hoia, he tino taonga. Ko te mihi tenei a Kanara Ropini (ko ia nei te upoko o nga ope hoia o te Tominiona i muri i a Tianara Koteri) i tona kitenga ai i te ope i te 23 o nga ra o Oketopa, 1914 :—

"Ki taku whakaaro he tino ope ataahua tenei, te roroa o te tangata, te pai o te whakatupu. Ina ata whakaakona tena ratou e tino tau hei hoia."

No nga nupepa o Akarana ko enei kupu i tuhia, i te kitenga ai i te ahua o nga ropu tuatahi i whakaeke ki te puni :—

"Ki te penei katoa te tu o te tangata me te hunga kua eke nei ki te marae, kei hea ake te ropu hoia : te nunui, te pakari o te tangata, he iwi kua taunga ki te whiti o te ra; kua matotoru nga kiri ki te pupuhi, i te hau te ua."

No te Hatarei te 24 o nga ra o Oketopa ka tae te Honore Hemi Arani, Minita mo te Whawhai, kia kite i te ope Maori. Ko te waahi o tana whai-korero i te marae e tuhi ki konei ko tenei :—

"Kei te whakapehapeha toku ngakau i te mea no Niu Tireni te iwi Maori tuatahi i whitiki i a ratou mo tenei pakanga-haunga hoki ano nga Maori o Inia, kua hoia noa atu era. Kaati, kia whakaaro ki to koutou ingoa pai ina tae koutou ki Ihipa, ki tehea atu waahi ranei o te ao e whakahaua ai koutou e Rore Kitini kia haere ki reira. Kia aha ai? Kia hoki rawa mai ai koutou ki to koutou whenua tupu, ka manaakitia koutou ki nga manaaki e tika ana mo tenei hanga mo te toa, mo koutou i tuku whakarere i o koutou tinana hei whakahere ki a te Kingi. Ka maaha ra te ngakau o te Kawanatanga, o te iwi nui hoki, i te mohio iho, ina whakawhiwhia koutou ki nga rakau o te riri, ki te matauranga hoki e tika ai i aua rakau, kahore he awangawanga mo koutou. Ki te kaha koutou ki te hopu i nga whakaakoranga, ko wai e hua ka hira ake pea to koutou ingoa pai i to o koutou hoa pakeha."

I mihi hoki a ia ki te tokomaha o nga tamariki kura i roto i taua ope, no Te Aute, no Waerengahika, no Tipene, no Hikurangi (Wairarapa), no Otaki, no Three Kings (te Kareti Weteriana i Akarana).

Kaati i konei tenei matenga o te kauwhau mo te ope matamua o te iwi Maori.

3. Te Tarainga i te Waka, Te Maanutanga.

Ko te kupu nui o te panuitanga i tukua e nga mema Maori ki te Kahiti ko tenei : "Kei te hiahiatia kia haere he ope hoia Maori ki Hamoa, ki Ihipa, ko te maha kia rima rau." Ko te kupu hoki tena i whakaaturia e te Kawanatanga. I whakamaramatia ano ki nga iwi, ki nga tai-tamariki hoki i whakauru nei i a ratou ki te ope, ko te haere a nga ope hoia Maori e haere ana ki te whakakapi i nga waahi e watea i nga ope pakeha e tukua ana ki te pakanga : ara he haere ta ratou ki te tiaki paraki.

Na, kei te whakapae etahi o nga iwi Maori, a kei te waiho e ratou hei take e arai ai ratou i a ratou tamariki i nga karangatanga ope o muri nei, he mea ata whakatakoto e te Komiti o nga Mema Maori, e te Kawanatanga ranei o enei moutere, e te Kawanatanga ranei o Ingarangi kia hunaia i te iwi Maori te whakaaro mo a ratou tamariki kia tukua ki roto ki te pakanga. Kei roto i tenei kauwhau e kitea ai te pohehe o tena whakapae.

Me whakamarama i te tuatahi te take i huia ai nga ope e rua, i meatia ai kia haere topu ki te waahi kotahi. I te wa ano i poroporoakitia ai nga tamariki nei i nga marae, i te wa i whakawhaitiria ai ki Akarana, ka whaikupu ratou, ka whaikupu hoki o ratou matua, kaua ratou e wehewehea. Ko te hiahia o ia iwi o ia iwi, kia haere whaiti a ratou tamariki ki te waahi kotahi : mehemea ki Hamoa, ki Hamoa katoa : mehemea ki Ihipa, ki Ihipa katoa. Ko te hiahia ia o nga tamariki ko Ihipa, ko te waahi e tata atu ana ki te ahi e ka mai ra i Oropi. Kahore o ratou hiahia ki te haere ki Hamoa, kua poko hoki te ahi i ka mai ra i reira, kua raupatutia te Tiamana i reira.

I te 21 o nga ra o Oketopa, 1914, ka tae a Ta Timi Kara, a Reri Kara (Heni Materoa), a Wi Pere, a Tame Parata ki te Minita mo te Whawhai ka tono ki a ia kia kaua nga tamariki e wehea, engari me tuku topu ki te waahi kotahi; ara ki Ihipa. Ko te whakahoki a te Minita, e kore e taea e ia te whakaae, i te mea kei te Kawanatanga o Ingarangi te tikanga. Engari mana e tuku ta ratou kupu ki te Kawana, ma te Kawana e tuku atu ki te Kawanatanga o Ingarangi.

I te 23 o nga ra o Oketopa ka tae te Minita mo te Whawhai kia kite i nga tamariki i to ratou puni. Na, i a ia i reira ka tae mai tetahi Komiti o nga tamariki ka tono ki a ia, kia tukua katoatia te 500 ki Ihipa, a kia whakaaetia kia haere tonu ratou ki roto ki te pakanga. Ka whakamarama te Minita, e hara i tenei Kawanatanga, e hara hoki i te Kawanatanga o Ingarangi ratou i karanga kia haere ki te whawhai; engari na te iwi Maori te tono, a hei whakatau mo ta ratou tono te whakaaetanga a te Kawanatanga o Ingarangi kia haere he ope kia 200 ki Ihipa. Na te Kawanatanga o Nui Tireni i tapiri te ope mo Hamoa, hei whakakapi i etahi o nga hoia pakeha i reira, kia watea ai era ki te haere ki te pakanga. Kaati kei te Kawanatanga o Ingarangi te Kupu mo ta ratou tono.

I te hokinga mai o te Minita i Akarana ka tohe nga Mema Maori kia raua ko te Pirimia kia whakaaetia te inoi a nga iwi Maori katoa, a nga hoia Maori hoki, kia tukua ratou ki Ihipa.

No te 28 o nga ra o Oketopa, 1914, ka waeatia e te Kawana ki a te Hekeretari o nga Koroni i Ranana (kia Hakota) Ko nga kupu enei o te waea :—

"Kanui te tohe o nga rangatira Maori, o nga mangai hoki o te iwi Maori kia haere katoa te ope Maori e 500 ki Ihipa, kaua ki Hamoa. E tino hiahia ana toku Kawanatanga kia ea ta ratou tono, a tera e koa mehemea ka rongo atu kua whakaaetia mai."

E ngaro atu ana te whakautu o tena waea ka pa he raruraru nui ki nga hoia. Ko te take o tena raruraru ko te huinga ai i nga iwi, ka hanumi o te tai-hauauru ki o te tai-rawhiti, o te tai-tokerau ki o etahi atu iwi. Ka noho kino nga tamariki i runga i tena ahua. Otiia no te wehenga i nga ope e rua, ara, i te ope ki Ihipa, i te ope mo Hamoa, katahi ka nui rawa te raruraru. Ko nga hoa, ko nga whanaunga i haere mai ra i te waahi kotahi, no iwi kotahi, ka titaritaria ki roto ki era afu tamariki tauhou. Ka takahia nga kupu o nga marae i mea mai ra, "Kia mau ki te ingoa o to koutou iwi : mauria atu te ingoa toa o o koutou tupuna." Kua kore e taea aua kupu i te mea kua kore e kitea nga rohe o tena iwi, o tena iwi. I runga i te tohe a nga Mema Maori ki te Minita mo te Whawhai ka whakaaetia kia whakatikaina. No te 6 o nga ra o Noema, ka whakatikaia tena take, katahi ka tau nga whakaaro o nga tamariki.

Ko te whakaroputanga ai tenei:—
A Kamupene (Tai-hauauru, Tai-tokerau me te Waipounamu).

Ropu (Platoon) 1.—Tamaki ki te Rerenga-wairua
Ropu 2.—Tamaki ki Parininihi, Hauraki, Maniapoto, Tuwharetoa, Tauranga.
Ropu 3.—Waitotara, Whanganui, Taihape ki Pamutana.
Ropu 4.—Horowhenua ki Poneke me te Waipounamu.

B. Kamupene (Tai-rawhiti).

Ropu 5.—Te Arawa.
Ropu 6.—Te Awaateatua ki Whangaparaoa, Waiapu.
Ropu 7.—Uawa ki Turanga ki te Paritu.
Ropu 8.—Te Mahia ki Heretaunga, ki Wairarapa.

I taua wa ano, ara, i te 7 o nga ra o Noema ka tae mai te waea a Hakota, Hekeretari mo nga Koroni, ki a te Kawana o Niu Tireni, e mea ana mai:—

"Kua whakaaetia kia haere katoa te ope Maori e 500 ki Ihipa."

Ko tenei kupu i whakaaturia e te Maahi, Pirimia, i tana whai-korero i Pukekohe. Na, ka rua ai take harakoa ma nga tamariki, tuatahi, kua whakaroputia ratou i runga i te ahua o nga kupu a nga kaumatua, tuarua, kua ea ta ratou tono kia kaua ratou e wehea, engari kia tukua ratou ki te waahi kotahi, ki Ihipa.

Heoi ra, i muri i tena ka mahi te hoia i ana mahi. Ka whakaakona e o ratou kai-whakaako ki nga karangaranga, ki nga haere, ki nga whakataki kokiri, ki nga hapai rakau a te iwi pakeha : ki te keri parepare, ki te hanga pa, ki te kokiri po, ki era atu mahi katoa e rite ana. Na, ka whaka-pakaritia o ratou tinana, ka whakamarotia nga waewae, pakapaka ana te tangata. E pa ma, he whakairo ano hoki to te tangata, ma ona tohunga ano e whakairo, kia matara te poho, kia maiangi te waewae, kia hikimata te tapuwae, kia tangatanga nga waahi katoa o te tinana.

He maha nga pakeha rangatira i tae kia kite i a ratou i te puni, i puta a ratou kupu mihi mo taua ope. Tera tetahi manuwhiri no Ahitereria ki te Tonga, ko T. Raeana, Tiamana o te Poari o nga Kura o tera whenua. I tae ia ki te puni i te 9 o nga ra o Noema, ka whaikupu ki a ratou penei :—

"I tino miharo tona ngakau i tona kitenga i te ataahua o te whakatupu o te iwi Maori: oho ana tona mauri, puata ana ona kanohi. Kua kite hoki a ia i te nuinga o nga iwi Maori, o nga iwi kiri-mangu, o tenei taha o te ao, kore rawa era atu iwi e taea te whakarite mai ki te ataahua o te iwi Maori, engari me tango rawa e ia i nga tai-tamariki whiri-whiri o te Ingarihi, o te Kotimana, o te Airihi e kitea ai he rite. E hari ana tona ngakau i tona kitenga i te piripono o te iwi Maori ki te kara o Ingarangi, me tona mohio hoki tera ratou e whakaheke i o ratou toto kia iri tonu taua kara, te tohu o nga tikanga papai o te ao. Kua kite nei a ia i a ratou, kei te whakawhetai tona ngakau ki te Atua mona i haere mai, i kite ai."

Ko nga whanaunga o nga tamariki nei e haere tonu ana kia kite i a ratou i nga marama e noho ana mai ratou i Akarana. Tera hoki te takuta, nga apiha hoki kei te kowhiri i nga mea e kitea ana he he nga tinana, he mate ranei, he kuware ranei. Ko etahi hoki o nga matua kei te kukume i a ratou na tamariki ki waho, ko etahi o nga wahine i a ratou tane. Ko etahi o nga tamariki i taki-omaoma Otira kei te puta mai etahi i runga i ena take maha, kei te whakakapia mai e nga tamariki uru hou. He tika i te roa rawa o te noho mai o nga tamariki i Akarana he nui to ratou hoha: na te hoha ka taki-omaoma etahi.

I tae mai te rongo i nga ra timatanga o Noema kua whakahoa te Taake ki te Tiamana raua ko te Auhitiria. I muri tata ka tae mai te rongo kua totohu i nga manuao o te Tiamana etahi o nga manuao o te Ingarihi ki te moana i te tai-hauauru o Amerika ki te Tonga. Otira no te wiki tuatahi o Tihema ka ngakia tena mate e tetahi tere manuao i tukua mai i Ingarangi. Ka mate i kona te nuinga o nga manuao o te Tiamana, e whakahaehae haere ana i enei moana o te ao. Ka toe ko etahi takitahi, a ko te rongo mai kei te kimi-hia e te Ingarihi, e te Tiapani kia whakangaromia rawatia nga manuao o te Tiamana i tenei taha o te ao, kia takoto marino ai enei moana. No te wiki tuatahi ano hoki o Tihema ka u te ope hoia tuatahi o Nui Tireni, o Ahitereria ki Ihipa. I te 17 o nga ra o Tihema ka tae ano te Minita mo te Whawhai ki te mataki i nga hoia Maori. He nui tona mihi mo to ratou hohoro ki te hopu i nga mahi a te hoia. Ko etahi o ana kupu i reira i penei :—

"Kahore au i te mohio ki nga mea e tupono mai a ko ako nei, e tutaki-a-kanohi ai koutou ki nga hoariri o Emepaea ; tena pea ka tutaki i a koutou ki te takiwa o Ihipa. A ina tupono mai ki a koutou, kei te tumanako au kia aranga o koutou ingoa. Ka tae koutou ki Ihipa, ka kite koutou i te huihuinga o nga iwi katoa i raro i te mana o Ingarangi, na, kia mahara kei heke to koutou tupu. Whakaatia te tu o te iwi Maori. Ko koutou te hunga whiriwhiri o roto i te iwi Maori, te tumuaki o nga iwi Maori kei raro i te ra e noho tahi ana me nga iwi pakeha. Kia maia, kia toa, kia hoki mai ai te rongo pai ki muri, ka koa matou ko o koutou matua, te hunga tiaki kainga."

I whakaotia i reira kia kirihimete tonu te ope ki te puni, engari ko o ratou whanaunga e haramai ki reira ratou. Na, i te kirihimete ka hui mai nga whanaunga, no nga iwi ano e noho tata ana ki Akarana. Ka takoto te hakari. Ka mata-kitaki te pakeha e taka ana te Maori i te hakari, e tao ana nga hangi poaka, manu, tuna, taewa, kumara, me era atu kai o a te Maori hakari. E kiia ana i te hukenga ai o nga hangi ka hui nga hoia, ka tatari kia kitea te ahua o te kai, te maoa, te mata ranei. Tino pai te maru o te kai. Na, ka noho tahi nga hoia me o ratou whanaunga, tane, wahine, tamariki. Kaore rawa e kiia he puni hoia e takatu ana mo te pakanga : me te mea nei ko nga hui Maori nunui ano o tena wa o te tau.

Tera ia i taua ra kei te hui te Hahi Mihinare ki Peawhai-rangi, ki te whakamahara i te ekenga o te rau tau o te unga o Te Matene ki Niu Tireni i te 25 o nga ra o Tihema, 1914. Kei reira tera o nga hui e whakanui ana i tera ra, i te tima-tanga ai o te kauwhau o te rongo pai o Ihu Karaiti ki Aotearoa. Kei reira te Pihopa o Akarana e kauwhau ana i te kaha o te iwi Maori ki te hopu haere i nga tikanga pakeha i roto i taua rau tau : he Minita Maori nga Minita o te Hahi : kua tu ki nga waahi katoa he whare karakia, na te iwi Maori i hanga : kua tu he kura mo nga tamariki Maori ki nga waahi katoa o nga motu e rua : kua puta ake i roto i aua kura he Minita, he mahita-kura, he neehi, he roia, he takuta, he apiha Kawanatanga, he Mema Paremata : a kei Akarana te huihui o nga hoia Maori, e 500, e takare ana kia tu-tahi me o ratou hoa pakeha ki te pakanga ki nga hoariri o Inga-rangi. E tika ana ra kia miharo tatou mo ena ahua.

I te wiki timatanga o te tau hou, ara i te 6 o nga ra o Hanuere, 1915, ka whakamanuwhiritia e nga hoia o ratou whanaunga, i haere mai i nga waahi katoa. Ko te kitenga whakamutunga tena o etahi i o ratou whanaunga. Ko te ra hoki i rewa atu ai ratou i Akarana kahore i whakaaturia e te Kawanatanga ki nga iwi Maori.

No taua wa ka tae mai te rongo kei te puhia e nga manuao a te Ingarihi raua ko te Wiwi nga pa o te Taake i te Taata-nera. I muri tata iho ka tae mai te rongo kei te whakaeke te Taake ki Ihipa, a hinga ana, i riro herehere mai etahi i nga ope a te Ingarihi. Ko te pakanga tuatahi tena i uru ai nga ope o Niu Tireni, o Ahitereria. Ka noho te maharahara i roto, ka tata rawa mai te pakanga ki te waahi e haere atu ana nga tamariki nei. Otira kore rawa he hokinga mai o o ratou whakaaro.

No te 10 o nga ra o Pepuere ka rewa mai te ope i te puni, ka heke iho ma Kuini Tiriti i Akarana ki te tima, ki te "Warimu," e tau ana i te waapu. E kiia ana kahore he whakanui a te taone o Akarana i a ratou, i tukua noatia.

No te Paraire ratou ka u ki Poneke, i ahu mai ma te moana. No te Hatarei te 13 o nga ra o Pepuere, 1915, ka u ratou, ka haere tahi me nga hoia pakeha i nga Tiriti o Poneke, tae noa atu ki te papa i Nutaone, i hui atu hoki nga iwi o te taone, nga whanaunga o nga hoia ki reira poroporoaki ai ki a ratou. Ko nga pakeha i kite i te ahua i te waewae o taua 500 kahore i te wareware: kei te huatau tonu ki te pai o taua ope, ki te nunui ki te pakari o te tangata, ki te rawe o te haere, ki te rite i a ratou o nga ahua katoa o nga tino ope hoia o te ao. Ko etahi e ki ana kei runga ake to ratou ahua i to nga ope hoia pakeha i kitea ki te papa i Nutaone. E tika ana ano ra kia pera. I tuku iho hoki ki a ratou nga mahi a o ratou tupuna, te haka, te tutu-ngarahu, te hoe-waka, te waiata, i ata whakaakona ai i era ra te rite o te hiki o te waewae, o te whiu o te ringa, o te hapai o te waiata. Ko taua ahua kei roto i a ratou, i a ratou ka ako nei i enei haka a te iwi pakeha.

No te 13 o nga ra o Pepuere, 1915, ka eke te ope Maori ki te tima nana i hari atu ratou ki Ihipa. No tetahi ra ake ka tino wehe atu ki te moana.

Hei konei mutu ai tenei matenga o ta tatou kauwhau. Hei tetahi upoko o tenei kauwhau ka whai atu ai i te ope ki te moana, whiti noa atu ki Ihipa, a tae noa atu ki Malta. Hei tetahi atu upoko ra ka whakataki ai i to ratou urunga ki te pakanga i te Taatanera.

I taia i runga i te Mana o te Kawanatanga o Niu Tireni, e HOANI MAKAE, Kai-ta a te Kawanatanga, Poneke.

A Description concerning the Maori Contingent of Aotearoa and Te Waipounamu who took part in the Great War*

Collated by the Committee of the Maori Members of Parliament

An Explanation

In consequence of the request made by the Maori Members of Parliament, which was supported by the Native chiefs who assembled in Wellington towards the beginning of September, 1915, the Government consented to print in the 'Kahiti' certain matters deemed necessary in connection with the Maori Contingent, who have taken part in the World's Great War, and also matters relating to other Maori Contingents who may hereafter take part in the war. This is a matter that might well have been considered at the commencement of the war. But whoever thought at that time that the flames would have spread to the four corners of the earth? It was only because Maori blood had been spilt, and pain had entered the hearts of many in different homes, that the idea arose that something should be done to commemorate the deeds of the brave who have fallen in this struggle. Hence it was thought that the facts relating to the enlisting of the First Maori Contingent, their departure from these Islands, their sojourn in Egypt, at Malta, their arrival at the front, and their casualty lists [sic].

The material has been collected from records in the office of the Minister of Defence, from Hansard, from telegrams from the front. These statements will be printed in a Supplementary 'Kahiti' from time to time. A list will be printed in the Kahiti showing the names of men who were afflicted, whether by disease or by bullets. It is the desire of the Minister of Defence and the Committee of Maori Members, who are assisting in matters pertaining to the Maori Contingents, that this description will enlighten the various tribes, who have sent their sons to the front and also those tribes who have not sent their sons: and further this will alleviate the sorrow of the relatives of those who have died or who have been wounded.

1. The reasons for the formation of a Maori Contingent.
On the 28th day of June, 1914, Arch-Duke Franz, the nephew of the Emperor of Austria, [was assassinated] at Sarajevo, a town in Bosnia, near Servia. He was a person who was reckoned to become Emperor on the death of the aged Emperor. A Society associated with Servia but belonging to the races under the dominion of Austria, was accused of his murder.

For one month after this murder, the world remained inactive. On the 27th day of July, 1914, the Government of Austria declared war against Servia. It was at this stage that Russia awoke to assist Servia, and Germany to assist Austria. When the 2nd of August, 1914 had been reached, the war had spread among the great nations of the world — on the one side were Germany and Austria, and on the other side were Russia, France and Servia. On the 3rd August Germany violated the neutrality of Belgium, the land that the English, the French and the Germans declared, in a Treaty made in 1839, that they, or any one of them, should not violate if war broke out. This was the reason for the entry of the English into

---

* This is the original unpublished translation. Minor corrections to punctuation, spelling, etc, have been made where necessary.

MAORI SOLDIERS IN THE MAKING: SNAPSHOTS OF THE TROOPS IN TRAINING AT THE NARROW NECK CAMP, TAKAPUNA, AUCKLAND, LAST WEEK.

WILSON & HORTON

this struggle. On the 4th August, 1914, the Government of England declared that it would wage war against Germany and assist France and Russia.

Hence the awakening of all the races under the sovereignty of King George V, King of England and Ireland, of many islands throughout the world, Emperor of India. Hence the awakening of the forces, the chiefs, the white races, the brown races and the dark-coloured races. The controversies of the people subsided, local disputes were suspended which can always be renewed as a cultivation is re-tilled, persons of rank stepped off their high positions in order to stand side by side with the people. When the call came to go to the war, the noise within the house became silent, the attention was riveted on the war that is confronting them. Now, when the Cabinet Ministers in London had come to a decision on the 4th August, 1914 and when the news had been cabled to the utmost corners of the earth, Canada in America awoke, so did South Africa and India and Australia and should we sleep on? No indeed. New Zealand was the first to send an Expeditionary Force across the water — the force which went to Samoa.

The Maori Race of Te Aotearoa and Te Waipounamu had a reputation for bravery in his fights of ancient days and also during the wars against the White Race. Wherefore during the first days of the present war, the people of both islands waited to hear the voice of the Maori people calling 'Let the Maori Race also go to put out the fire that is raging afar off'. They did not have to wait long. On the 6th day of August, telegrams were received by the Government, by Maori Members of Parliament from Te Arawa, Ngati Apa, Ngati Kahungunu at Wairoa, declaring their desire of seeing a Maori force going to the war. On the same day the contents of a telegram appeared in the newspapers at Gisborne declaring that the students at Te Raukahikatea had applied to be allowed to go to the war. Several other telegrams were received by the Government and Maori Members of Parliament to the same effect. We make no mention of telegrams received offering hundreds from certain tribes — that is all wind and words. The most important feature is this, the voice of such a small race is heard crying out to be allowed to enter the war of great nations, of the world.

The four Maori Members of Parliament were in Parliament listening, together with their old man Sir James Carroll. They were listening to the tramp of European feet: they were listening to hear the voice of the tribes behind them: they could not say anything because the tribes were silent, because this was a thing new to them, which they and the tribes did not even dream of. If they happened to be at the courtyards of both Islands and at meetings at which matters of moment were discussed, they would certainly have not wasted any time letting the Government know that the thoughts of the Maori Race are these or those. Now, when information came that some of the tribes were alert and are asking to be allowed to take part in the war, the Maori Members were enabled to ask the Government to give effect to the wishes of the tribes that they should take part in matters pertaining to the war.

The Government's reply was this: it is the wish of the Government of England that the Maoris should not take part in the wars of the White Race against a White Race. After this word was received that an army of Indian Troops had landed in France on their way to assist England and that a force of Algerian troops from Africa had also arrived at the seat of war to assist the French, that is that the restriction that Native races should not take part in the wars of the White races against the White races had been lifted. The Kings, the Princes and the Chiefs of India had offered the Native troops of that land: they themselves asked that they should be allowed to go to the war. It was not the Government of England who ordered them to go. When this news came through, a second request was made to the Government. The reply of Mr. Massey, the Prime Minister, was as follows:

'I am exceedingly pleased with the request that the wishes of these subjects of the King to be allowed to go to the war be granted. There is an embargo that a Native force should not take part in wars between the White races. But as Native troops from India have arrived in Europe, who will shortly enter into the war, a way has been paved for the offer of the Maori people. We must not forget that our Maori friends are our equals in the sight of the law. Why then should they be deprived of the privilege of fighting and upholding the Empire when assailed by the enemy? This is my own personal opinion, but I will place this matter before His Excellency the Governor.'

This speech was delivered on the 1st September, 1914. On the 10th September the Premier was asked whether he had anything further to say in regard to the request of the Maori people. The Premier replied that he had or rather the Governor had sent a request to the Government of England. Word had been received, but he was not able to make it public at that time. On the 16th September the Premier made public the communication received from the Government of England, namely, that that Government had agreed that a Maori Contingent of two hundred men should go to Egypt. After that the consent of the Government of England was received to a second Maori Contingent — one consisting of 250 men to go to Egypt and the other of 250 men also to go to Samoa. This statement was communicated by the Minister of Defence to the Maori Members and he delegated to the Committee of such Members and Sir James Carroll certain powers of action up to such time as the Maori soldiers got into the Camp allotted to them.

The tribes will see the reasons why a Native Contingent was called together, namely:
(1) Because of the call that had come to all the races under the United Kingdom of England and Ireland, and the Dominions under the King of England;
(2) Because of the reputation of the Maori Race for bravery, although a small race, it was hoped that the Maori Race would not be backward in coming forward;
(3) Because of the offer of certain tribes of the Maori Race to go and take part in the war. It was then thought that all parts of Aotearoa and Te Waipounamu were imbued with the same feeling;

The First Maori Contingent parade through Auckland on 10 February 1915. WILSON & HORTON

(4) Because of the knowledge that other Native Races more numerous than the Maoris had arrived at the front;

(5) Because of the blood of their brave ancestors, who were ever ready to fight, which was coursing through the veins of their descendants and could not be kept under.

Perhaps if the voices of certain Maori tribes had not been heard, a separate Maori Contingent would not have been called together, but young Maori men would have joined individually the European Forces of New Zealand as their blood could not be kept under.

2. *The collecting together of the First Maori Contingent.*
When the consent of the Government of England had been received permitting a Maori Force to go and after certain powers had been delegated by the Minister of Defence to the Maori Members and Sir James Carroll and after the Contingent had arrived in the camp allotted to them, the Maori Members and Sir James Carroll went to the office of the Hon. Dr. Pomare on the 18th September, 1914.

Their Committee decided that each Member should send the call to his own district. He should appoint a person, a committee of his people or an officer, who should select young men desirous of enlisting in the Contingent, to assemble those who had been selected at certain places and to accompany them to the camp allotted to them.

Now, in order that the course to be pursued by each Member in his district might be perfectly understood, the number to be selected from each district was decided upon, that is, from the Electoral district. The quota to be contributed by each district is as follows:

District.	*Member.*	*Number.*
Tai-Tokerau	P. H. Te Rangihiroa	100
Tai-Hauauru	Hon. Maui Pomare	180
Tai-Rawhiti	Hon. A. T. Ngata	180
Te Waipounamu	Taare Parata	40

It was also decided that if the quota to be contributed by one district could not be made up by that district, it should be made up by another district.

The joint call of the Maori Members and Sir James Carroll was expressed per medium of a certain notice in the Kahiti at Wellington which was issued on the 22nd September, 1914. The notice is as follows:

Wellington,
Tuesday, September 22, 1914
Notice.
This is a notice that it is desired that a Maori Contingent numbering 500 men should be sent to Samoa and to Egypt. Wherefore, this is a call to the Maoris and their descendants in Aotearoa and Te Waipounamu to assist this call. Persons between the ages of twenty one and forty years will be selected. They should be men of good health, strong and upright and men who are unencumbered. It is hoped that the name of the Maori Race, though small, should be heard of in the midst of the many nations who uphold the sovereignty of King George the Fifth. It should also be understood that the length of their service as soldiers will be the duration of the war.

O! people, gird yourselves!
Whiti! Whiti! E!

  James Carroll,)
  Apirana Ngata,)
  Taare Parata,) Management Committee
  Te Rangihiroa,)
  Maui Pomare,)

You, O! Tribes! remember how this call was answered. You saw your young men girding their loins in each courtyard. Men from the North Cape to Tamaki, from Tamaki to Parininihi, thence along to Raukawa and across to Te Waipounamu, yea, even to the Chatham Islands, from Turakirae to te Matau-a-Maui, to Port Ahuriri, Mohaka, Te Wairoa, Te Mahia to Gisborne, from Toka-a-Taiau to Tawhiti, from Tawhiti to Patangata, thence to Whakatane, from Kohi to Whakapaukorero by way of Te Kaokaoroa, from Maketu to Nga Kuri-a-Wharei, thence to Moehau, thence to and round Hauraki and along the seacoast to Whangarei, Kororareka, Whangaroa, Mangonui to Parengarenga, including the islands, the bays, the rivers and the forests on the mainland. Men came from Whanganui, from Taupo, from Waipa, from the Lakes of the Arawas in answer to the call made to the Maori people. 'O! people! gird your loins! Whiti! Whiti! E!'

Only one month was allowed by the Minister of Defence within which to collect the five hundred men. If the call had come while the Maoris were assembled together in their courtyards, it would have been an easy matter to collect a force together. However, this was done in consequence of the great efforts of certain groups and persons in each of the various districts. Notwithstanding the differences of opinion among the Medical men as to the fitness or otherwise of the young recruits and notwithstanding the distances some of them have had to come, the state of the roads, the number of conveyances some have had to take, every requirement of the Minister was complied with. It would be well at this stage for the Committee of the Maori Members to congratulate and thank those persons who collected the First Maori Contingent: it was they who made the work light; it was they who enabled the call upon the Maori people to be answered. Theirs was not an easy task. It was they who saw the young men pleading to their parents, the wives crying for their husbands: it was they who were smitten by the tongues of those whose feelings had been hurt and who were under the misapprehension that some person had persuaded their sons to go.

It would not be possible to give here the farewell speeches made at each courtyard by each tribe to their sons. You remember those because it was you who welcomed and farewelled them.

However, on Saturday, the 17th October the First Unit arrived in the Camp at Avondale, near the Auckland–Kaipara railway line: the Maori name of that place is Waiatarua. Some of the men composing that unit were from Mangonui, some from Auckland. Tents had already been put up on the Race course and the buildings belonging to the Club had been offered for the use of the camp: it was a pretty place and was eminently suitable for Military Camp purposes. From the 17th October to the 22nd the men who were selected continued to arrive in the Camp allotted to them. On the 19th the men from the South Island arrived 50 in number, 36 from Hauraki and Ngati Maniapoto. On the morning of the following Tuesday 92 arrived from the West Coast, from Whanganui, from Ngati Apa, from Manawatu, from Ngati-Raukawa, from Ngati-Toa: in the afternoon of the same day there arrived the advance guard of the Tai-rawhiti, the Arawas, the Ngati-Awa, the Whakatohea, the people of the East Coast as far as Tikirau, 90 in number. On the morning of Wednesday the 21st the force from Gisborne to Waiapu arrived: in the afternoon those from Hawke's Bay and some from the North of Auckland arrived. The last unit arrived on the 22nd. They were from Wairarapa, from Ngati-Kahungunu at Wairoa. We make no mention of individual men who came singly afterwards, but those already mentioned were the units of some dimensions. Now, it only took the conveyances of the Pakeha one week to collect these five hundred men and put them in one place.

The Maori Members saw that Contingent as a whole, when they arrived at the Camp at Auckland, afterwards when they had had some training as soldiers and just before they left for those distant lands. The process was somewhat like a totara post under the chisel of the professional carver. While it is a log, the inexperienced eye cannot conceive what carving could be produced from it. The professional carver on the other hand looks at it and pictures in his mind where the head will be and the hands and the legs. After a while when the chips and saw-dust have fallen, the novice will detect the transformation of the log. When excavations are made and the scientific touches of the artist have been applied, the log becomes a distinct block of wood. As soon as the dust and the shavings have been brushed aside and the 'paua' have been placed in their proper places, behold! the wood is looking at you with open eyes. Alas! how wonderful are thy works, O! Carver! But it is the same totara log; whilst growing in the forest, it was not considered of any value. But when part of the 'whare', what better property could you have.

The position regarding your children was the same. While they were moving about in front of your houses, their suitability to carry fire arms could not be judged. The material is there for they are the descendants of their ancestors and of the braves of the past. When they arrived at the camp at Waiatarua, they were examined by the Military experts and found to be the right stuff. On seeing the force on the 23rd October, 1914, Colonel Robin (Officer Commanding the Dominion Forces after General Godley's departure) made a statement as follows:

'In my opinion this is a fine body of men, clean and stalwart. With training they will make excellent soldiers.'

The Auckland Newspapers, on seeing the first batches of men who arrived in camp, commented as follows:

'If the stamina of the men already in camp can be taken as a criterion of the whole, they should turn out to be a useful body of soldiers, the majority of them being strongly built and used to outdoor life.'

On Saturday the 24th day of October the Hon. James Allen, Minister of Defence, went to see the Maori Contingent. A portion only of his speech, which was delivered at the camp, is given here:

'I am proud of the fact that New Zealand was the first Overseas possession next to India to raise a body of Natives at this crisis. I would urge you to acquit yourselves in Egypt or wherever Lord Kitchener might send you, so that on your return to New Zealand you might be proudly met as men who had done their duty to the Empire, fearlessly and well. The Government and people wish to feel that they can repose the utmost confidence in you. The troops would be well equipped, well trained and self-reliant. You might even turn out better soldiers than your Pakeha brothers if you chose.'

He also remarked on the fact that several of the men composing the troop were educated young men from Te Aute, Waerongahika, St. Stephens, Hikurangi (Wairarapa), Otaki and Three Kings (Wesleyan College at Auckland) Colleges.

This concludes the description regarding the First Maori Contingent.

3. The construction of the canoe and its departure.

The most important matter in the notice which was sent by the Maori Members to be printed in the Kahiti is this: 'It is desired that a Maori contingent should be sent to Samoa, to Egypt, consisting of 500 men.' That is what the Government announced. It was explained to the various tribes and to the young men who enlisted in the contingent that the Maori contingents were being sent to take the places made vacant by the European forces who would be sent to the front: that is, they were going to do garrison duty.

Now, some of the Maori people are making accusations, and are using this matter as an excuse for preventing their sons from joining the reinforcements, that the Committee of Maori Members, the Government of these Islands, the Government of England, are deliberately hiding from the Maori people the intention to send their sons to the front.

It will be seen from this description that these accusations are groundless.

First of all let us explain why the two forces were amalgamated and why it was ordered to proceed to the one destination. At the time farewells were being given to these young men at their various homes, and when they were being assembled at Auckland, they asked, and their parents asked that they should not be separated. It was the desire of each tribe that their sons should go together to the one destination: whether to Samoa, they should all go to Samoa: whether to Egypt, they should all go to Egypt. The young men wished to be sent to Egypt, a place which is close to the fire now raging in Europe. They did not wish to go to Samoa as the fire which raged there had been put out, the Germans there having been conquered.

On the 21st day of October, 1914, Sir James Carroll, Lady Carroll, Wi Pere and Taare Parata went to see the Minister of Defence and asked him not to separate these young men, but to send them as one force to the one destination, that is, to Egypt. The Minister replied that he could not consent to this as the matter was in the hands of the Government of England. But, he said, he would refer their request to His Excellency the Governor for submission to the British Government.

On the 23rd of October the Minister of Defence went to the camp to see these young men. Now, while he was there, a committee of these men came to him and asked that the whole of the 500 should be sent to Egypt and that they should be allowed to go to the front. The Minister explained to them that it was not this Government, nor the Government of England who called upon them to go to the War; but it was the Maori people who asked, and in order to comply with their request, the British Government agreed that a contingent of 200 should be sent to Egypt. It was the Government of New Zealand who added the contingent for Samoa to take the place of the European soldiers there and so enable them to go to the front. However, he said, the Government of England had the sole decision in regard to their request.

When the Minister returned from Auckland the Maori Members implored him and the Prime Minister to grant the request of the whole of the Maori people, and the Maori soldiers that they should be sent to Egypt.

On the 28th of October, 1914, His Excellency the Governor cabled to the Secretary of State for the Colonies in London (Harcourt). The cable was in these words:

'Leading representatives of Maori race are very anxious that whole Native contingent 500 strong should be sent to Egypt and that none should be sent to Samoan Islands. My Government particularly desire to accede to their request and would be glad to know if arrangements can be made to this effect.'

Before the receipt of the reply to this cable, trouble arose in connection with the soldiers. The cause of this trouble was on account of the mixing up of members of the various tribes, men from the West Coast being mixed up with those of the East Coast and those of the north of Auckland district being mixed up with those of other tribes. This position was most unsatisfactory to the young men. But when the two forces were separated, that is, the force for Egypt and the force for Samoa, the dissatisfaction was increased. Friends and relatives who came from the one place and belonging to the one tribe were scattered among other and strange men. This did not conform with the sentiments expressed at the 'maraes' — 'Uphold the name of your race: take with you the reputation of your ancestors for bravery.' These words could not be carried out because the various tribes were mixed up. In consequence of the request of the Maori Members to the Minister of Defence, it was agreed to form groups of the various tribes. On the 6th of November, this intention was carried out and gave satisfaction to the young men. The grouping was as follows:

A. COMPANY. (West Coast, North of Auckland and South Island).
Platoon 1. Men from Tamaki to the North Cape.
Platoon 2. Men from Tamaki to Parininihi, Hauraki, Maniapoto, Tuwharetoa, Tauranga.
Platoon 3. Men from Waitotara, Whanganui, Taihape to Palmerston North.
Platoon 4. Men from Horowhenua to Wellington and the South Island.

B. COMPANY. (East Coast).
Platoon 5. Men from Te Arawa.
Platoon 6. Men from Te Awaateatua to Whangaparaoa, Waiapu.
Platoon 7. Men from Tolaga Bay to Gisborne and Paritu.
Platoon 8. Men from Te Mahia to Hawke's Bay and Wairarapa.

During the same time, that is, on the 7th November, a cable was received from Mr. Harcourt, Secretary of State for the Colonies, to His Excellency the Governor in these words:

'It has been agreed that the whole of the Maori contingent of 500 strong should go to Egypt.'

The Right Hon. Mr. Massey, the Premier, announced this in his speech at Pukekohe. This gave the young men a further cause for satisfaction, the first was their grouping in accordance with the desire of their elders, and the second was the fulfilment of their request that they should [not] be separated but they should all go to the one destination, to Egypt.

So after that the soldiers went to work. They were taught to be soldiers and were given military training.

Many Europeans of importance went to see them in camp. They praised the troops. A visitor from South Australia — Mr. T. Ryan, Chairman of the Education Board of that land — who went to the camp on the 9th November, addressed them and said that:

'He was surprised at finding such splendid physique among the Maoris; it was an eye opener to him to find them such a splendid stamp of men. He had come in contact with nearly all the dark races south of the equator and he could not compare them with the Maoris at all, but he must compare them with all that was best among the English, Scotch and Irish. He rejoiced to see the Maoris so loyal to the British flag which he knew they would fight for to the last. Now that he had seen them, he thanked God he had come.'

The relatives of these young men continually went to see them during their stay in Auckland. The Doctor and the Officers were weeding out those whose constitutions were not fit, who were afflicted with disease or ignorance. Some of the parents were taking their sons from the force, and some wives, their husbands. Some of the young men ran away. Nevertheless while some were extricating themselves, other new recruits were filling their places. It is true that owing to their long stay in Auckland, they got tired and in consequence some ran away.

During the beginning of November news arrived that the Turks had sided with the Germans and the Austrians. Soon afterwards news came that the German warships had sunk some of the English men-of-war on the south-west coast of America. However, during the first week in December that score was wiped off by squadron sent out from England. Several of the German warships were destroyed there, which were a menace to the oceans at this end of the world. A few were left and were being pursued by the English and the Japanese with the intention of entirely destroying the German warships on this side of the globe so as to clear these seas. It was also during the first week in December when the Expeditionary Force of New Zealand and Australia landed in Egypt.

Members of the First Maori Contingent on the Wellington wharf, February 1915.
ALEXANDER TURNBULL LIBRARY

1st N.Z. Maori Contingent

Embarkation Roll
Wellington N.Z.
14.2.15

	Officers	Rank & File
	15	494
	Total	509

Disembarkation Roll
Port Suez 26.3.15

Left in Hospital Albany W.A. 1
Died at Sea   1
                                         14   493
Transferred from W.M.R. 3rd Reinf. 1
                                         15   493 = 508

Marching in State
Anzac. 3.7.15
Appointed Commandant - Convales.
Camp - Malta   1} 1
Promoted 2nd Lieuts Zeitoun   2}
N.C.O's promoted 2nd Lieuts   2} 32
Less In Hospital Egypt & Malta 30}
                                         16   461 = 477

Te Ope Tuatahi

Ready to sail. Te Hokowhitu a Tu on the SS. *Wairrimoo*, Wellington, February 1915.
ALEXANDER TURNBULL LIBRARY

On the 17th of December the Minister of Defence again went to see the Native troops. He was greatly pleased with the progress they had made in their training. Some of his words on that occasion were as follow:

'I cannot say what will happen in the future when you will come face to face with the enemy of the Empire; you may meet him in the vicinity of Egypt. And when you do meet him, I hope you will make a name for yourselves. When you arrive in Egypt, you will see there assembled the races under the sovereignty of England and remember that you must not lose your dignity. Show the pride of the Maori race. You are the selected representatives of the Maori people, the chief of the dark races living under the sun and alongside the white races. Be strong, be brave so that your good reputation may come back to us, and gladden our hearts and the hearts of your parents, who remain at home.'

It was then decided that the troops should spend Christmas in the camp, but their relatives should come there to see them. Now, at Christmas time, their relatives, who lived near Auckland, assembled. The feast was spread. The Europeans watched the Maoris preparing their feast, cooking pork, poultry, eels, potatoes, kumaras and other food of the Maori in 'Hangis'. It is stated that, when the 'hangis' were unearthed, the soldiers assembled to see whether the food was cooked or not. The food was properly cooked. Then the soldiers and their relatives, men, women and children sat together. It could not be said that it was a military camp: it was more like a Maori meeting peculiar to this time of the year.

During the same day a meeting of the Church of England was being held at the Bay of Islands to commemorate the centenary of the arrival of the Rev. Marsden to New Zealand on the 25th day of December, 1814. That meeting was held to commemorate the day of the advent of Christianity to Aotearoa. The Bishop of Auckland was there preaching about the progress made by the Maori people in assimilating European learning and ways within that period of one hundred years: there were Native clergymen in the Church; Churches had been built everywhere by the Maori people: schools at which Maori children were taught have been erected everywhere on both Islands: clergymen, schoolmasters, nurses, solicitors, doctors, Government officers, members of Parliament have emerged from these schools: and in Auckland 500 soldiers were assembled and anxious to stand shoulder to shoulder with their European friends and fight against the foes of England. We have every reason to marvel at such progress.

During the beginning of the New Year, that is, on the 6th January, 1915, the soldiers entertained their relatives who had come from everywhere. This was the last meeting of some of the soldiers with their relatives. The date of their departure from Auckland was not made known to the Maori people by the Government.

It was during this time when news arrived that English and French warships were bombarding the Turkish forts at the Dardanelles. A little while afterwards news came to the effect that the Turks were moving against Egypt. On the 6th February the Turks were attacked in Egypt and were defeated and some were made prisoners by the English. This was the first battle in which the Expeditionary Forces of New Zealand and Australia took part. Anxiety was felt that the War was getting very near to where these young men were going. Nevertheless they never thought of turning back.

On the 10th February the Maori contingent marched from their camp through Queen Street in Auckland to the transport — the *Wairrimoo* — which was lying alongside the wharf. It is stated that Auckland City did not do them honour, they were sent off without any public demonstration.

On Friday they landed in Wellington, they went by sea. On Saturday the 13th February, 1915, they landed and marched through the streets of Wellington with the European soldiers to the Newtown Park, the townspeople and the relatives of the soldiers having assembled there to bid them farewell. The Europeans, who had seen that 500 march, have never forgotten: they still speak in high praise of them, of the splendid condition of the men, of their marching and of their general appearance which compared favourably with the best troops in the world. Some went as far as to say they were even better than the white soldiers seen at Newtown Park. It is only right that it should be so. The heritage of their ancestors had been inherited by them, such as the haka, the tutu-ngarahu, canoe-paddling, singing the performance of which in those days meant the rhythmical motion of the legs and swinging of the arms and the singing of the 'waiata'. That quality was already in them while they were learning these 'hakas' of the white races.

On the 13th February, 1915, the Maori contingent embarked on the transport which took them to Egypt. On the following day they sailed out to sea.

We will here conclude the description under this heading.

Under another heading we will describe their journey on the sea up to their arrival in Egypt and Malta. We will describe under yet another heading their entry into the War at the Dardanelles.

CHAPTER TWO

THE WAR PARTY SAILS

Let us continue the story of Te Hokowhitu a Tu after it sailed from New Zealand. The original plan in 1914 had been for half of the Maori Contingent to go to Samoa as garrison. Colonel Robert Logan, the Administrator of Samoa, objected to this, and the Maori themselves wished to remain together. It was then agreed that the contingent would join the New Zealand Expeditionary Force in Egypt, and it sailed from Wellington on the SS *Wairrimoo* on 14 February 1915.

Pirimi Tahiwi wrote to his family in Otaki: The boys are in excellent condition, all well and eating like elephants . . . We have a band on board and its not bad at all. We got the instruments in Wellington — 2 Euphoniums, 1 baritone, 2 tenor horns — 2 trombones, 2 E flat basses — and 2 drums, 2 1st Cornets and 2 2nd Cornets — Lieuts Stainton and Tahiwi musical directors and joint conductors . . .[1]

Meanwhile James Allen, the Minister of Defence, wrote to Major-General Sir

E te ope tuatahi
No Aotearoa,
No Te Wai-
  pounamu,
No nga tai e wha.
Ko koutou ena
E nga rau e rima,
Ko te Hokowhitu
  toa
A Tu-mata-uenga
  . . .

We greet our first
  war band
From Aotearoa,
From the Island of
  Greenstone:
We sing of our
  warriors,
Our gallant Five
  Hundred
The chosen heroes
Of Tu-mata-uenga
The Angry-Eyed
  War God . . .

'Te Ope Tuatahi'

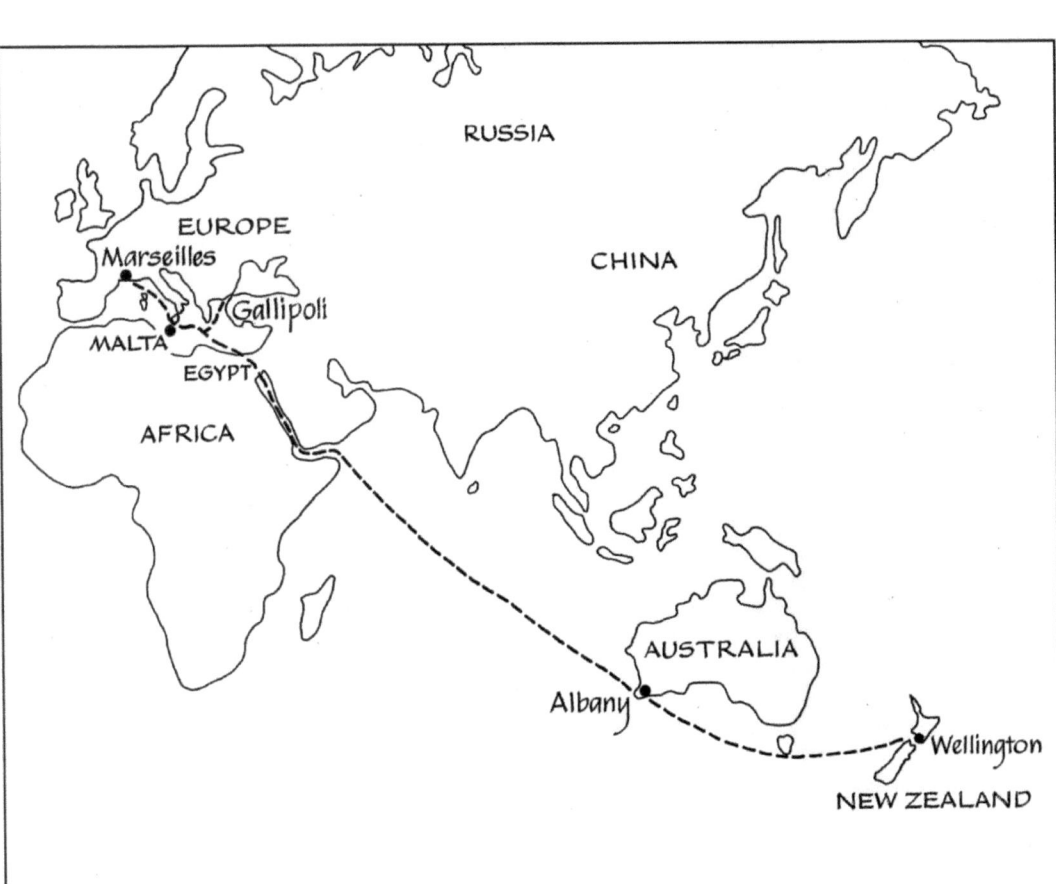

The voyages of Te Hokowhitu a Tu.

ABOVE: Officers of the First Maori Contingent. *Back Row:* Lieutenants Stainton, Hetet, Tikao, Walker, Nerito, Kaipara, Coupar. *Front Row:* Lieutenant Ferris, Chaplain Wainohu, Dr Buck, Captain Ennis, Major A H Herbert, Captains Pitt, Dansey, Jones, Tahiwi. WILSON & HORTON

LEFT: First leave in Cairo. Two sergeants of the Maori Contingent, April 1915. QUEEN ELIZABETH II ARMY MEMORIAL MUSEUM

OPPOSITE ABOVE: The haka of the First Maori Contingent, Egypt, 3 April 1915. NZ FILM ARCHIVE

OPPOSITE BELOW: The Maori Contingent in Egypt before sailing for Malta. WILSON & HORTON

Officers of the First Maori Contingent in Malta.
ALEXANDER TURNBULL LIBRARY

Alexander Godley, who commanded the New Zealand Expeditionary Force: Although they are a coloured race I think it would be apparent on their arrival that they are different to the ordinary coloured race . . . The only thing I am afraid of, however, is that possibly they may be weaker than the pakeha in respect to temptations.[2]

Fewer in number than an infantry battalion and raising real doubts about its ability to sustain the losses that an infantry battalion would face, the First Maori Contingent was recruited to be a pioneer battalion, providing the skilled labour for the New Zealand Expeditionary Force. Both Godley and the senior officers of the New Zealand Expeditionary Force were sceptical about the worth of the Maori Contingent, but it was on its way and Godley recommended that it go to Malta as garrison where the Maori could do further training. There was no thought that it would be needed at the Dardanelles in its pioneer role. Sending it to Malta seemed to be the easy answer to get rid of an awkward late arrival while the rest of the force was busily preparing for the Dardanelles.

The contingent arrived in Egypt on 26 March 1915 in time to take part in the final parade of the New Zealand and Australian Division (which included the units of the New Zealand Expeditionary Force) which was about to sail for Gallipoli. A film survives of this parade and also of the haka staged for the British High Commissioner to Egypt, Sir Henry McMahon, on 3 April 1915.

The Maori Contingent, having joined the Expeditionary Force, naturally wanted to go with it and fight for the Dardanelles, which everyone was talking about. After all, the badge the contingent wore on their hats and jacket collars told of their background and pride: 'a taiaha and a tewhatewha crossed through a crown, with the motto "Te Hokowhitu a Tu" signifying the 140 warriors of the war god Tu'.[3] The film shows the haka of the men of the Ngati Porou from the East Coast and the Arawa from Rotorua. The taua is demonstrating its willingness to fight, and the officers of the contingent, with Chaplain Henare Wainohu prominent in his white collar, watch from the flank. After the haka the contingent second-in-command and Medical Officer Major Peter Buck (Te Rangi Hiroa) made an impassioned plea for the Maori to be sent to Gallipoli. 'Our ancestors', he said,

were a warlike people, constantly sending out war parties on their intertribal campaigns. The members of this war party would be ashamed to face their people at the conclusion of the war if they were to be confined entirely to garrison duty and not be given an opportunity of proving their mettle at the front.

I speak now not so much as a soldier, but as a representative of the old Maori chiefs who would have spoken to you had they the opportunity. I voice their views and the thoughts that are in them. If we transgress the rules and forms that govern soldiers, then forgive us, for we speak as Maoris. We would sooner die from the bullets of the enemy than from sickness and disease — for what says the Maori proverb? Man should die fighting hard like the struggling ururoa (shark), and not tamely submitting like the lazy tarakihi, which submits without a struggle. Though we are only a handful, the remnant of the remnant of a people, yet we consider that we are the old New Zealanders. No division can truly be called a New Zealand Division unless it numbers Maoris amongst its ranks. [Loud applause from the members of the New Zealand battalions who were looking on.] We, therefore, ask you, as the old chiefs of our

Trench digging in Malta. Roger Dansey with Peter Buck behind and Second-Lieutenants Hiroti and Tikao.
ALEXANDER TURNBULL LIBRARY

people would ask you, to give us an opportunity for active service with our white kinsmen from New Zealand. Give us a chance.[4]

The spirit of his plea was admired, but the authorities had made their plans and the Maori were sent to Malta for training and garrison duties. It seemed to the contingent that they were a travelling show, 'a kind of Williamson company' as one of the soldiers said. Like the J C Williamson Theatre Company they had entertainment value as performers for the dignitaries; however, they were not considered good enough to fight. On Malta they drilled and trained in mounting frustration as word of the landing on 25 April 1915 reached them and the wounded from the Dardanelles arrived at the Malta hospitals.

CHAPTER THREE

THE MAORI CONTINGENT ON GALLIPOLI

> Whatever you do remember you have the mana, the honour and the good name of the Maori People in your keeping this night... Do your duty to the last, and whatever comes never turn your backs on the enemy.
>
> CHAPLAIN WAINOHU'S ADDRESS BEFORE
> THE NIGHT ATTACK 6 AUGUST 1915[5]

The stalemate of Gallipoli and the heavy losses within the Anzac Corps in the first months saw the Maori Contingent sent to reinforce the depleted New Zealand brigades. They landed at Anzac Cove on 3 July 1915, and joined men who in number and physical strength were a shadow of the force that had landed in April 1915.

The Maori were attached to the New Zealand Mounted Rifles Brigade on the northern flank of the Anzac perimeter, manning a line from Russell's Top, down Walker's Ridge and along North Beach to the outposts at Fisherman's Hut. The New Zealanders they joined had become professional the hard way, facing an enemy who knew the land and the trade of soldiering, and who made the invader pay for any carelessness with lives.

The Maori were employed as pioneers, and the photographs show them clearing the spoil from the mine-workings below Quinn's Post and dragging watertanks up onto the spurs of Plugge's Plateau. They risked rifle fire, endured heat, lice, and flies; they lived with the stench of death in their nostrils, ate bully beef and biscuits, and eked out the ration of one gallon of water per man per day, shipped in from Egypt and tainted by the kerosene that the cans had previously held. They suffered from the dysentery that afflicted everyone, and in the evenings they watched the sunset over Imbros and dreamed of other shores. From their base at the No. 1 Outpost on North Beach, soon known as the Maori Pa, they dug the Great Sap or communication trench that etched its way, 8 feet deep and wide enough to carry two stretchers side by side, along the beach from Walker's Ridge to the low foothills on the coast that made up Nos 1, 2 and 3 Outposts. These were the northerly limits of the Anzac perimeter and the jumping-off point for the August offensive.

There were Maori already ashore before the Maori Contingent arrived. The nominal rolls and casualty lists of both the infantry and mounted rifles of the New Zealand Expeditionary Force show they were in every unit from the 6th Haurakis, the 11th Taranakis, and the Auckland and Wellington Mounted Rifles, with names like Bird, Black, Skerret and Grace. They had enlisted with their mates in the companies of the provincial battalions, not conscious or concerned about race, only keen to take part in this war before it ended.

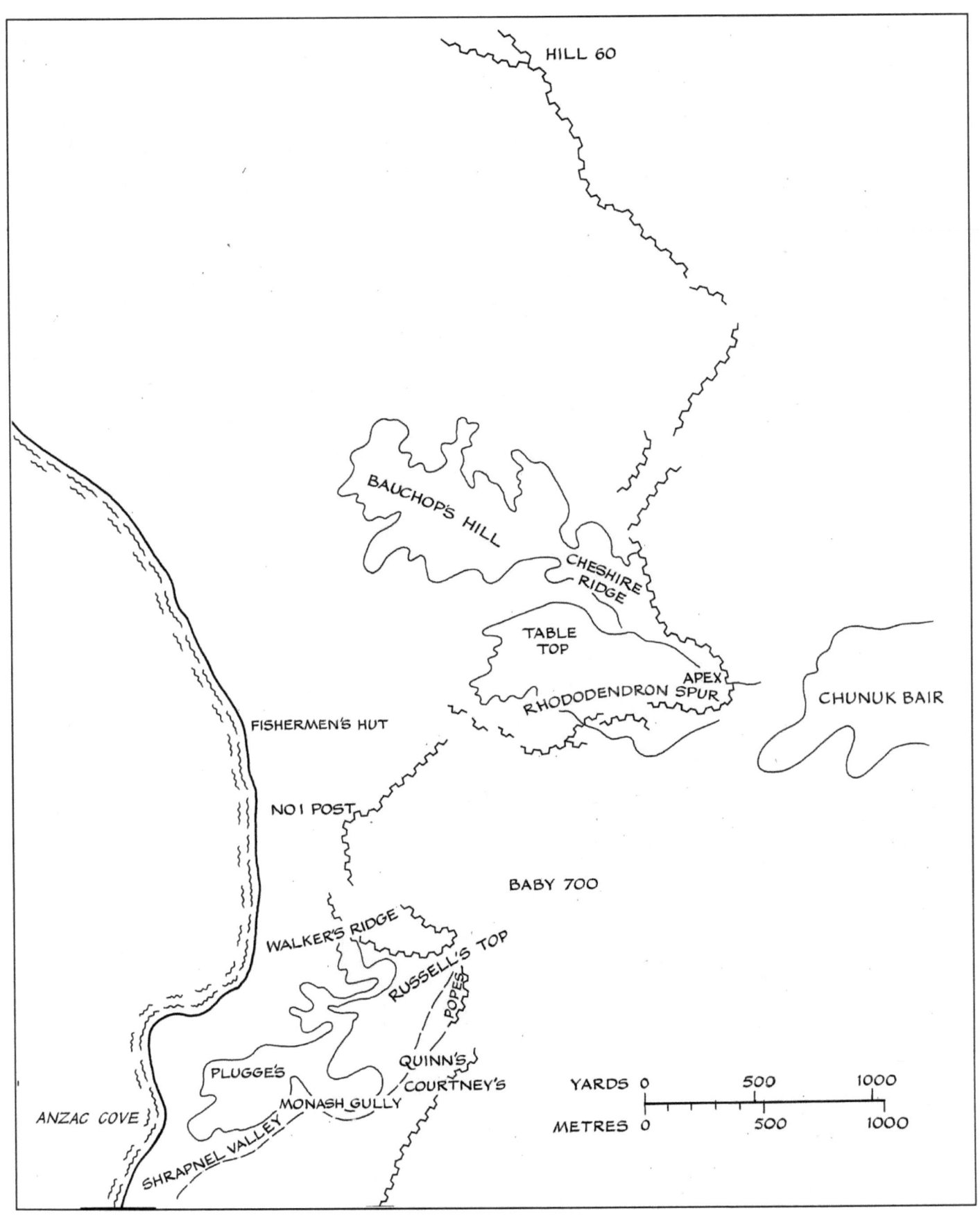

Te Hokowhitu a Tu on Gallipoli.

ABOVE: Men of the Maori Contingent drag water tanks on to Plugge's Plateau.
AUSTRALIAN WAR MEMORIAL

LEFT: Number One Outpost, sometimes known as the Maori Pa, garrisoned by the Maori Contingent. J C READ COLLECTION, ALEXANDER TURNBULL LIBRARY

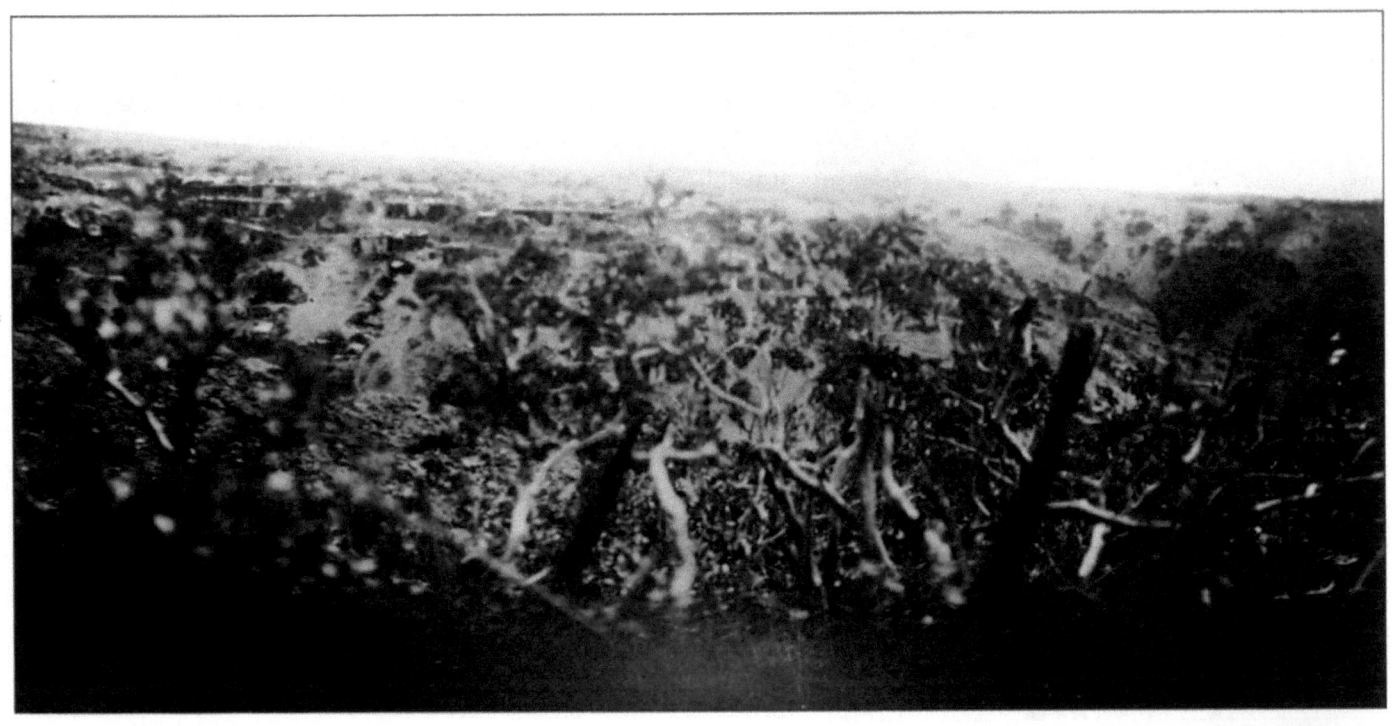

ABOVE: View from a sniper's possie occupied by one of Grace's crack shots looking towards the dugouts on Pope's with the Turkish held skyline beyond. QUEEN ELIZABETH II ARMY MEMORIAL MUSEUM

RIGHT: Men of the Maori Contingent clearing earth from the mine tunnels at Quinn's Post. QUEEN ELIZABETH II ARMY MEMORIAL MUSEUM

One of the outstanding New Zealand soldiers on Gallipoli was a young officer with the Wellington Infantry Battalion. Second Lieutenant Thomas 'Army' Grace, an old boy of Wellington College, was a noted sportsman who had toured Australia and New Zealand with Parata's Maori rugby team in 1913 and 1914. He was also a crack shot. Lieutenant-Colonel W G Malone, who commanded the Wellington Battalion, put Grace in charge of his best marksmen and told him to clean out the Turkish snipers at the head of Monash Gully, who were picking off the supply parties working to the front line. The Australian historian C E W Bean wrote:

> Grace's snipers, posted throughout the valley, placed a barrier as impenetrable as any earthwork between the traffic in Monash Valley and the Turks whose trenches overlooked it. Thence forward, provided the snipers were first warned, even a convoy of mules could go to the supply depot near the head of the gully at midday, without a shot being fired at it.[6]

Lieutenant T M Grace, Wellington Battalion, one of the outstanding New Zealand soldiers on Gallipoli. WILSON & HORTON

Grace led by example, and raided and sniped the Turkish posts with his scouts. He also died with them on Chunuk Bair on 8 August 1915 during the August offensive to seize the critical heights.

The August offensive started with a night advance by the New Zealand Mounted Rifles Brigade to take the foothills and open the way to the top of the heights. In this battle the men of the Maori Contingent were divided by platoons among the regiments of the New Zealand Mounted Rifles. It was a night attack with rifle and bayonet, and the anxious watchers within the Anzac perimeter could follow the story of the New Zealand success by the battle-cry of the Maori as each trench was taken: 'Ka mate, ka mate! Ka ora, ka ora!' (We may die, we may die! We may live, we may live!),[7] and by the receding flashes of the rifle and machine-gun fire as the Turks were driven back up the slopes towards the crest.

Private Peter Tahitahi took part in that attack:

> There were dead Turks in the trenches, some of them were half dead, just laying there — you could feel it when you tramped on them — breathing. We just turned the bayonet with the rifle round and finished them off.[8]

Buck and Wainohu, as doctor and chaplain to the contingent, moved with it in the advance, and in the heat of battle established the first-aid post at the head of Chailak Dere close to the front line on the slopes below Chunuk Bair:

> We dug a terrace with our entrenching tools into the left bank to get protection from the shrapnel. At the back it was barely three feet deep, and just long enough to accommodate the wounded men lying flat on the ground . . . There was fearful slaughter, and the wounded came pouring down so that our first-aid post was filled to overflowing. We dressed their wounds and, whenever there was a lull in the firing from the left, we sent the walking wounded down the stream.[9]

The Maori Contingent on Gallipoli

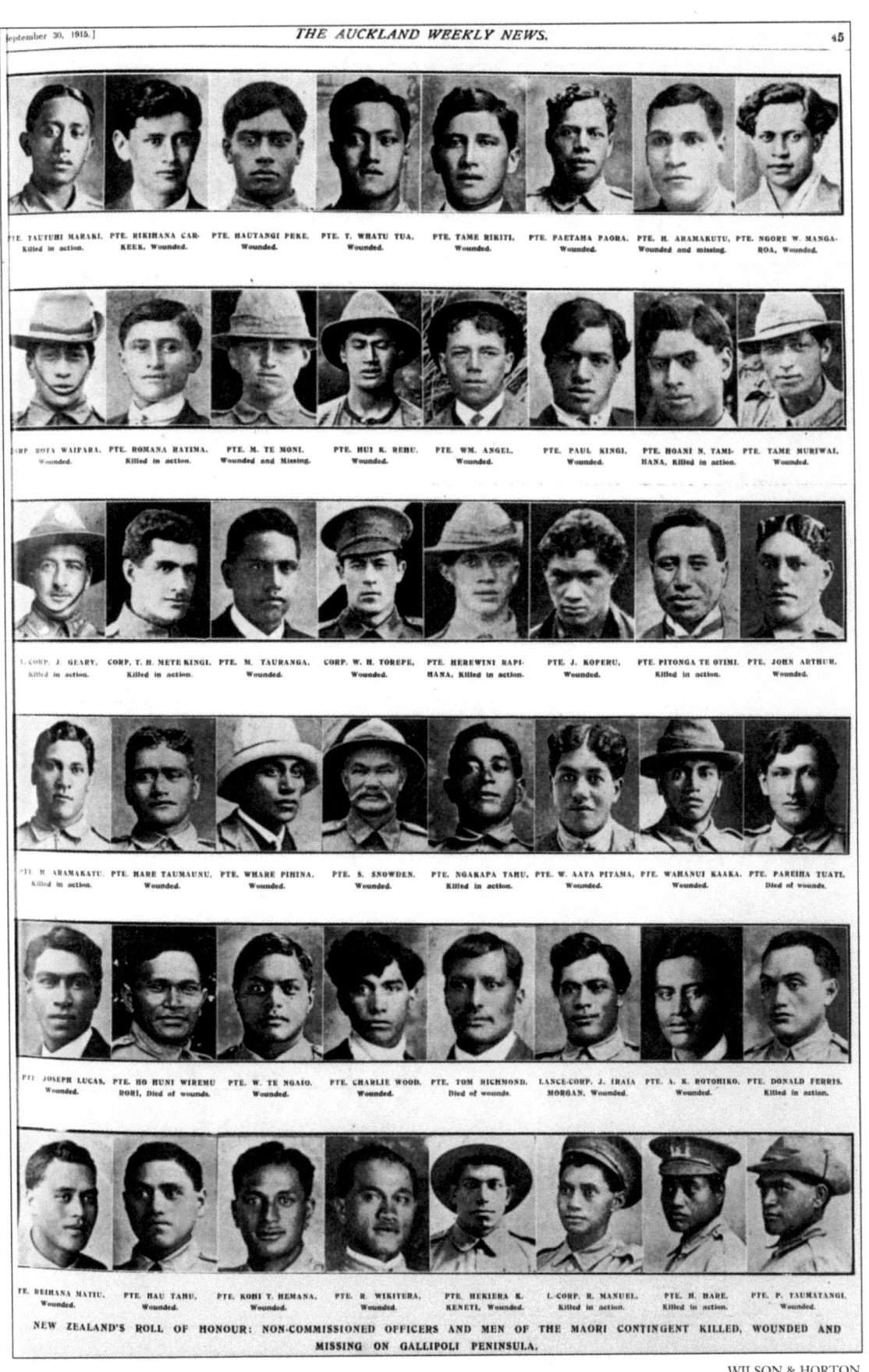

NEW ZEALAND'S ROLL OF HONOUR: NON-COMMISSIONED OFFICERS AND MEN OF THE MAORI CONTINGENT KILLED, WOUNDED AND MISSING ON GALLIPOLI PENINSULA.

WILSON & HORTON

1st N.Z. Maori Contingent.

Marching in State.
Anzac
3.7.15

Officers	Rank & File
16	461

Total
477

Marching out State
Evacuation Anzac.
14.12.15.

Officers	Rank & File
2	132

Total
134

New Zealand Maori Contingent Nominal Roll, WA1 97/3/16. NATIONAL ARCHIVES OF NEW ZEALAND

	Officers	Rank & File
Returned to N.Z.	4	
Sent to Various Hospitals	6	228
Wounded	3	123
Transferred	1	
On leave from Sarpi Camp 5.10.15 Mudros	2	
Killed in action		32
Died in Hospital		18
	16	401
Rank & File continuously on Gallipoli Peninsular		60
	16	461
Transferred to Maori Contg. 1 Officer) 2nd Lt Bright		Total
Wounded 1		477

	Officers	Rank & File
Promoted Officers (from the Ranks&F)	2	
Rank & File continuously on Gallipoli Peninsular		60
Returned to duty on G. Peninsular		72
	2	132
		Total
		134

The New Zealand losses were cripplingly heavy. Maori losses numbered 17 killed, 89 wounded and two missing. This does not include the men with dysentery and enteric fever who were evacuated as they broke down, exhausted, in August.

The weakened contingent were committed again in late August to seize Hill 60 as part of the Mounted Rifles, and were destroyed as fighting units. The Maori losses in the two battles of August led Godley, the New Zealand commander, to split the contingent among the four battalions of the New Zealand Infantry Brigade. This was partly due to a lack of numbers in both the Maori Contingent and in the infantry battalions. The casualties of August had reduced the battalions from 1,000 to 100–200 men.

The roll book of the Maori Contingent, its pages of indelible pencil and ink entries stained with water and sweat, record the struggle. Of the 16 officers and 461 rank and file, 60 alone remained on the peninsula to be rested at Mudros (on the island of Lemnos) in September 1915. Returning sick and wounded built this up to two officers and 132 men by the time Anzac was evacuated on 14 December 1915. Buck would receive a Distinguished Service Order for his work on Gallipoli, Lieutenant William Stainton a Military Cross, and Chaplain Henare Wainohu the Serbian Order of the White Eagle. Seven Military Medals were also awarded to the contingent. Buck wrote afterwards:

All who have come through the Gallipoli Campaign, where pakeha and Maori have shared the fatigue, danger, and incessant vigil of the trenches, side by side, recognise that the Maori is a better man than they gave him credit for, and have admitted him to full fellowship and equality.[10]

An equality of the trenches was admitted within the New Zealand force but there was also shame. There were tensions between Major A H Herbert, the Maori Contingent commander, and his Maori officers. Buck and Wainohu had provided an important bridge but the strain of the August fighting had broken this link and four Maori officers were returned to New Zealand: Captain W T Pitt on medical grounds and Lieutenants R Dansey, T Hiroti and T Hetet for unsatisfactory performance. Dansey in particular had shown outstanding bravery in the August offensive, yet despite pleas from the contingent officers, including Buck and Wainohu, the military hierarchy supported Herbert's actions.

There was sadness and anger among the remaining officers and men. Their bravery was praised but the split-up announced by Godley meant they had lost their identity as a contingent, and some of their officers were in disgrace. Their feelings were shared by Maori politicians and elders in New Zealand who, while proud that the Maori were fighting as part of the New Zealand Infantry Brigade, were concerned that the parcelling out of Maori platoons among the infantry battalions would put an end to their special sense of identity. They asked that the Maori Contingent be re-formed as a unit when the 2nd Maori Contingent of 300 men arrived. They also asked that the three officers sent home in disgrace be allowed to return. Faced with a refusal by Maori elders to recruit further reinforcements, and growing disquiet over the grounds for the officers' removal, Godley agreed. Dansey, Hiroti and Hetet rejoined the Pioneers in France, and justified their return with their deeds.

CHAPTER FOUR

FORMING THE NEW ZEALAND PIONEER BATTALION

On 20 February 1916 the New Zealand Pioneer Battalion was formed as a unit of the New Zealand Division which was formed in Egypt after the evacuation of New Zealanders from Gallipoli in December 1915. It was made up of the men of the original Maori Contingent, the 2nd and 3rd Maori Contingents, and men of the Otago Mounted Rifles whose unit strength had been reduced from a 600-strong regiment to that of a mounted squadron. The Otagos thus became the Pakeha half of the Pioneers. The old badge of the Maori Contingent was put away and a regimental badge of the New Zealand Pioneers adopted which was a Maori warrior's face above the crossed pick and axe, flanked by fernleaf fronds and the words 'NZ Pioneers'.

The Pioneer Battalion that sailed from Egypt for France was not a fighting unit but a labour force trained and organised to work on engineering tasks, digging trenches, building roads, laying light railways, and the other hundred and one labouring jobs an army needs to do.

It was an interesting mix of fiercely proud provincial and indigenous groups: men from Otago and Southland, Maori, and Pacific Islanders — including 125 Niue Islanders and 45 Rarotongans. The battalion was organised into four companies, each with two Maori and two Pakeha platoons. 'A' Company had Nos 1 and 2 Platoons (Northland and Waikato) with Nos 3 and 4 Platoons (7 Squadron OMR); 'B' Company, Nos 5 and 6 Platoons (North Island West Coast, Wanganui and Wellington) with Nos 7 and 8 Platoons (5 Squadron OMR); 'C' Company, Nos 9 and 10 Platoons (Bay of Plenty, East Coast, Taupo and South Island) with Nos 11 and 12 Platoons (12 Squadron OMR); and 'D' Company, Nos 13 and 14 Platoons (Poverty Bay, Wairoa, Hawke's Bay and Wairarapa) with Nos 15 and 16 Platoons (a mixture of NZ Mounted Rifles). The Otago Mounted Rifles were as angry as the Maori at losing their identity, and they fiercely resented becoming 'pioneers'. With such proudly independent elements, the unit needed the best of leadership — and it got it.

Major George Augustus King, a regular officer of the New Zealand Staff Corps, was appointed Commanding Officer. Formerly staff captain of the New Zealand Mounted Rifles Brigade, King was highly thought of by Major-General Sir Andrew Russell, the New Zealand Divisional Commander. Russell recognised the potentially explosive mixture in the pioneer unit and gave its command to one of his most able men. King himself was unhappy at being plucked out of his Mounted Rifles, but there was no option: 'We will have to go whether we like it or not.'[12]

Major Peter Buck became the second-in-command. Buck had the personality, leadership skills and mana to command both Maori and Pakeha. Initially, company commanders were Pakeha and the company second-in-commands were officers of the Maori Contingents. By October 1917 almost all the company commanders were Maori.

Ko koe Niu Tireni
Te kuini o te ao
Arohaina nei e au
Ko koe tangihia
Ko koe e mihia
Ko koe te kainga
  pai
Te au taku moe
Te aroha kia koe
I te roa o te ra

Chorus
Ka whai mai ra
Te aroha
A huri noa te ao
Ka whai mai ra
Te aroha
A huri noa te ao

Marching Song of the New Zealand Pioneer Battalion[11]

ABOVE: Farewelling the Second Contingent outside the Auckland town hall. WILSON & HORTON

LEFT: Niue Islanders in training to join the Pioneers. WILSON & HORTON

LEFT BELOW: Tongans were also part of the mix of all races in the Pioneer Battalion. WILSON & HORTON

OPPOSITE ABOVE: Wellington farewells the Second Maori Contingent. AUCKLAND WEEKLY NEWS

OPPOSITE BELOW: In New Zealand, young men went to Territorial Camps and waited to turn 21. ALEXANDER TURNBULL LIBRARY

The Maori had been to Egypt, Malta and the Dardanelles, and were back in Egypt again. Now the word was France, but even their commanding officer was unsure where they would end up next. 'Everyone says we are going to France next but am not believing anything . . . and will not believe it until we get there.'[13]

Regtl No	Rank	Name	Coy	Religion	
511	Pte	Kaanga Te Kutu	A	Meo	
512	Pte	Te Awarau Hou Karaka	B	C.E.	Base FP 24.8.15
513	"	Poipoi Pita	B	"	FP 9/9/15
514	S.S.M.	Stewart James Douglas	HQ	"	To N.Z.M.R. Bde 24/8/15
515	R.S.M.	Singery Edward	HQ	"	W. To N.Z.M.R. Bde 24/8/15
516	Pte	Tauri William Hoani	A	"	FP Alexandria 27.6.15
517	"	Hakopa Kotuku Horima	MG	"	K. 9.8.15
518	Sgt	Broughton Edward Renata	B	C.C.	
~~519~~	~~Pte~~	~~Ferris Donald~~ (Mickrugs)	MG	C.C.	Killed 8.8.15
520		Jones Francis Moncur		"	medically unfit 5
521	Pte	Ranawa Matiu	B	C.E.	R 9/9/15
522	Pte	Broughton Maurice	A	R.C.	K.4.8.15
523	Pte	Peke Hautangi	A	C.E.	K 6.8.15 Rejoined 24.11.15
~~524~~	~~Pte~~	~~Baker Whare~~		"	Killed 21.8.15
525	Pte	Rapona Kiri	B	"	
526	Pte	Rotoatara Kipa	B	"	W. 21.8.15
527	Pte	Paora Reihana	A	"	
52Y					
528	Pte	Kingi Karauria	B	C.E.	Returned duty. Base FP 24.8.15 Hosp 23.12.15
529	Pte	Renata Re	B	"	W 28/7/15
530	Pte	Rauhiti Huki	B	"	FP 9/9/15 Reported dead 14/10/15
531	Pte	Savage James	B	"	
532	Pte	Hiroti Jack	A	"	R 6/10/15
~~533~~		~~Kereopa John~~			medically unfit 5. 2.15
534	Pte	Ngarangione Huki	B	Mor	W 21.8.15
535	Pte	Samihana Wi	B	"	W 9/9/15
536	Pte	Hape Hona	B	C.E.	
537	Pte	Kinita Paki	B	"	FP 6/10/15
538	Lieut	Jones Edward Albert Mills	B	"	FP 12/10/15
539	Q.M.S.	Hamilton D'Arcy Eagle	HQ	"	Base Hsp. 4.8.12 Returned duty 11-10-12
540	Pte	Rapana Samuel	A	"	

A page from the Roll book of the Maori Contingent on Gallipoli. NATIONAL ARCHIVES OF NEW ZEALAND

KO TE KAHITI O NIU TIRENI.

Reg. No.	Rank.	Name.	Name and Address of Next-of-kin.	Casualty.
16/176	Private	Herewini, Hohepa	Ruahuihui Herewini, Ngapuna, Rotorua	Died of wounds at Anzac, 21/9/15.
16/978	,,	Heta, William	Thomas Heta, (father), Poroti	Sick. Admitted Pont de Koubbeh Hosp., 14/1/16.
16/325	,,	Hetaraka, Hurae	Timoti Hetaraka, Peria, Mangonui	Died of dysentery, 16/8/15.
16/326	,,	Hetaraka, Peretiti	Hetaraka Heta, Whatuwhiwhi, Mangonui	Slightly sick. Disembarked Malta, Ship "Grampion," 2/10/15.
16/446	Corporal	Hetet, Tuheka Taonui	John Taonui Hetet, Te Kuiti, Auckland	Slightly sick. Disembarked Malta, Hosp. Ship "Neveralia," 18/9/15.
16/375	Private	Himiona, Akuhata	Teone Himiona, Aorangi, Feilding	Gunshot wound, knee.
16/190	,,	Hirini, Mohi	Mrs. Repora Whango (mother), Whakatane, Bay of Plenty	Slightly sick. Disembarked Malta, Hosp. Ship "Galeka," 24/11/15.
16/182	,,	Hoani, Pita	Petera Haeriteao (cousin), Tu Ngapuna, Rotorua	Sick. Admitted Pont de Koubbeh Hosp., 7/2/16.
16/327	,,	Hohaia, Wiki	Hura Hohaia, Peria, Mangonui	Returned to front from Cairo.
16/229	,,	Hohepa, Ahere te Koari	Pera Hohepa, Puketapu, Wharerangi, Napier	Wounded. Arrived at Beaufort War Hosp., Fishpond, Bristol.
16/328	,,	Hohipa, Tawi	Wakarua Hohipa, Pukepoto, Auckland	Wounded. Admitted 1st Aust. Gen. Hosp., Heliopolis, 11/8/15.
16/510	,,	Honeycombe, Charles	Charles Honeycombe, Mamaku, Rotorua	Slightly sick. Disembarked Malta, Hosp. Ship "Ascanius," 31/8/15.
16/548	Sergeant	Hovell, Charles Harry Pireka	C. W. Hovell, J.P. (father), Kennedy's Bay	Sick. Admitted Pont de Koubbeh Hosp., 14/1/16.
16/556	Private	Hovell, George Woodward	C. W. Hovell, Kennedy's Bay	Died of wounds, King George's Hosp., London, 20/10/15.
16/330	,,	Howell, Hemi	Mrs. M. Howell, Main Road, Taradale, Napier	Sick. Admitted Clearing Hosp., Eastleigh.
16/451	,,	Ihaka, Maihi	Ihaka Hura (father), Whangape	Slightly sick. Admitted 2nd West Gen. Hosp., Manchester.
	Captain	Jones, Albert Edward Miles	Mrs. E. Jones (mother), 3 Kingsdale Read, Mosley Hill, Liverpool, Eng.	Sick. On furlough, London.
16/331	Private	Kaaka, Wahanui	Tewiki Harawira, Awanui	Slightly wounded. Disembarked Malta from Hosp. Ship "Itonus," 14/8/15.
16/8	,,	Kainga, Tamihana	Mrs. Kate Kainga, Wairoa, Hawke's Bay	Slightly wounded. Disembarked Malta, Hosp. Ship "Dunlace Castle," 27/9/15.
	Lieutenant	Kaipara, Aitimi Pitara	Mrs. Monika Kaipara, Waiotapu, Rotorua	Seriously ill. Disembarked Malta from Hosp. Ship "Somali," 31/7/15.
16/148	Private	Kaipara, Hori	P. T. K. Mokonuiarangi (father), Waiotapu	Sick, enteric. Out of danger, 4/11/15.
16/147	,,	Kakukore, Charlie	Heni Eruana Owhata, Rotorua	Sick. On furlough, Eng.
16/332	,,	Kamariera, Ngorama	Turuhine Kamariera, Huria, Mangonui	Sick. Returned to front.
16/395	,,	Kanapu, Tamehana	Kanapu Haerehura, Springvale Road, Wanganui	Wounded. Discharged from Hosp. convalescent, Alexandria.
16/630	,,	Karaitiana, Rutene	Rangi Karaitiana (brother), Hastings	Discharged convalescent, Alexandria.
16/453	,,	Karati, Wiremu	Hone Kaiati, Thames	Slightly sick. Disembarked from Hosp. Ship "Karoo," 19/8/15.
16/270	,,	Karauti, Abraham	Horo Karauti (brother), Ohau	Sick, enteric. Out of danger, Gen. Hosp., Alexandria, 19/1/16.
16/121	,,	Karehana, Wiremu	John Karehana, Raukokore, Bay of Plenty	Sick. Recovered.
16/271	,,	Karetai, Stewart	Joseph Karetai, Otakou	Killed in action, 21/8/15.
16/595	,,	Karetai, Sydney George	Joseph Karetai, Otakou, Dunedin	Sick. Admitted Lord Derby Hosp., Warrington.
16/95	,,	Kawhia, Eruera	Raniera Tuhoro Kawhia (father), Kahukioia, Port Awanui	Sick. On furlough, London.
16/13	,,	Keneti, Hekiera Kupara	Mrs. Maria T. Keneti, Tokomaru Bay	Slightly wounded. Disembarked Malta from Hosp. Ship "Sicilia," 28/7/15.
16/275	Sergeant	Kingi, John Henry	Wiramina Kingi, Hastings	Wounded. Admitted 1st Gen. Hosp., Birmingham.
16/528	Private	Kingi, Karauria	Tuteari Kingi, Te Karaka, Gisborne	Sick. Discharged from hosp., Alexandria, convalescent.
16/573	,,	Kingi, Paul	Tu Te Ari, Te Karaka	Wounded. Out of danger, 20/11/15.
16/152	,,	Kingi, Raiona	Tauhu Kingi, Te Puke	Wounded. Admitted 19th Gen. Hosp., Alexandria.
16/537	,,	Kinita, Paki	Rangi Karuita, Muripara, Rotorua	Wounded. Admitted hosp., Heliopolis, 11/1/16.
16/156	,,	Kipa, Hori	Meri Rewhiti, Kopu, Thames	Wounded, hand.

The Gallipoli casualty lists were published in the *Kahiti*.

CHAPTER FIVE

THE NEW ZEALAND PIONEER BATTALION IN FRANCE

E haere ana 'hau
Ki runga o Wiwi
Ki reira 'hau nei,
E tangi ai.
Me mihi kau atu
I te nuku o te
  whenua,
Hei konei ra e,
E te tau pumau.

And now I am
  leaving
For France's red
  war fields.
There I'll
  remember;
My heart will send
  greetings
O'er far land and
  ocean
To my own
  constant love.

'Te Ope Tuatahi'

On 9 April 1916 the Pioneers reached Marseilles. A long and uncomfortable train trip was endured until they reached their billeting area in northern France. The green fields looked better than the desert sands, but the nights were cold for men fresh from Egypt. Administration was a muddle, there was no pay, and the French looked askance at these savage-looking New Zealanders. Billets were dirty and the first job was to set to and clean them out. It was cold and wet, and the one blanket issued per man did little to help. Maybe the bleak climate explains why the battalion shared with the rest of the Division a fondness for alcohol and for being absent without leave. King cracked down hard:

My crowd are doing very good work and everyone is pleased with them, but the Maoris are a nuisance every pay day as about two beers and a tune on the piano seems to make them drunk and they get very noisy, so have been handing out 28 days in the clink pretty freely to discourage them.[14]

For everyone it was straight to work, and Maori with forestry experience were sent off on a tree-felling party in the Forêt de Nieppe. Cowan records that the trees were 'felled in the French style, no standing butt was left; the tree was cut level with the ground and the top of the stump showing was carefully trimmed so as to leave a rounded surface, which would not hold water'.[15] The British officer commanding the forestry work was full of praise and wrote to King that he 'never had a better party in the Forest, although there have been up to nearly 10,000 different men working in it at various times'.[16]

Intense rivalry arose within the New Zealand gangs as there were champion axemen in the ranks. Competitions were held with money changing hands. In May 1915 the 2nd Army Competition involved every engineer and pioneer unit from the Canadian, Australian, New Zealand, and British forces as well as local French civilians. As the routine orders show, the New Zealand Pioneers held their own. Rewiri, Tamaki, and Bannister won the tree felling by nine minutes from the second-placed Australians, with the Canadians third. In the cross-cut saw the Canadians won, with the Pioneers Butler and Tamaki second; the Australians won the log chop with the Pioneers second. A New Zealander, Poutou, won best axemanship. The New Zealanders also won a competition against the French *bucherons* or woodsmen, with both teams cutting French style.

King was pleased with the way his Pioneers were settling in:

Gen. Russell was round this morning and is very pleased with the way our people are working — says this battalion does more work than two Infantry Bat[talio]ns. Am very pleased and so are the men and they have been behaving themselves very much better lately and I haven't had an orderly room for nearly a fortnight now, which is a good job. I hate having to hand out punishments so generally give them a good dose to keep them from coming up again.[17]

Routine orders record the settling in of the battalion, the strictures on dress and saluting, the placing of estaminets out of bounds during certain hours of the day, and indicate that most of the men were adapting to conditions in France.

However, it was soon obvious that the Niue Islanders could not stand the cold weather, most of them collapsing on the first march on the paved roads. By June 1916, after two months' service, they were returned to Niue. In the same month the battalion was reorganised into two Maori and two Pakeha companies — with 'A' and 'C' the Maori companies, and 'B' and 'D' the Pakeha. Language led to the battalion church parades separating the congregation by race rather than religion, Roman Catholics being the single exception:

For Maories [sic]. At 8.45 a.m. at the same place as last Sunday . . .
For Pakehas at 8.45 a.m . . . [18]

The Pioneers made themselves at home. Every stray French mongrel that came sniffing around the billets was adopted by the men. The films and photographs show visiting dignitaries, from the British Commander-in-Chief General Haig to the New Zealand Prime Minister W F Massey, being informally escorted by a proud collection of terriers during the inspection of a guard inevitably drawn from one of the Maori companies. The Pioneers were a divisional unit, not part of a brigade, and that usually meant being billeted close to the Divisional Headquarters and providing more than a fair share of picquets and

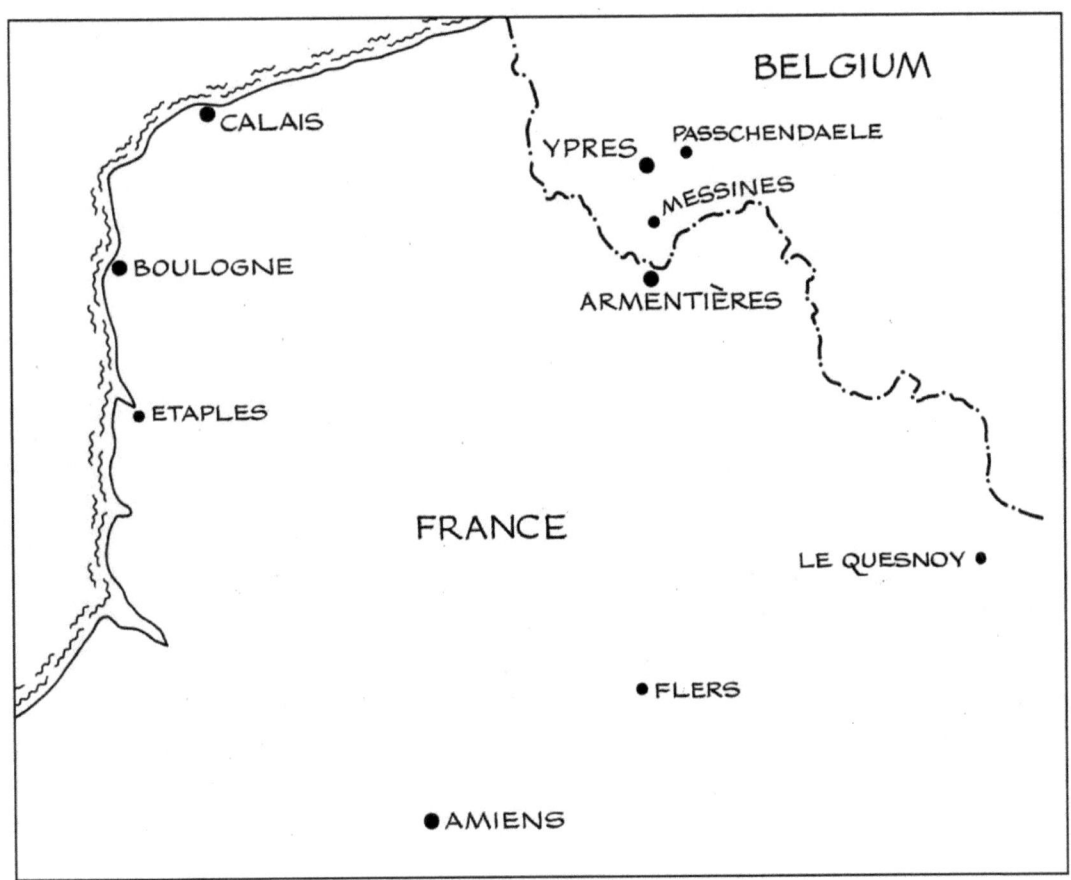

The Pioneers on the Western Front.

guards. In every film that survives of a VIP visit to the New Zealand Division, the Pioneers feature. Buck was usually made guard commander and escorted various British cabinet ministers as well as Massey and Sir Joseph Ward, the Minister of Finance in the coalition government, around the ranks of the Maori soldiers.

The New Zealanders had an ability to get on good terms with the locals. The *Chronicles of the N.Z.E.F.* are full of the fractured attempts at French that the soldiers used in the estaminets and billets. The songs and the haka captivated and delighted the French public, and open-air concerts were sometimes held in the local square. The *Chronicles* on one occasion noted that a hall was cleared of young women because of the ferocity of these New Zealand 'dances'. Men would help at the village pumps and were fascinated by the differences in farming techniques — and it was not just the presence of the women working in the fields that had parties of men at rest behind the lines giving a hand with the harvesting and stacking the stooks. Farm work was a chance to get away from the business of war, and provided an important link with a life in New Zealand that now seemed so unreal.

Buying bread from a French woman. Note that the Maori soldier is a member of the Canterbury Battalion. Maori soldiers were encouraged to transfer to the Maori Pioneer Battalion, but many elected to stay with the battalions in which they first enlisted. H SERIES, QUEEN ELIZABETH II ARMY MEMORIAL MUSEUM

Pioneer batmen bringing up the officers' luggage.
IMPERIAL WAR MUSEUM

New Zealand Engineers at work.
QUEEN ELIZABETH II ARMY MEMORIAL MUSEUM

The Pioneers had the thankless task of providing the firing party to shoot Private Frank Hughes of the Canterbury Battalion on 25 August 1916. Hughes was the first of five New Zealanders to be shot during the First World War. Normally the firing party was detailed from the condemned man's own battalion. In Hughes' case, Russell directed that the Pioneers do the killing, most probably because they were the closest unit to the New Zealand Divisional Headquarters where Hughes was imprisoned. Sergeant A E M Rhind of New Zealand Divisional Headquarters recorded in his diary:

This morning at 5 am the first N.Z. soldier was shot for desertion. The firing party came from the Pioneers. I have just seen them marching back into town, so I suppose it's all over now. It will have a great effect on some of the men . . .[19]

On 15 May 1916 the Pioneers moved into the combat zone at Armentières. They ran the Divisional Trench Warfare School, teaching the non-commissioned officers of the Division the latest techniques in trench building, and wiring methods. Nights saw Pioneer working parties going into the front line and the first combat casualties. Two officers were killed in May and there was a constant flow of wounded from the nightly artillery fire which, as King wrote, 'smashed things up a bit'.[20]

The other battalions of the New Zealand Division at Armentières were carrying out trench raids, and the Pioneers also wanted a share. Sir Andrew Russell, the Divisional Commander, agreed that they could make a raid. Fifty men were picked from each Maori company and trained under Captain Roger Dansey. A raid on the German trenches was planned, with the object of capturing machine guns and trench mortars, taking two prisoners for identification, and killing as many Germans as possible. Dansey carefully trained his raiding party. It was to be swift and silent. Orders detailed:

'No rifles and bayonets will be taken. Officers and sappers will carry revolvers. Other ranks will be armed with meres . . . Only Maori will be spoken by all parties after leaving starting point.'[21]

It was not unusual for raiding parties to make their own clubs and cudgels. This is the only record of meres being taken. The Maori language would be used again as a means of securing secrecy of speech both in the Second World War with the 28th Maori Battalion and in operations in Borneo in the 1960s by the 1st Battalion Royal New Zealand Infantry Regiment.

The raid, mounted on the night of 9 July 1916, was a failure. The wire in front of the German trench was found to be uncut as the Maori crawled across No Man's Land. One man was killed and three were wounded as the party retired to their trench. Another attempt, made the following night, was also unsuccessful. This was the last of the Pioneer's large-scale raids, although small patrols were mounted throughout July 1916. Raiding was not their job; theirs was the hard graft of digging trenches in the combat zone, laying railway tracks and plank roads, building casualty clearing posts and bunkers. It was heavy work in dirty and dangerous conditions and, like the infantry around them, they suffered from tactics of attrition, as artillery and sniper fire steadily increased their numbers of dead and wounded.

CHAPTER SIX

THE DIGGERS ON THE SOMME

Your boys have proved beyond a doubt what the race is capable of.
DR MAUI POMARE TO TE RANGI HIROA
(MAJOR PETER BUCK)

In late August 1916 the Pioneers were the first unit of the New Zealand Division to move to the Somme battlefield that had been fought over since 1 July. The New Zealand Division was to be part of the so-called Third Battle of the Somme and part of the British XV Corps in the attack on the German defensive position around the village of Flers. The Pioneers found themselves billeted among the South African and German dead in Delville Wood. The ground was a muddy horror with the woods marked by the bared stumps of splintered trees. Shelling went on day and night, gas shells being mixed with the shrapnel and high explosives. During this the Pioneers started digging what was to become the famous communication trench named 'Turk Lane', forward through the shell holes towards the front line. The platoons worked in relays under gas and shell fire that produced a steady trickle of casualties. Buck wrote, 'Dead men, German and English, everywhere in the trench, in the sides of the trench and about in the open, unburied, and smell fearful.'[22] The men dug on.

The New Zealand Pioneers' work in building the communication trenches — first 'Turk Lane' and then its companion 'Fish Alley' — would earn them the sobriquet the 'Diggers'. The British units they served coined the term on account of the Pioneers' exploits as the 'Digging Battalion'. 'Digger' was adopted by the rest of the New Zealand Division in 1916. By 1917 the name had spread from the New Zealand Division to the Australian Divisions in the two Anzac Corps (somewhat ironically, it might be said, for the Australians never set great store by the pick and shovel, and this was always a cause of complaint when the Pioneers took over from an Australian unit!).

The Somme gave the New Zealanders a reputation as fighting soldiers. It was hard won. On 15 September 1916, the day of the New Zealand attack, Pioneer casualties were 12 killed and 40 wounded, most of them from 'B' Company. Mortally wounded, Lieutenant Henare Kohere of Ngati Porou asked that his cousin Lieutenant Pekama Kaa be given command of the Ngati Porou platoon, and it was done.[23] Kaa himself would die in August 1917. Seriously wounded along with several of his platoon, he refused to be shifted until his men were carried to safety; he was killed by a shell before he was moved. As a friend wrote at the time:

To our limited vision, it seems as if an officer like this can ill be spared; but the example of his life lived, and finally given for others will always be of inestimable value to those who knew him. Heoi, e oku teina, kia whai kaha koutou i roto i te Ariki.[24]

These words would equally apply to the generation of Maori and Pakeha who earned a reputation for New Zealand in France and who were killed or maimed there, or who returned to Aotearoa, shadows in health and spirit of the men who went away. King was proud of his men:

'I think my crowd have made a fairly good name for themselves since we started on this job. We have been here 33 days now and are being relieved in three days so expect we have seen all we will of the Great Offensive.'[25]

The measuring stick of performance had once been the British Divisions, but after the Somme the New Zealanders knew the British had had their match. King wrote:

It has all been most interesting but rather solid both for work and casualties — our part in the offensive started on 15th [September] and I have already lost over 200 men while the Infantry have lost over 50% all round, but have done magnificently and wiped the eye of all the British Divisions round here — we are farther ahead than any other Div. and have never given anything up once we have captured it.[26]

After the battle, King explained:

My people were detailed to push Communication trenches through to the captured positions as soon as they were sure and we came in for a lot of shell fire as Fritz put up a barrage on our line of work and I lost poor old Harris, 'B' Coy commander and about 50 others — it kept getting hotter and they were blowing in the trench as fast as it was dug so I pulled the Coy out till it quietened [sic] again a bit. The other Coys did not catch it so badly and only lost a few men.
    All the time my crowd chased up the firing line with communication trenches and Turk Lane (our masterpiece) is just about the longest trench in France and is certainly the best on the Somme.[27]

Maui Pomare wrote to Peter Buck after the Somme:

I agree with you that the training, the influence, and the discipline that the men are receiving at the Front

Advancing on the Somme. IMPERIAL WAR MUSEUM

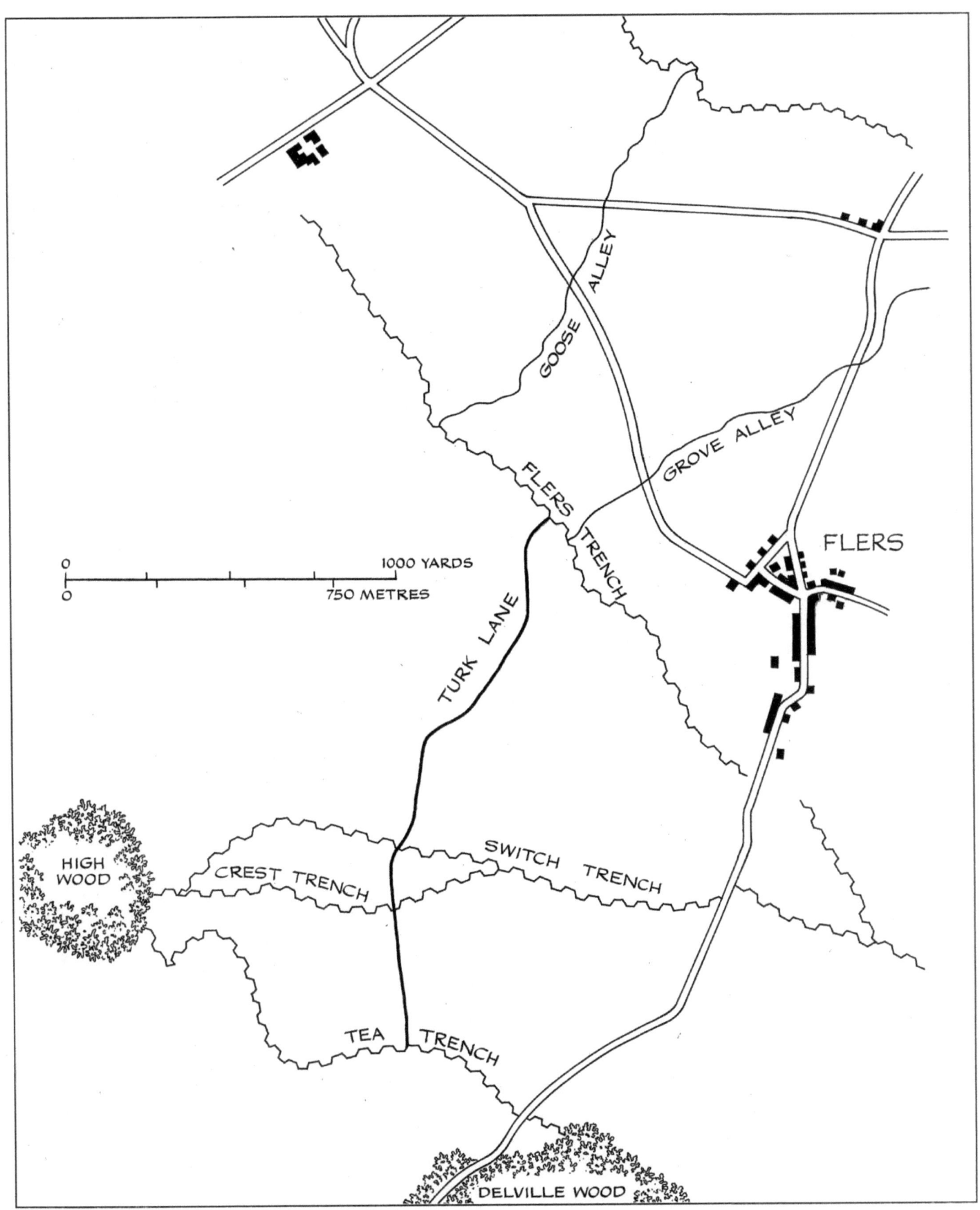

Turk Lane — the Pioneers' masterpiece of the Somme Battle.

will mean a great awakening for the Maoris, and I agree with your sentiment that 'what matters if we are wiped out, for it is a damned sight better to go out in a big thing than to fritter away in idle security at home.' Your boys have proved beyond a doubt what the race is capable of.[28]

The Somme saw the battalion honoured. Russell ordered that it receive the same quota of honours and awards as an infantry battalion: two Distinguished Conduct Medals and 10 Military Medals. He 'told us that no Division had ever been so well served by its Pioneers as the N.Z.Div. had been and that in the way of honours we are to be treated the same as the Infantry which pleased the men greatly.'[29] It did not work out like that, even though King put his men in for the two DCMs and 10 Military Medals. Godley, the Corps Commander, 'turned them down and only gave five'.

The New Zealanders suffered 7,408 casualties on the Somme and the decimated New Zealand Division, including the Pioneers, needed to be rebuilt: 'The Div. has lost a big crowd of men one way and another and those that are left need a good spell as they are pretty done up.'[30]

But by November 1916 it was work as usual. Their commanding officer noted:

Things are pretty quiet around here so far as the Fritz is concerned but I am kept pretty busy, as my people are scattered all over the area on various jobs and it takes an awful long time to go round and see what they are all doing.

Besides the ordinary routine jobs on roads, drainage and trenches in the Divisional area, I have got over 300 men on detachment jobs and they are working all over the country for miles. The men are very comfortable and are keeping very fit — all have been given [gum]boots to work in and stacks of clothes and dry socks issued every day.[31]

On another occasion King wrote: 'I have found that the Maori is quite all right and happy so long as you keep his puku well filled and give him a football to knock about in his spare time — when he has any.'[32] These words apply to every New Zealand soldier, and indeed every soldier, then and now.

The New Zealanders were far from saints. They got drunk, chased women and featured in the venereal disease statistics. King accepted this as the reality of soldiering:

The men are behaving wonderfully well considering the amount of beer there is to be had (French beer), but I got some awful stiffs in the last draft of reinforcements and have just run a couple in for 28 days clink and put two more up for Courtmartial for getting drunk and smashing up an estaminet (beer-shop), and I hope they get a couple of years each, then I won't be bothered with them again! It's funny that the latest reinforcements should always try to run the show — the old hands very seldom get into bad trouble. I think people in N.Z. must make too much of the men coming away now, as they always have a big opinion of themselves.[33]

The Somme showed the difficulties of keeping units up to strength in manpower, and it was obvious that the Maori reinforcements could not sustain the 30–50 percent casualties suffered by the infantry battalions. Efforts were made to post Maori serving with the infantry units to the Pioneers, but these were not successful because the Maori infantrymen wanted to stay with the men and the battalion they had originally joined.

It was in France that many New Zealanders saw the Maori not only as a soldier but also as an individual person for the first time. It was a long way to come for such a lesson. The two Pakeha companies of the Pioneers and the infantry battalions now realised that Maori were more than figures of curiosity and amusement, which is how they were usually portrayed in the New Zealand press. On the Somme the Pioneers were held in awe for the work they did. It seems ironic that New Zealanders had to go to Gallipoli and France to find out about themselves and each other.

After the efforts of the Somme, Christmas 1916 was eagerly looked forward to:

The Coys have all been buying pigs for a Xmas feed, as there are no turkeys or geese here, and are fattening them up on scraps of the tucker and keeping them in pens near the dugouts where the picquets can see them in case anyone takes a fancy to them. Each Coy. has three of them (big white ones) and we have a small one for Headquarters. Also I have given one for a Prize to the platoon which collects the most derelict gear and tools before the 20th. The waste here in stores and tools is something awful and the people we took over from have left dumps of tools and wire and ammunition all over the place, and it seems a darn shame to see them rotting, so am encouraging the young gentlemen to bring them in by means of the pig. They will probably steal all the Infantry and Engineers' tools to make a good catch, but it will help to make these people more careful about leaving them about.[34]

Cowan records that 'Christmas was spent peacefully in good winter quarters', and the men enjoyed a dinner of pigs and fowls steam-cooked in hangis, which was 'tino pai'.[35] Equally important, 20 cases of toheroa would arrive from New Zealand in February 1917. In the

The Regimental Butcher. IMPERIAL WAR MUSEUM

meantime routine work continued 'We are messing along in the mud and fog, patching roads and trenches and cleaning out ditches and building breastworks and barbed wire entanglements to annoy Fritz if he comes here in the Summer.'[36]

The Pioneers endured and looked forward to going home. King wrote:

> Our Regimental Butcher, Pura, is an old chap and a regular old-time Maori who has visions and dreams, etc. The other day he was not well — had sciatica or something — so Buck went along to see him.
>
> He said he was very glad to see Buck, as [he] wanted to tell him of a vision that had come to him — said that the spirits of many people came to him during the night and that the spirit of the Colonel [King, the Commanding Officer] frequently came to him.
>
> In the last dream he was in the front line trench with the Colonel and many others (all spirits) when a man from the German line came over and asked for terms of peace.
>
> Then the spirit of the Colonel stood up and said, 'When you have given back all the land that you have taken and repaid all the money which has been spent and paid for all the blood that has been spilt, then I will stay my hand and only then. If there is a Chief among you big enough to accept these terms, then there will be peace.'
>
> The German returned to his lines to see about the terms and after a time he returned carrying something in his hand — he stood in front of the spirit of the Colonel and started to pull this thing out (like a concertina). He stretched it to the full extent of his arms and then started to let it close again, and something told him (Pura) that if it came back to its original size then there would be peace. However it was only about half shut when it broke in pieces and fell from the German's hand and he returned to his trench.[37]

King recorded that Pura 'was greatly troubled by this dream and wanted Buck to interpret it for him, which, however, he couldn't do, so the old chap is waiting for another vision to come'.

Peace was two years in the future and King would not see it.

CHAPTER SEVEN

THE PIONEERS IN 1917

The year 1917 saw the growing strength of Maori numbers in the Pioneer Battalion with 'A', 'C' and 'D' companies Maori and 'B' now the single Pakeha company. King wrote about his 'menagerie' of a battalion: 'We have got Pakehas, Maoris, Rarotongans, Niueans, Fijians and Samoans here already, not to mention an odd Tahitian, and it's too much of a good thing, so have asked for only Maoris in future — the others arn't much good.'[39]

The climate was proving too tough for the other Pacific Islanders and they were gradually all returned to New Zealand. The Rarotongans, however, went to Sinai and Palestine where they gave excellent service.

Long-serving senior non-commissioned officers, including Sergeant-Majors P H Mete Kingi, T Roto-a-Tara, and R J Kemp, were commissioned to fill the officer establishment.

The New Zealanders moved north to prepare for the attack on Messines, and the Pioneers went with them, building the hutted camps, the bomb-proof dug-outs on Hill 63 facing Messines and putting down the light railways to bring forward stores and ammunition for the attack. The move had its frustrations, and King wrote: 'I don't know why it should be so, but every section we take over seems to be in a rotten state through idleness of the previous people, and we only just get time to straighten things up when we move again.'[40]

The approach of summer made up for poor billets and German shelling:

There is a nightingale in the bush just across the road from us who sings all night, but he is a very much over-rated bird and makes a noise much like a blackbird — any tui with a cold could sing him out of business in half an hour.[41]

In the New Zealand attack on the town of Messines on 7 June 1917, the Pioneers were tasked with linking the newly captured Messines Ridge to the existing front line by digging communication trenches, as they had done on the Somme, and also extending the light railway lines onto the new position. King wrote of his battalion's achievements:

I started out my crowd about 7 a.m. digging two communication trenches from our old front line to the new one past Messines and running a tram line forward for ammunition stores and water and to bring out the wounded.

One job got hung up owing to shelling but the other two were pushed on straight away and by evening we had two trenches and the tram into Fritz's old second line and nearly half way to our new front line.[42]

It was done despite heavy shelling and casualties. The battalion had 17 men killed, 88 wounded, 45 gassed, and five known exhaustion cases — a total of 155. Nevertheless, it completed 5,000 yards of trench digging and considerable distances of light railway lines. At the end of June the men were pulled out of the line to rest. As King noted in the war diary: 'No work for anyone and a damn good job.'[43]

He roa te wa ki
  Tipirere
He tino mamao
He roa te wa ki
  Tipirere
Ki taku kotiro
E noho Pikatiri
Hei kona Rehita
  Koea
He mamao rawa
  Tipirere
Ka tae ahau

It is an old friend in new guise, and the last word of the first line will tell you that it is none other than 'Tipperary', But what is the tongue that it is sung in, and what of the men that sing it.[38]

Te Hokowhitu A Tu

OPPOSITE ABOVE: The New Zealand Division training for the attack on Messines.
QUEEN ELIZABETH II ARMY MEMORIAL MUSEUM

OPPOSITE BELOW: The Pioneers playing 'bingo' or 'housie', the only gambling legally allowed in the British Armies in France.
ALEXANDER TURNBULL LIBRARY

RIGHT: 'You can't do anything without getting your photo taken.' The Maori Pioneer Battalion.
ALEXANDER TURNBULL LIBRARY

BELOW: A formal afternoon tea for members of the Maori Contingent with King George V looking on.
ALEXANDER TURNBULL LIBRARY

Te Hokowhitu A Tu

Reinforcements, Wanganui and West Coast (North Island) Platoons, Maori Pioneer Battalion
BACK ROW: N Taiaroa, H Tangiuru, N Potaka, R Tamakehu, H Erueti, D Te Huna, K Te Huia
THIRD ROW: Kahukura, T Hiri, P Timoti, Rangi (the bugler), W Rangitauira, C Tawhati, D Tonihi,
P Haami, Tom Kingi, R Wheato, T Kaiwhare
SECOND ROW: W Taputoro, K Huirua, R Marumaru, T Te Hina, P Katene, A Phillips
SEATED: Rangi Pokiha, Pirihira Kingi, R Tapa, R Tuatini, Mrs Tuatini, Lieutenant H Omana,
Sergeant J Omana, B Stubbings, Hori Tinirau

This photograph was taken at Wanganui in about 1917. The above names were obtained from a copy of the photograph displayed in the marae hall on the Koriniti Marae, Whanganui River. The photograph had been placed there by Mr Rangi Pokiha, a veteran of the Pioneer Battalion, and elder of the Ngati Pamoana tribe of Koriniti. Mr Rangi Pokiha was my grandfather, having adopted my father. Mr Pokiha was the last surviving member of this group, and he died in Wanganui, in February 1980, aged 84 years. My Great Grand Uncle, Tom Kingi (third row) was the only other long surviving member who predeceased Pokiha in the late 1970s. Pirihira Kingi, a sister of Tom Kingi, was my Great Grandmother. There were two brothers in the group, the Omanas in the front row.
(Account by Major Shayne R Gilbert, RNZIR New Zealand Army)
F J DENTON COLLECTION, ALEXANDER TURNBULL LIBRARY

'My crowd have already landed two Military Crosses, one Meritorious Service Medal and five Military Medals for the last stunt, and more to come, so we are really not doing so badly for a mob of navvies.'[44]

In July 1917 the Pioneers, along with the 3rd New Zealand Rifle Brigade, were attached to the First French Army to assist in digging in positions and telephone cable for the French artillery brigades:

Major Peter Buck escorts Sir Walter Long, Secretary of State for Colonies, on an inspection of a Pioneer Battalion guard on 9 March 1917. NZ FILM ARCHIVE

When we came here first everyone thought we were Yanks because of our hats — they had never seen a Colonial before.

Our boys are getting very friendly with the other troops round here and their language is getting more mixed every day — It's quite a common thing to hear a man use three or four languages in the one sentence at any time and now it's getting worse.[45]

The sector was quiet and the men worked well. It was the single close contact with the *poilu* during the war. The French Army commander, General Anthoine, inspected the battalion and promised that the two Pioneers, Privates C T Richards and Puia Tamihana, wounded when they were with the French, would receive the Croix de Guerre, and they did. The Pioneers also enjoyed working with the French farmworkers, now mostly women and old men, in the fields of potatoes and grain. It was a welcome touch of home.

CHAPTER EIGHT

THE NEW ZEALAND (MAORI) PIONEER BATTALION

> We are completing the Pioneer Battalion with a 4th Maori Company of Maoris, which will make it an entirely Maori Unit, and the Maoris are very anxious that this fact should be recognized by altering its designation and calling it 'The New Zealand Maori Pioneer Battalion', which I think will be only a fitting tribute to the Maori Race.
> MAJOR-GENERAL SIR ANDREW RUSSELL[46]

On 27 August 1917 Lieutenant-Colonel King was transferred to command the 1st Battalion Canterbury Regiment. His last task was to arrange for 'B' Company, the last Pakeha company in the Pioneer Battalion, to be posted to other units in the Division. There were enough Maori reinforcements to fill all four companies, and as the infantry battalions urgently needed reinforcements most of the Pakeha veterans in 'B' Company went there, though some rejoined the Mounted Rifles. As Captain F M Twisleton, the 'B' Company commander, noted, the rearrangements finally broke up those Otago Mounteds who had been part of the Pioneers since its beginning. Twisleton was among those who rejoined the Mounted Rifles in Palestine and he would be killed there. The Otago Mounted Rifles never published a regimental history of the First World War; however, for 18 months its members were an integral part of the Pioneer Battalion and King's thoughts mirrored their own: 'I am feeling rather sad about leaving this crowd, as they are a very fine lot of boys in spite of making me wild sometimes, and have worked very hard for me.'[47]

Four days later, on 1 September 1917, the battalion became a full Maori unit and as Cowan wrote: 'the old name was restored — the New Zealand (Maori) Pioneer Battalion, and the proud badge was re-adopted.'[48]

On the day that the New Zealand (Maori) Pioneer Battalion was formed it was trekking out of the Messines sector after a prolonged period of hard work and casualties. On 14 September 1917 the New Zealand Division paraded before the Commander-in-Chief, Field Marshal Sir Douglas Haig, and a surviving film shows the Pioneers parading as a complete Maori unit for the first time since the original contingent arrived in Egypt in March 1915.

Lieutenant-Colonel C G Saxby replaced King as commanding officer. Badge collecting was the rage, and the unit badge was in short supply. Routine orders stressed that:

'Men are to be warned that on no account are they to part with their badges and any man found without the badges will be charged under Section 24[2] of the Army Act and ordered to suffer stoppage of pay to replace the badges at the rate of 5/- per set in addition to such other punishment as may be deemed necessary.'[49]

Five shillings was a day's pay for a soldier and as each man usually made an allotment of 2/- a day, the badge swopping craze that the New Zealanders indulged in could become an expensive exercise if caught.

October 1917 saw the Maori Battalion working before Passchendaele in the mud and swamps of Gravenstafel and below Belle Vue Spur. It was a botched battle in which wounded men died of gas gangrene from lying out for days in the mud or drowned as the shell holes filled with rain. The Pioneers tried to keep the roads open by laying planks to give the guns purchase, but this, like Passchendaele itself, was a lost cause. Teams of Pioneers a hundred strong would drag the gun teams forward as horses sank up to their bellies in the mud. Exhausted men would slump down grey-faced and sleep in the rain, and the captured German pillboxes that dotted the slopes became islands of sanctuary in a vast desolate ocean of mud. After the failed New Zealand attack of 12 October the men of the battalion recovered the body of their former Commanding Officer, Lieutenant-Colonel George King, killed by British supporting artillery fire. On 14 October 1917 they buried him in front of the battered ramparts of Ypres:

I do not think I will ever forget that service, a cloudless sky and an aeroplane scrap overhead, the shallow grave, the body sewn in a blanket and covered with the New Zealand flag, the surpliced Padre, the short impressive burial service and finishing up with the beautiful Maori lament for a fallen chief, 'Piko nei te Matenga' ['When our heads are bowed with woe'] sung by the Maoris present, and with its beautiful harmonies and perfect tune, it seemed to me the most feeling tribute they could offer.[50]

The area around Ypres known as the Salient remained the home of the battalion through the Christmas of 1917. But there was time out of the line, and before Christmas came the battalion sports which featured the mules in the New Zealand Pioneer Grand National Steeplechase: 'No spurs or whips were allowed. C Company's "Pioneer Stew" led the field to the turn, where he was challenged by D Company's crack mule "Pork and Beans" which after a desperate finish won by a head.'[51]

At the end of 1917 the battalion was 928 strong. The last of the Rarotongans left in January to join the Rarotongan Company in Palestine, and in the same month, Major Peter Buck was transferred to the Medical Corps. This was a hard parting, for he had been identified as kaumatua, and with Padre Wainohu had sustained the spirit of the unit.

Experience had hardened the battalion, knitting the men together in a way that only happens in war. Rules were dictated by the practicalities of what would keep them alive. Losing one's way at night in the wastes of the Salient was always a problem but routine orders directed that the 'practice of carrying blazing sticks of cordite about at night as torches is dangerous, it must be discontinued at once'. This was ignored, as was a directive forbidding non-commissioned officers and soldiers to carry revolvers. A Luger or Mauser pistol was every man's dream, and the only safe place to carry it was on one's person. In 1918 it could be dangerous getting into an argument with Maori Pioneer veterans in the estaminets, as most were armed:

Complaints have been received from neighbouring divisions that the troops of this Division have been in the habit of entering their Areas . . . [and] behaved in a most unbecoming manner by getting drunk and using filthy and obscene language. They have broken into cafes, and jeered at cavalrymen for being so far behind the Line.[52]

Te Hokowhitu A Tu

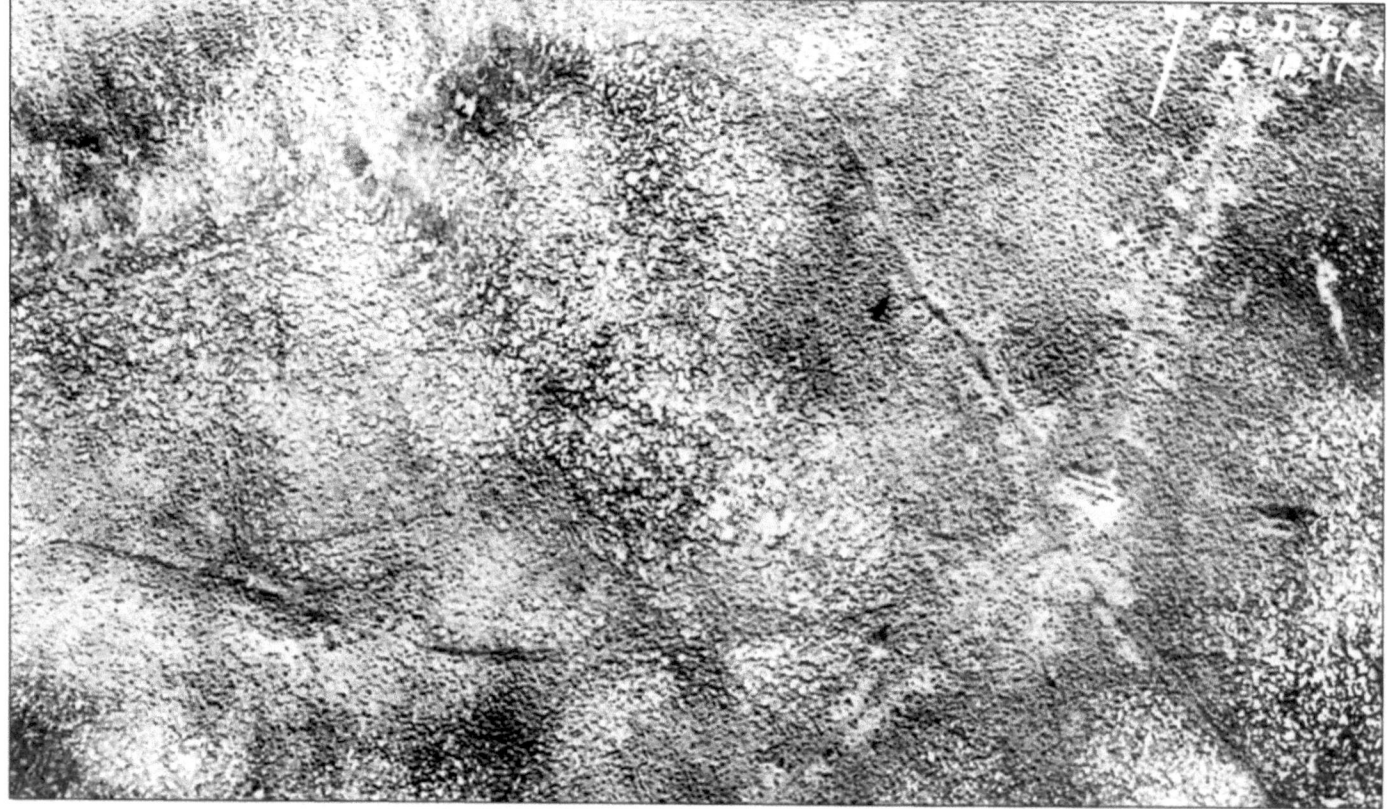

OPPOSITE: Passchendaele, before (above) and after (below).
QUEEN ELIZABETH II ARMY MEMORIAL MUSEUM

ABOVE: 'Piko nei te Matenga' — 'When our heads are bowed with woe'. The burial of Lieutenant-Colonel G A King, Ypres, 14 October 1917.
QUEEN ELIZABETH II ARMY MEMORIAL MUSEUM

RIGHT: The anti-aircraft guard of the Maori Pioneer Battalion.
ALEXANDER TURNBULL LIBRARY

TE RORU  HONORE.

I mate turoro.—Prvt. K. Auwha.
Taotu kei nga Hohipera.—Taumaha, Prvts. J. Hakaraia, A. Pene, R. Horomona, K. Harehuru, Lieut. K. Ehau. Ahua pai, Prvts. H. Tehau, R. W. Kanara, J. H. Paraone, J. W. Tepene, W. Hohepa, Corp. L. Kepa.

Reta a Henare Wainohu ki te Pihopa.

I TE Hui Topu i tu nei ki Omaahu, tera tetahi motini e ki ana:

"Kia puta atu he mihi ma tenei hui ki te minita e mahi mai ra i roto i nga hoia Maori i te marae o te pakanga, a kia riro hoki mana e whakaputa atu ki a tatou tamariki hoia ta tatou mihi ki a ratou, me te pumau hoki o tatou ngakau ki te inoi ki te Atua kia manaakitia ratou i a ratou mahi pai ki to ratou Kingi me to ratou whenua.

"Kia tukua atu e te Pihopa tenei motini ki te minita o nga hoia Maori.

"Kia puta ano hoki he mihi aroha ma tenei hui ki nga whanaunga o nga mea kua mate i roto i tenei whawhai.

Kua tae tenei motini ki nga parepare o Wiwi, a tenei hoki te whakahoki mai a Wepiha i tuku mai ai ki te Pihopa o Waiapu:

Ki taku Ariki Pihopa.

KO to reta aroha i tuhia mai nei e koe i te 26 o nga ra o Aperira, nonanahi nei ka tae mai ki a au. Nui atu taku koa mo te taenga mai o to reta ki ahau, me taku whakamihi ki nga kupu o te motini i pāhitia nei e te Hui Topu i tu nei ki Omaahu i te 23 o nga ra o Aperira. E mihi atu ana ki nga mema o te Hui Topu mo ta ratou manaaki me to ratou aroha kia 'matou ko aku hoa apiha me nga hoia kua whakaritea nei ko ahau hei matua mo ratou. Ka nui to matou koa mo te kupu whakaatu mai kei te inoi tonu koutou mo matou. He oranga ngakau mo matou tena kupu kei te inoi koutou mo matou. Ka nui te pai me te kaha o nga tamariki Maori e noho atu nei. Ki taku titiro nui atu nga painga kua puta atu ki te iwi Maori i runga i nga ahuatanga maha o tenei whawhai. He nui nga akoranga pai kua homai ki ahau me aku tamariki, akoranga kaore nei e mau mai i a matou ahakoa tae ki te 100 nga tau e noho ana i Niu Tirani na. Katahi tonu matou ka hoki mai i te whawhai i Messines. Na matou ara na Niu Tirani te taone o Messines i riro mai ai. Kaore i nui rawa o matou i matemate, engari te Tiamana he parekura nui rawa. Mo te mihi mai mo te honore moku e kiia nei ko te Ekara Ma (White Eagle) kaore ahau e mohio ana he aha te take i homai ai taua honore moku i te mea kei te mahi tonu ahau i nga mahi e tika ana hei whakahaere maku me taku awhina haere i te Hokowhitu a Tu. Kaore ahau e mahi ana mo tetahi honore moku. Ko aku tamariki ke kei te mahi nui a mo matou tahi tenei

A sample page from the 'Kahiti', showing a roll of honour and a letter.

Laying plank roads through the mud.
QUEEN ELIZABETH II ARMY MEMORIAL MUSEUM

Rugby football was a consuming passion, as it was in every New Zealand unit. The unit diary notes that in the battalion intercompany rugby the Maori side defeated the Pakeha 50–3. Four members of the Pioneers, Company Sergeant Major Rogers, Sergeants F Barclay, B Geary and Private P Tapsell were chosen for the divisional trials in February 1918, and Geary was selected for the divisional side that played a French Army selection in Paris. Success in rugby was as important to the Division as success in battle, and the haka was an integral part of the challenge. The divisional team made a final tour of France in late 1918, and the film of the game against a French selection at the Parc de Prince in Paris shows a young Maori soldier in New Zealand uniform walking onto the field to lead the footballers in the traditional haka to start a game that New Zealand won.

CHAPTER NINE

DIGGING TO VICTORY

A battle is only the culminating point of a long laborious series of working operations, and the best man for the job is the bushman, he can do quickly and efficiently any kind of engineering work.
CAPTAIN FRANCIS M TWISLETON

The year of the German Push was 1918. At the beginning of March, Captain P Tahiwi wrote: 'We have not had a spell yet — it seems as if we're here for the season. "No rest for the wicked" eh? However, we are still carrying on as usual and keeping the big war going.'[53]

As part of the New Zealand Division, the Pioneers were rushed to the Somme in late March where they laid kilometre on kilometre of barbed wire between the hastily evacuated French villages. As Lieutenant-Colonel C G Saxby complained:

> . . . have since been deluged with claims for the frightful excesses our men did not commit . . . One platoon, though accused of consuming between 2 a.m. and 8 a.m. 10 bags of flour, 2000 kilos of potatoes, 200 kilos of grain, and all a French gentleman's furniture, did not show any excessive corpulence, while it was a mystery what another platoon had done with 1,000 francs worth of straw they were accused of annexing as bedding.[54]

The accusations may have been exaggerated but the 'Walkers' or 'Henares' as they were known in the Division were not completely blameless. Saxby, their Commanding Officer, took a certain pride in their initiative when it came to salvage, noting on one occasion in 1918 that 'the boys got busy pinching iron from the very irate Tommies, and were soon coming in from all directions with sufficient material to house twice their number'.[55]

Souveniring was a New Zealand trait, and one that was constantly decried in routine orders: 'All ranks are forbidden to remove from German prisoners any personal belongings, including watches and other jewellery, iron crosses, money, identity discs, pay books, and articles of personal clothing.' Even the excuse that the items were gifts of gratitude for taking their owner prisoner was not seen as valid.[56]

Keeping the roads open, bridge repair and crater filling were the tasks of the Pioneers during the advance in the Summer of 1918. The Maori Battalion, at 900 men, was stronger than any equivalent Dominion infantry battalion, and by November 1918 it was difficult for some British and Australian brigades to muster this bayonet strength in the four infantry battalions of a brigade. The New Zealand Division also maintained its strength in the last year of the war.

In New Zealand the government had introduced conscription with the 1916 Military Service Act, and extended it to include Maori in June 1917. This was not made necessary because of any lack of numbers within the battalion in France. From 1917 onwards numbers

ABOVE: The Pioneer cookhouse.
RSA COLLECTION, ALEXANDER TURNBULL LIBRARY

RIGHT: Mealtime in the frontline trench within 250 yards of the enemy, the New Zealand faces a mix of Maori and Pakeha. La Signy Farm, 6 April 1918.
RSA COLLECTION, ALEXANDER TURNBULL LIBRARY

were not a problem; rather it was a response to the wishes of Te Arawa, Ngati Porou, and Nga Puhi, tribes who resented that the Waikato were not doing their share.

For the Maori Pioneer Battalion, the war ended in triumph and frustration. On 4 November 1918 the New Zealanders surrounded and captured the old fortified town of Le Quesnoy, Brigadier-General Herbert Hart noted in his diary that one Maori soldier had got tired of being a Pioneer and joined one of the battalions of the New Zealand Rifle Brigade in the assault on the town walls.

When Le Quesnoy surrendered after the New Zealanders had entered the town, the German Imperial Standard flying from the Town Hall was replaced by a Union Jack, and it is fitting that it was one of the consecrated flags of the Maori Pioneer Battalion, presented by the Maori school children of Otaki and Levin, that was raised on the flagstaff. This was one of three flags presented to the Pioneer Battalion: the school children had presented two and the other had been presented by the Ngai Tahu people of Kaiapoi for use on the triumphal march into Berlin. The flags had been held for safekeeping at Divisional headquarters, and it was time one at least was unfurled over Le Quesnoy. The Maori Pioneer Battalion would never march through Berlin, but to the townspeople of Le Quesnoy the New Zealanders had triumphed.

As part of the New Zealand Division, the Pioneers were to join the Rhine Garrison and they trekked towards the German frontier in the last weeks of December 1918. Everyone wanted to go home; the thought of garrisoning Germany was not a popular one, but the job had to be done. On 20 December 1918 the battalion reached the German frontier, where it was to entrain for Cologne the next day. Instead, it was halted and told by the New Zealand Divisional Commander, Sir Andrew Russell, that the move to Germany for the Maori Pioneers had been cancelled and the battalion was to go home via Dunkirk. This was not a New Zealand decision but one taken by the British authorities. It seemed that with the signing of the Armistice, the old rules once again applied and native troops would not be used to garrison Germany. The men resented this attitude, but welcomed the thought of going home.

ABOVE: Sir Joseph Ward and Hemi light up, France 1918. NZ FILM ARCHIVE
BELOW: Mr William Massey, the New Zealand Prime Minister, and Sir Joseph Ward receive a haka from the Pioneers. RSA COLLECTION, ALEXANDER TURNBULL LIBRARY

The New Zealand Maori Pioneer Battalion filling up a mine crater in front of the Beauvois Church, France, 15 October 1918. RSA COLLECTION, ALEXANDER TURNBULL LIBRARY

New Zealanders at the 'Tote' at the horse races during a break from the front, Louvencourt, 30 July 1918. ALEXANDER TURNBULL LIBRARY

TURE WHAKARITE MAHI HOIA, 1916.
MILITARY SERVICE ACT, 1916.

REHITATANGA I NGA MAORI HEI HOIA.
ENROLMENT OF MAORIS.

PANUITANGA.
NOTICE.

KO nga tane Maori katoa kei waenganui i te 20 me te 46 tau te pakeke tenei ka whakahaua kia haere atu ki te teihana pirihimana tutata ki o ratou kainga kia tuhituhia ratou ki roto ki te rehita o te Rahui Ope Hoia o Niu Tireni mo te Pakanga i mua mai o te 20 o nga ra o Pepuere, 1918.

Ko te whiu—E rima tekau pauna, e toru marama ranei ki te herehere.

Kua whakaturia nga Apiha Pirihimana katoa hei Apiha Rehita, a kua whakamanaia ratou hei tuhituhi ki roto ki te rehita i nga Maori katoa e noho ana i roto i o ratou takiwa kua rite nga tau mo te mahi hoia.

Ki te nuku tetahi Maori Tangata Rahui ki tetahi atu kainga noho ai me tere tonu tana whakaatu ki te Kaitatau a te Kawanatanga (Government Statistician), Poneke, kei te nuku ia ki tetahi atu kainga; ko nga whooma (forms) mo taua mahi kei nga poutapeta katoa e takoto ana.

Ko te whiu—E rua tekau pauna.

He mea whakahau.

MALCOLM FRASER,
Kai-tatau a te Kawanatanga.
Government Statistician.

Poneke,
31 o Hanuere, 1918.

ALL male Maoris between the ages of 20 and 46 are required to attend at the nearest police-station and make application for enrolment in the New Zealand Expeditionary Force Reserve on or before 20th February, 1918.

Penalty—Fifty pounds or three months imprisonment.

All Police Officers have been appointed Registration Officers, and are empowered to enrol all Maoris of military age in their respective districts.

Any Maori Reservist changing his place of abode is required to immediately notify the Government Statistician, Wellington, thereof. Forms for this purpose are provided at all post-offices.

Penalty—Twenty pounds.

By order.

MALCOLM FRASER,
Government Statistician.

Wellington,
31st January, 1918.

Troops of the Maori Pioneer Battalion doing improvement work on trenches near Gommecourt, France, 25 July 1918. ALEXANDER TURNBULL LIBRARY

There were disciplinary problems in the battalion at Rouen when an officer was shot and killed by a soldier on New Year's Eve and two soldiers were convicted of rape. Nothing seemed as it should be. Good men who deserved to see New Zealand again died of Spanish influenza, including Lieutenant-Colonel Saxby on leave in England. He was succeeded by Lieutenant-Colonel W O Ennis, a member of the original Maori Contingent.

Further disciplinary problems arose in England. In February 1919 at Sling Camp the Pioneers raided a British battalion's lines in search of beer:

A party of Maoris about 20 or 30 strong have just broken into our canteen, stolen a 36 gallon cask of Ale, and are now rolling it towards the Amesbury Road . . . Some of them have pistols and are covering their retirement down the road. Our men are very much disturbed and are turning out.[57]

The British battalion drew arms and ammunition out of the armoury and a running fight ensued with two British soldiers wounded. This was a raid in the old style, even if it did nothing for relationships with neighbouring units. Finally, after months of frustration, the battalion sailed on the *Westmoreland* in March 1919.

CHAPTER TEN

THE RETURN

Toia mai
Te waka
Kumea mai
Te waka
Ki te urunga
Te waka
Ki te moenga
Te waka
Ki te takotoranga
I takoto ai
Te waka

Oh haul away
The war canoe!
Oh hither draw
Our grand canoe!
To the resting
  place,
To the sleeping
  place,
To the abiding
  place —
Our great canoe.
Oh haul away!
For home comes
  our canoe!

Toia Mai

The New Zealand (Maori) Pioneer Battalion was the only battalion of the New Zealand Expeditionary Force to return to New Zealand as a complete unit, and its welcome was the welcome that the New Zealand Division never received because it came home shipload by shipload. The Pioneers paraded through Auckland to a tumultuous reception. A Hui Aroha was held in the Auckland Domain and everywhere the battalion was fêted. Similar welcomes were held in Rotorua and Gisborne. Te Hokowhitu a Tu had come home, and before the battalion dispersed to a hundred maraes and towns, a Maori Pioneer rugby team toured New Zealand in 1919 for a series of provincial games. The war canoe and its crew had returned.

The soldiers of the New Zealand Expeditionary Force had discovered the Maori were like themselves, with all the strengths and weaknesses that make New Zealanders New Zealanders. But this was not recognised at home, where few understood the real achievements of the New Zealand Division. They did not recognise the strength of the bonds that had been forged among its members in those years overseas, nor did they see the Maori Pioneer Battalion for what it was: an outstanding unit, not easy to command but responsive to good leadership. Its reputation has been overshadowed by its successor in the Second World War, the 28th Maori Battalion, yet the second built on the spirit and experience of the first. Each was only as good as its leadership at the time. Each was important in forcing a recognition of Maori worth on a complacent and unresponsive Pakeha society.

Armistice celebrations, Levin, 13 November 1918.
ADKIN COLLECTION, ALEXANDER TURNBULL LIBRARY

The Return

The reception for the Maori Battalion at the Gisborne racecourse.
AUCKLAND PUBLIC LIBRARY

Putiki Pa, scene of the Wanganui welcome to the returned Maori Battalion.
AUCKLAND PUBLIC LIBRARY

The cost of war: New Zealanders in the Kia Ora Club, Brockenhurst.
QUALIS ALBUM, QUEEN ELIZABETH II ARMY MEMORIAL MUSEUM

An English churchyard and the names of New Zealand dead.
ALEXANDER TURNBULL LIBRARY

A total of 2,227 Maori and 458 Pacific Islanders served with the unit in its various guises from First Maori Contingent to Maori Pioneer Battalion: 336 died on active service and 734 were wounded. The numbers of Pakeha who served with the battalion from February 1916 to September 1917 are not known but are numbered in the hundreds. After the war, the temporary wooden crosses that marked the New Zealand grave sites in France and Flanders were replaced by stone headstones etched with the Silver Fern. All those who served with the Pioneers in France, both Maori and Pakeha, were retrospectively identified as being part of the New Zealand (Maori) Pioneer Battalion. It is fittingly so. As Lieutenant-Colonel King said, for most of its life the battalion was a 'menagerie' of a unit comprising men of different races and social backgrounds who, brought together in the waste and tragedy of war, came to see each other as New Zealanders.

The Prince of Wales decorating members of the Maori Pioneer Battalion, Rotorua, 1920.
RAMSDEN PAPERS, ALEXANDER TURNBULL LIBRARY

CHAPTER ELEVEN

THE KING'S COLOUR OF THE NEW ZEALAND (MAORI) PIONEER BATTALION

> His Majesty the King has been graciously pleased to approve of the Presentation of a silk Union Flag to . . . each Battalion of Overseas Troops . . . which has served abroad during the War. . . these Flags which will represent the King's Colour, are to be consecrated and to be granted all the salutes and compliments authorized to be paid to Colours.
> ARMY COUNCIL INSTRUCTION NO. 444 OF 1919

Thirteen silk Union Jacks came to New Zealand in 1919 and were distributed to the senior surviving officers of the three battalions of the Auckland, Wellington, Canterbury and Otago Regiments and to the New Zealand (Maori) Pioneer Battalion. Each flag was to be embroidered with the unit's name and number. This was done for all the infantry battalions and the colours were presented, dedicated and then laid up for safekeeping in cathedrals and museums throughout the country.

The last Commanding Officer of the Pioneer Battalion, Lieutenant-Colonel W O Ennis DSO, was living in Westport and agreed to arrange for the embroidering of the battalion's flag, but he died in an accident in Auckland in 1926 before anything was done. In 1939 his widow passed the flag into the care of the Army Department, which in 1946 deposited it in the Dominion Museum, where it remained forgotten.

The King's colour was not the first flag the Pioneer Battalion received. As mentioned earlier, Ngai Tahu of Kaiapoi had presented a flag that they asked be used on the triumphal march to Berlin. The district nurse at Otaki, a Nurse Lewis, had also organised the Maori children of Otaki and Levin to raise money for an ambulance and two flags. The flags were consecrated and sent to the battalion with the wish that they be returned to the district after the war; one was to be placed in Rangiatea church at Otaki and the other in the District High School at Levin. It was one of these flags that flew at Le Quesnoy. Both flags were eventually returned to Otaki and were presented to schools in the district, the flag presented to the people of Le Quesnoy having been replaced by another from the New Zealand government. The fate of the flag presented by Ngai Tahu of Kaiapoi is not known.

In 1988 the late Sir James Henare lamented the fact that the 28th Maori Battalion did not receive a colour and enquired whether such an award was too late. It was, but Sir James's query initiated a search for the King's colour of the Pioneer Battalion. It was assumed that the colour would be identified by the embroidered name of the battalion in the centre of the silk Union Jack, but nothing was found to match this description.

The King's Colour of the New Zealand (Maori) Pioneer Battalion

Sir Charles Bennett, last surviving Maori Commanding Officer of the 28th Maori Battalion, presents the King's Colour of the New Zealand (Maori) Pioneer Battalion to the New Zealand Army in December 1993.
BRUCE CONNEW

Veterans of the 28th (Maori) Battalion honour their predecessors, December 1993.
BRUCE CONNEW

It was only the efforts of Major Wally Fraser MBE that brought success. He carefully researched the history, description and details of the colour. Then together with Mr Michael Fitzgerald, Curator of History at the Museum of New Zealand, he examined the flags held by the museum. As Fraser records:

On my arrival [Mr Fitzgerald] produced a colour on a pike. When it was unfurled we compared it with photographs of the Wellington Regiment's colours . . . There is no doubt in my mind that the colour held by the museum is one of the 13 originally received in 1919, and is the New Zealand (Maori) Pioneer Battalion Colour deposited by Army Headquarters in 1946.[58]

The museum released the colour to the care of the New Zealand Army. Conservation advice from museum staff was obtained and the title of the battalion was embroidered on the silk of the Union Jack. In December 1993 the presentation and dedication of the flag to the New Zealand Army finally carried out King George V's directions of 1919.

There is no longer a Maori unit because Maori and Pakeha are indistinguishable as soldiers of the New Zealand Army. There is no one alive today who served with the New Zealand Pioneer Battalion. Yet, just as a book like this records their story, so their colours symbolise the spirit of the thousands of Maori and Pakeha who were Pioneers in the First World War.

The Nominal Rolls of the Maori Contingents and Reinforcements 1914–18

The names that follow are the published lists of the 31 Maori drafts that sailed from New Zealand between 14 February 1915 and 3 October 1918. The roll of the Second Maori Contingent which sailed on the SS *Waitemata* on 19 September 1915 could not be located, and was made up from the consolidated rolls which did not include individual occupations.

First	Maori Contingent,	sailed	14	February	1915
Second	"	"	19	September	1915
Third	"	"	5	February	1916
Fourth	"	"	6	May	1916
Fifth	"	"	29	July	1916

[There was no Sixth Maori Contingent or Reinforcement]

Seventh	Maori Reinforcements	"	19	August	1916
Eighth	"	"	23	September	1916
Ninth	"	"	11	October	1916
10th	"	"	15	November	1916
11th	"	"	16	November	1916
12th	"	"	2	January	1917
13th	"	"	19	January	1917
14th	"	"	16	February	1917
15th	"	"	3	April	1917
16th	"	"	26	April	1917
17th	"	"	26	April	1917
18th	"	"	12	June	1917
19th	"	"	16	July	1917
20th	"	"	26	July	1917
21st	"	"	15	August	1917
22nd	"	"	13	October	1917
23rd	"	"	17	November	1917
24th	"	"	22	November	1917
25th	"	"	31	December	1917
26th	"	"	8	February	1918
27th	"	"	3	March	1918
28th	"	"	23	April	1918
29th	"	"	9	May	1918
30th	"	"	13	June	1918
31st	"	"	17	August	1918
32nd	"	"	3	October	1918

NEW ZEALAND MAORI CONTINGENT.—NOMINAL ROLL.

Reg. No.	Rank.	Name.	Occupation.	Next-of-kin.
\multicolumn{5}{c}{HEADQUARTERS STAFF.}				
16/575	Lieut. (temp. Major)	Peacock, Henry	N.Z.S.C.	Mrs. H. Peacock, Tainui Road, Devonport.
16/582	Captain	Ennis, William Oliver	Railway Employee	Sarah Louise Ennis, care of W. H. Whittaker, Thames Street, Invercargill.
16/544	,,	Mabin, Frederick Burton	Civil Servant	Mrs. Beatrice Constance Mabin, care of J. Kelling, Nile Street East, Nelson.
16/593	..	Buck, Peter Rangihiroa (Medical Officer)	Medical Practitioner	Mrs. Margaret Buck, care of Mrs. Wilson, Manor Street, Milton.
16/545	Reverend	Wainohu, Henare (Chaplain)	Clerk in Holy Orders	Mrs. Erana Wainohu, Mohaka.
16/515	Staff S.M.	Tingey, Edward	Soldier	Mrs. Bertha Tingey, 24 Richmond Street, Ponsonby, Auckland.
16/539	Q.M. Sergt.	Hamilton-D'Arcy, Eagle	Farmer	Mrs. Vera Mary D'Arcy-Hamilton, Takapuna, Auckland.
16/514	,,	Stewart, James Douglas	Soldier	James Stewart, Hemp Expert, Department of Agriculture, Wellington.
		A COMPANY.		
16/317	Lieutenant	Dansey, Roger Ingram	Engineer	Daisy Sarah Dansey, Selkirk Street, Roslyn, Dunedin.
16/304	,,	Tahiwi, Pirimi	Schoolmaster	Rawiri Rota Tahiwi, Otaki.
16/445	2nd Lieut.	Hetet, Thomas	Clerk	Mr. H. M. Hetet, Te Kuiti.
16/392	,,	Hiroti, Turu	Civil Servant	Katarina Hiroti, Wanganui.
16/260	,,	Coupar, Simon James Stuart	Manager	James Stuart Coupar, Colac Bay.
16/390	Coy. S.M.	Eva, John	Gymnastic Instructor	Aquilla Clapshaw, Cricket-bat Merchant, London.
16/403	Coy. Q.M.S.	Mete Kingi, Paki Hoani	Farmer	Hoani Mete Kingi, Wanganui.
16/252	Sergeant	Bevan, Matthew	Chauffeur	M. Bevan, Merton.
16/262	,,	Davis, William	Sheep-farmer	Mrs. A. W. Taituha, care of Mr. J. J. Davis, Salvation Army, Blenheim.
16/322	,,	Harawira, Kahi	Linesman	Taki Moana Harawira, Te Kao, North Auckland.
16/323	,,	Heath, Arthur	Labourer	Paki Haimona, Ahipara.
16/268	,,	Jacob, Hohepa	Farmer	Hoani McMillan, Koputaroa.
16/336	,,	Leaf, Harding Waipuke	,,	Henry Leaf, Whirinaki, Hokianga.
16/338	,,	Maaka, Nikora Hohepa	Carpenter	Hohepa Maaka, Okere Falls, Rotorua.
16/420	,,	Pehimana, Ngawakataurua Tetahua	Farmer	Pehimana Tetahua, Patea.
16/386	,,	Tauri, Whetu	Clerk	Hoani Tauri, Putiki, Wanganui.
16/227	,,	Tikao, John Charles	Farmer	H. Tare Tikao, Rapaki, Lyttelton.
16/446	Corporal	Hetet, Tuheka Taonui	Carpenter	John Taonui Hetet, Te Kuiti.
16/393	,,	Karehana, Herewini	Farmer	Karehana Tauranga, Awahuri, Feilding.
16/276	,,	Lucas, Joseph	Machinist	Wiki Toria, Buller Bridge, Westport.
16/477	,,	te Moananui, Mikaera	Farmer	Tihitapu te Moananui, Paeroa.
16/409	,,	Paurini, James Waru	,,	Taiaha Paurini, Takaanu.
16/211	,,	Pohio, Henry Huru	Labourer	James Iraia Pohio, Tuahiwi, Kaiapoi.
16/191	,,	Torepe, William Himiona	,,	H. Torepe, Temuka.
16/382	,,	Wakarua, Herewini	Farmer	Mrs. Wakarua, Waitotara.
16/307	,,	te Whao, Thomas	Labourer	John te Whao, Puketeraki.
16/434	Lance-Corpl.	Angel, Richard	Farmer	William Henry Angel, Whangarei.
16/255	,,	Cameron, Edward	,,	Mrs. William Potiki, Bluff.
16/489	,,	Keepa, Kenny	,,	Kate Mohoaonui, Tokaanu.
16/455	,,	Kingi, Paani	Blacksmith	Paraki Kingi, Maraeroa, Hokianga.
16/340	,,	Manuel, Richard	Farmer	Manuel Walter, Te Kao, North Auckland.
16/383	,,	Mete Kingi, Teira Hoani	Labourer	Hoani Mete Kingi, Raetahi, Putiki, Wanganui.
16/344	,,	Morgan, Joseph Iraia	,,	Iwingaro J. Morgan, Whirinaki, Hokianga.
16/298	,,	Tahiwi, Henare Kima	Grocer	Ria Tahiwi, Otaki.
16/308	,,	Woods, George	Labourer	Thomas Woods, Puketeraki.
16/379	Bugler	Hiroti, Rangihiwinui	Farmer	Matawai Hiroti, Gonville, Wanganui.
16/463	,,	Netana, John	,,	Rihari Netana, Kihikihi.
16/486	,,	Wi, Thomas	,,	Wi Kio, Te Kuiti.
16/310	Private	Adams, James	Mill Hand	Riperi Adams, Whangape.
16/432	,,	Amohanga, Te Rohe	Farmer	Te Amohanga Hauparoa, Hangatiki.
16/583	,,	Angel, Edward	,,	W. H. Angel, Matakohe.
16/550	,,	Angel, William	Farm Labourer	W. H. Angel, Matakohe, Northern Wairoa.
16/381	,,	Aperahama, Hone	Farrier	Te Rewai Hohepa, Te Ihupuku, Waitotara.
16/250	,,	Armstrong, Alexander	Shepherd	Mrs. J. Armstrong, Otaki.
16/251	,,	Arthur, John	Labourer	D. Arthur, Waikawa, Picton.
16/305	,,	te Au, David	Fisherman	Ratimira te Au, Colac Bay.
16/311	,,	Auhana, Reweti	Labourer	J. Housham, Hohoura.
16/230	,,	Bannister, Tuhuru	,,	J. W. Bannister, Jacob's River, Bruce Bay.
16/435	,,	Barton, Whare	Farmer	Teaohau Rohutu, Tokaanu, Kihikihi.
16/389	,,	Bennett, William Rakeipoho	..	Mr. H. D. Bennett, P.O. Box 20, Taihape.
16/253	,,	Bragg, George Henry	Seaman	Mr. John Bragg, Half-moon Bay.

The Nominal Rolls of the Maori Contingents and Reinforcements 1914–1918

Reg. No.	Rank	Name	Occupation	Next-of-kin
\multicolumn{5}{c}{A COMPANY—*continued*.}				
16/313	Private	Brass, Rata	Labourer	Mere Paraihe, Ahipara.
16/594	,,	Breen, Claude Clarence	Clerk	Eunice Phœbe Breen, Coromandel.
16/522	,,	Broughton, Maurice	Labourer	Motete Paratene, Masterton.
16/314	,,	Brown, Harvey	Bushman	Mr. W. Brown, Dargaville.
16/315	,,	Busby, Haimona	None	Riapo Puhipi, Pukepoto.
16/256	,,	Carkeek, Rikihana	Clerk	Maraea Rikihana, Otaki.
16/436	,,	Cash, Henry	Miller	Ihaia Cash, Tangowahine.
16/258	,,	Cootes, David	Labourer	Mrs. Elizabeth Cootes, Otaki.
16/263	,,	Daymond, Henry	Farmer	Mr. Inia Tuwhata, Chatham Islands.
16/264	,,	Donaldson, George Thomas	Labourer	James Donaldson, Tuatapere, Otago.
16/373	,,	Duff, Matene Rangiamohia	Farmer	Mark Williams, Ngawaka, Taihape.
16/438	,,	Edwards, Charles	Drainer	Te Porana, Okauia.
16/319	,,	Edwards, Edward John	Farmer	Teddy Edwards, Whangarei.
16/265	,,	Ellison, Piri	Coachman	Hera Ellison, Waikanae.
16/439	,,	Emery, Peter	Farmer	Rangi Auraki Emery, Timawhae.
16/433	,,	Emery, Thomas	,,	Mrs. Wipaia, Kihikihi.
16/318	,,	Erueti, Aperahama	Bushman	Mr. Eru Patuone, Mangatacore, Mangonui.
16/212	,,	Flutey, Robert Henry	Labourer	Charles Flutey, Woodend.
16/587	,,	Gardiner, George	Engineer	Karehana Gardiner, Tauranga.
16/320	,,	Graham, Robert	Labourer	Ngainanga Mare, Ahipara.
16/441	,,	Grey, Daniel	Contractor	Pare Grey, Motueka.
16/442	,,	Haira, Rima	Farmer	Mikahiara Rima, Kaihu.
16/266	,,	Hapeta, Wiremu	Labourer	Utiku Hapeta, Otaki.
16/267	,,	Harding, Joseph	Fisherman	Charles Harding, Hokitika.
16/370	,,	Hare, Heremaia	Farmer	Hariata Maru, Te Kao, North Auckland.
16/581	,,	Hawkins, Henry	Labourer	John Martin Hawkins, Hastings.
16/391	,,	Hekiera, Remihana	Farmer	Hekiera Terangi, Otorohanga.
16/444	,,	Hemana, Kohi Tatana	,,	Tatana Hemana, Batley, Kaipara.
16/324	,,	Hemi, Rihari	,,	Rapana Hemi, Naumai, Northern Wairoa.
16/269	,,	Heremaia, John Hopa	,,	Mrs. Kiri Hopa, Levin.
16/325	,,	Hetaraka, Hurae	Labourer	Timoti Hetaraka, Peria, Mangonui.
16/326	,,	Hetaraka, Peretiti	Gum-digger	Hetaraka Heta, Whatuwhiwhi, Mangonui.
16/447	,,	Hika, Thomas Poutama	Farmer	Pei Hika, Kakariki, Rangitikei.
16/375	,,	Himiona, Akuhata	,,	Teone Himiona, Aorangi, Feilding.
16/448	,,	Hira, Rawiri	Bushman	Hura Waera, Coromandel.
16/532	,,	Hiroti, Jack	Chemist	Katarina Hiroti, Wanganui.
16/327	,,	Hohaia, Wiki	Farmer	Hura Hohaia, Peria, Mangonui.
16/328	,,	Hohipa, Tawi	,,	Wakarua Hohipa, Pukepoto.
16/329	,,	Hokai, Tumamao	Labourer	Hokai Puku, Whangape.
16/548	,,	Hovell, Charles Harry Pirika	Contractor	C. W. Hovell, J.P., Kennedy's Bay.
16/556	,,	Hovell, George Woodward	Clerk	C. W. Hovell, J.P., Kennedy's Bay.
16/330	,,	Howell, Hemi	Labourer	Mrs. M. Howell, Main Road, Taradale.
16/451	,,	Ihaka, Maihi	,,	Ihaka Hura, Whangape.
16/452	,,	Ihaka, Rewiri	Mill Hand	Ihaka Rewiri, Whangape.
16/240	,,	Johnson, William	Labourer	C. Johnson, Lakeside, Selwyn.
16/331	,,	Kaaka, Wahanui	Gum-digger	Tewiki Harawira, Awanui.
16/511	,,	Kaanga, Te Kuru	Farmer	Poreti Turoa, Raetihi.
16/332	,,	Kamariera, Ngarama	Labourer	Turuhira Kamariera, Huria, Mangonui.
16/395	,,	Kanapu, Tamehana	None	Kanapu Haerehuka, Springvale Road, Wanganui.
16/333	,,	Kanara, Henare	Labourer	Ripene Kanara, Awanui.
16/334	,,	Kapa, Ihaka	,,	Matiu Kapa, Kaikohe.
16/453	,,	Karati, Wiremu	Shearer	Hone Karati, Thames.
16/270	,,	Karauti, Abraham	Farmer	Horo Karauti, Ohau.
16/394	,,	Karena, Wero Mohi	Farm Labourer	Mohi Karena, Omahu.
16/271	,,	Karetai, Stewart	Labourer	Joseph Karetai, Otakou.
16/585	,,	Karetai, Sydney George	,,	Joseph Karetai, Otakou.
16/396	,,	Kerei, Hawea	Farmer	Kerei Pohiahia, Tokaanu.
16/456	,,	Kipa, Hori	Butcher	Awhimate Kipa, Kopu, Thames.
16/272	,,	Koeti, Butler	Labourer	Mary Koeti, Arahura.
16/335	,,	Koperu, John	,,	Koperu Paki, Maungatautari.
16/398	,,	Kora, Te Aurahi	,,	Kora, Aitutaki, Cook Islands.
16/380	,,	te Korowhiti, Wiremu	Gardener	Taruhae te Korowhiti, Parihaka, New Plymouth.
16/273	,,	Kotua, Hohepa Tuainani	Labourer	Mrs. H. Kotua, Croixelles.
16/399	,,	Kumeroa, Te Aohau	Farmer	Kumeroa Tetana, Parikino, Upper Wanganui River.
16/503	,,	Leef, Charlie	Carpenter	Parani Pereriwhi, Whirinaki, Hokianga.
16/502	,,	Leef, Robert	Labourer	Parani Pereriwhi, Whirinaki, Hokianga.
16/277	,,	Lucas, Robert	,,	Miss Phylis Lucas, Westport.
16/337	,,	Luke, Thomas	,,	Paharu Luke, Pukepoto.
16/339	,,	Manga, Pute	,,	Manga Pute, Rarotonga.
16/400	,,	Mangaroa, Ngore William	Student	Thompson Mangaroa, Taumarunui.
16/238	,,	Manihera, Anatipa	Farmer	James Manihera, Rapaki, Lyttelton.
16/189	,,	Manihera, Waitere	Contractor	Elizabeth Manihera, Rapaki, Lyttelton.
16/341	,,	Marsh, Manuera	None	Robert T. Marsh, Whangape.
16/241	,,	Martin, George Edward	Labourer	Mary Martin, Henley.
16/401	,,	Mateparae, Rawiri	Farmer	Manawa Wharepapa, Turangaarere, Taihape.
16/342	,,	Materoa, Poihakena	Seaman	Huihui Terakataha, Orakei.
16/460	,,	Matiu, Hone	Bushman	Heimona Matiu, Kaihu, Northern Wairoa.
16/546	,,	Matiu, Hone	,,	Iwingaro Matiu, Hokianga.
16/343	,,	Matiu, Reihana	Farrier	Kiriona Kiripini Matiu, Whatuwhiwhi.
16/543	,,	Matthew, John	Labourer	Matekitua, Te Papatapu, via Te Mata.
16/402	,,	Meihana, Paneta Otene	Wool-classer	Waengarangi Otene, Hastings.
16/385	,,	Mete Kingi, Henare	Labourer	Hoani Mete Kingi, Putiki, Wanganui.

Reg. No.	Rank.	Name.	Occupation.	Next-of-kin.
		A COMPANY—continued.		
16/278	Private	Mira, William	Labourer	Henry Mutu Mira, Otaki.
16/478	,,	te Moananui, Mutu	Farmer	Hirama te Moananui, Paeroa.
16/222	,,	Mokomoko, Nopera Hapi	Labourer	Tione Mokomoko, Tuahiwi.
16/555	,,	Moore, Sunny	Bushman	Miss Emily Moore, Parua Bay, Whangarei.
16/374	,,	Morehu, John	Farmer	Mrs. Huirangi Morehu, Waitara.
16/279	,,	Morgan, George	Labourer	Mrs. Raiha Morgan, Gisborne.
16/280	,,	Morrell, Kelly	,,	Mrs. Doris Elliott Morrell, Kaikoura.
16/281	,,	Morrell, Thomas	,,	John Morrell, Te Haumi, Oaro.
16/475	,,	Muriwai, Tame	Bushman	Muriwai Hepehi, Hokianga.
16/462	,,	Nathan, Louis	Farmer	Ruru Nathan, Maropiu.
16/404	,,	Nehemia, Hiroti	,,	Nehemia Teurumingi, Parikino, Wanganui River.
16/214	,,	Ngamuka, Hahi	Labourer	Kata Ngamuka, Porirua.
16/464	,,	Nihoniho, Henry	,,	H. Nihoniho, Waipiro Bay.
16/192	,,	Nopera, Raha	,,	Nohi Nopera, Temuka.
16/465	,,	Ormsby, William	Blacksmith	Messrs. Howarth and Arrowsmith, Solicitors, Otorohanga.
16/466	,,	Otene, Jack	Driver	Mrs. E. Thompson, Kihikihi.
16/405	,,	Otene, Rangi	Chauffeur	Pae Otene, Hastings.
16/362	,,	te Paa, Neri	Bushman	Wiki te Paa, Ripia, North Wairoa.
16/554	,,	te Paa, Richard	Coachbuilder	Mrs. K. Mutu, Naumai.
16/221	,,	Paipeta, Henare	None	Mrs. G. Paipeta, Rapaki.
16/497	,,	Paki, Jack	Farmer	Emeri Paki, Rangiotu, Palmerston North.
16/495	,,	Paki, Rangi	Carpenter	Emeri Paki, Rangiotu, Palmerston North.
16/576	,,	Paora, Raniera Ngapo	Farmer	Mrs. Louisa Ngapo Paora, Kennedy's Bay.
16/527	,,	Paora, Reihana	Ironworker	Poheri te Warutu, Mangapehi.
16/408	,,	Paora, Tauri	Farmer	Paora Tokoahu, Taupo.
16/346	,,	Para, Paki Whetu	Bushman	Whetu Para, Kaikohe.
16/407	,,	Paranihi, Tau	Settler	Wairakau Paranihi, Taumarunui.
16/282	,,	Parata, Rau	Labourer	Tata Parata, Porirua.
16/347	,,	Paratene, Mita	Blacksmith	Puti W. Paratene, Ahipara.
16/523	,,	Peke, Hautangi	Farmer	Ihipera Ahurei, Paeroa.
16/283	,,	Peneamene, Tieke	Farm Labourer	Hohepa Peneamene, Morven.
16/284	,,	Peneamene, Tumaru	,,	Hohepa Peneamene, Morven.
16/469	,,	Pera, William	Mill Hand	H. Pera, Opotiki.
16/3 2	,,	Pereka, John Haru	Farmer	Taiharuru Pereka, Te Karaka.
16/547	,,	Peri, Wiremu Tuuru	Bushfeller	Hauri Tuuru Peri, Waima, Hokianga.
16/577	,,	Pirika, Hura	Bushman	Pirika Waara, Coromandel.
16/220	,,	Pitama, Te Kirikaihau	Labourer	Hariata Pitama, Tuahiwi.
16/197	,,	Pitama, Wiremu Aata	,,	Hariata Pitama, Tuahiwi.
16/348	,,	Poa, George	Seaman	Mere Morgan, Mangakahia, Whangarei.
16/589	,,	Pohe, Thomas	Labourer	Pohe Hona, Rotorua.
16/494	,,	Pohio, Thomas	Farmer	Benjamin Pohio, Otaki Railway.
16/410	,,	Popoki, Te Ao	Bushman	Mr. Popoki Kurupae, Puketerata, Taupo.
16/287	,,	Porete, August Paani	Labourer	Paani Porete, Hillgrove.
16/388	,,	Potonga, Tame	Farmer	Kaioha Potonga, Waitotara.
16/378	,,	Rahui, Pare	Bushman	Ngapine H. Panapa, Ahikiwi, Northern Wairoa.
16/449	,,	Rangi, Horima	Farmer	Enoaka Rangi, Otorohanga.
16/232	,,	Ran in, Albert Hepi	,,	Hoani Ngapua, Kaikohe.
16/588	,,	Ransfield, Daniel	,,	Issac Ransfield, Manakau.
16/288	,,	Ransfield, Richard	,,	Haimona Ranapiri, Ohau.
16/542	,,	Ranui, Paeahi	,,	Tawehe Edwards, Kawhia.
16/540	,,	Rapana, Samuel	,,	Ngaone Toere, Waeegaehu.
16/579	,,	Rapata, Hira	Drover	Henare Natana Hira, Ahipara.
16/580	,,	Rapihana, Herewini	Farmer	Wiremu Rapihana, Pukepoto.
16/376	,,	Rata, Haki	Labourer	Te Rata, Ongarue.
16/492	,,	Rehu, Hui Kai	Fireman	Jennie Rehu, Kaiapoi.
16/558	,,	Rewha, Huirua	Farmer	Temamae Rewha, Russell.
16/352	,,	Rewiri, Taoho	Bushman	Moe Taoho, Rawene.
16/289	,,	Rickus, William	Labourer	J. Rickus, Temuka.
16/412	,,	Rikiti, Tame	Rabbiter	Joseph Rikiti, Taupo.
16/377	,,	Rikona, Hoani	Bushman	Ngakotaku Rikona, Tauranga.
16/290	,,	Roach, Howard	Law Clerk	Mrs. T. Roach, Jubilee Road, Otaki.
16/354	,,	Rogers, Augustus	Fitter	Charles Rogers, Maketu.
16/501	,,	Ropata, Jack	Farmer	Metapara Ropata, Tangahoe, Otaki.
16/291	,,	Ropata, Jerry	Labourer	Metapara Ropata, Otaki Railway.
16/199	,,	Ropata, Pahia	Engineer	Ngaruti Parata, Otaki.
16/578	,,	Rukingi, Henare	Student	Haurangi Rukingi, Ohinemutu.
16/226	,,	Ruru, Shed	Labourer	Huihana Ruru, Port Levy, Lyttelton.
16/293	,,	Ryan, George	,,	Phillip Ryan, Tuatapere, Southland.
16/170	,,	Savage, Thomas	,,	Thomas Savage, care of R. G. M. Park, Wanganui.
16/590	,,	Sidney, Thomas Philip	,,	Albert Hiki Sidney, Gisborne.
16/591	,,	Sidney, William	,,	Tuahine Haereone Sidney, Tolaga Bay.
16/294	,,	Simeon, Dick	,,	Mrs. Putiputi Simeon, Levin.
16/295	,,	Simeon, Frederick Taylor	Railwayman	Frederick P. Simeon, 77 Nairn Street, Wellington.
16/296	,,	Simeon, James Michael	Tailor	F. P. Simeon, 77 Nairn Street, Wellington.
16/471	,,	Smith, Kaa	Mill Hand	Mr. J. W. Smith, Rangiahua, Hokianga.
16/472	,,	Smith, William	Labourer	Ramari Smith, Mapuna, North Wairoa.
16/473	,,	Solomon, Rai	Farmer	Re Kanere, Otaua.
16/297	,,	Stewart, Thomas	,,	Nota Stewart, Waikanae.
16/414	,,	Stubbing, Benjamin	Labourer	Mr. F. Stubbing, Rangiwaea, Ruanui.
16/415	,,	Sullivan, Hoani	Farmer	Tahi Sullivan, Waitotara.
16/356	,,	Tahitahi, John	Bushman	Tukua Tahitahi, Ahipara.

Reg. No.	Rank	Name	Occupation	Next-of-kin
		A COMPANY—continued.		
16/357	Private	Tahitahi, Pita	Labourer	Tahitahi Tohuora, Ahipara.
16/358	,,	Tahu, Ngakapa	,,	Taimana Tahu, Te Kopuru.
16/228	,,	Tainui, Tuhuru	Engineer	I. Tainui, Arahura, Hokitika.
16/474	,,	Taka, William	Waterman	Taka, William, Mercer.
16/454	,,	Tamaki, Karena	Surveyor	Tamaki, Tamehana, Pirongia.
16/418	,,	Tamarapa, Waikohari	Cowman	Mr. Tamarapa, Ohangai.
16/359	,,	Tamihana, Rapi	Seaman	Huhana Marupo, Awanui, North Auckland.
16/419	,,	Tamou, Kimi	Farmer	Mangu Kimi Tamou, Waitotara.
16/360	,,	Taua, Matini	,,	Wiremu Hoani Taua, Whatuwhiwhi.
16/361	,,	Taumatangi, Paratene	,,	Paratene Kapa, Te Kao.
16/476	,,	Taupaki, Te Aotutahanga	Fireman	Raiha te Irikowhau, Paeroa.
16/516	,,	Tauri, William Hoani	Clerk	Hoani Tauri, Putiki, Wanganui.
16/213	,,	Tauwhare, Pita	Law Clerk	Tini Tauwhare, Mount Eden (care of C. E. Falwasser, Tendern Avenue).
16/193	,,	Teihoka, Joseph	Labourer	Mere Teihoka, Taumutu, Leeston.
16/299	,,	Thompson, Rangi	,,	Rebecca Thompson, Wanganui.
16/363	,,	Tiatoa, Pita	Bushman	Ripeka Tiatoa, Te Ahuahu, Bay of Islands.
16/417	,,	Ticketahi, Kotuku	Farmer	Ticketahi, Tawake Ariki, Waitotara.
16/364	,,	Tiini, Hopa	,,	Tiini, Heta, Peria, Mangonui.
16/303	,,	Timuiha, John	,,	Whawhai Hatana, Ohau.
16/423	,,	Toi Toi, Materepo	Labourer	Toi Toi, Tauranga.
16/480	,,	Tua, James	,,	Areta Tuatini, Hangatiki.
16/424	,,	Tua, Te Whatu	,,	Parekahungi, Maroa, Oruanui.
16/425	,,	Tukaki, Teme	Farmer	Ngarae Tukaki, Tauranga.
16/365	,,	Tuoro, Kawhena	Labourer	Hana Hotai, Otaua, Hokianga.
16/595	,,	Wade, Kiri	Farmer	
16/481	,,	Wahanui, Kohatu Hari Hemara	,,	Hari Hemara, Otorohanga.
16/488	,,	Wahanui, Thomas	,,	Hemara Wahanui, Otorohanga.
16/482	,,	Wahia, Moa	Bushman	Ani Ngarae, Matakana.
16/426	,,	Wahia, Thomas	Farmer	Wahia te Moananui, Tauranga.
16/541	,,	Waitford, Albert Victor	Chauffeur	Edward Berry Waitford, Waikaraka, Whangarei.
16/301	,,	Waiti, William	Labourer	Mr. Davis Waiti, Hitaua, Picton.
16/367	,,	Waitohi, Riwhi	Farmer	Mere Honeware, Rangiahua, Hokianga.
16/427	,,	Warahi, Rua	Settler	Tematewai Maria, Kaimananui, Taumarunui.
16/483	,,	Warren, Thomas	Bushman	Hari Taiteore, Puru, Thames.
16/368	,,	Waru, Henare	Labourer	Waru Puku, Whangape.
16/369	,,	Waru, Kopa	,,	Waru Puku, Whangape.
16/592	,,	Wellman, George Christie	Miner	Mrs. John Drummond, Henley.
16/421	,,	te Whare, Tajawhiao	Rabbiter	Mirima te Whare, Taupo.
16/384	,,	Wharemate, Turi	Labourer	Katarina Huiaiti, Opunake.
16/422	,,	te Whata, Wiremu	Rabbiter	te Whata, Wiremu, Taupo.
16/188	,,	Whitau, Puaka	Labourer	Rahera Whitau, Temuka.
16/231	,,	Whitau, Tuapaoa	,,	Rahera Whitau, Temuka.
16/485	,,	Wi, Patihana	Timber-rafter	Piri Paora, Ripia, Northern Wairoa.
16/428	,,	Wikatene, Rakateitei	Rabbiter	Rina Aramoana, Waitahuna.
16/371	,,	Wikitera, Robert	Bushman	Wikitera Reone, Whangape.
16/306	,,	Williams, James	Labourer	John William Tipene, Otakou, Otago.
16/498	,,	Wiremu, Niheta	Chauffeur	Mokai Keroru Niheta Wiremu, Pariroa, Patea.
16/487	,,	Wirihana, Ihaka	Labourer	Ihaka Hura, Whangape.
16/429	,,	Wi Rihia, Davis	Farmer	Wi Rihia, Tokaanu, Taupo.
16/430	,,	Wi Rihia, George	,,	Mr. Wi Rihia, Tokaanu.
16/431	,,	Wood, Charlie	Farrier	Raukau Hono Toka, Tauranga.
		B COMPANY.		
16/499	Captain	Pitt, William Tutepuaki	Civil Servant	Mrs. K. R. Pitt, care of W. Rogers, Ohinemutu.
16/50	Lieutenant	Ferris, James Paumea	Sheep-farmer	C. W. Ferris, jun., Wainui, Gisborne.
16/538	,,	Jones, Albert Edward Mills	Schoolmaster	Mrs. E. Jones, 3 Kingsdale Road, Moseley Hill, Liverpool, England.
16/90	,,	Stainton, William Houkamau	Teacher	W. G. Stainton, Gwavis, Tikokino.
16/10	2nd Lieut.	Kaipara, Autini Pitara	Interpreter	Monica Kaipara, Waiotapu.
16/187	Coy. S.M.	Walker, William Huatahi	Farmer	Kaneta W. Poihipi, Rotoiti, Rotorua.
16/124	Coy. Q.M.S.	te Awarau, Hatara Matehe	Student	Emma Matehe, Waipiro Bay.
16/518	Sergeant	Broughton, Edward Renata Muhunga	Land Agent	Mrs. Atiria Broughton, Fernhill, Hawke's Bay.
16/93	,,	Delamere, Heremia	Farmer	Edward Delamere, Omaio, Opotiki.
16/61	,,	te Hau, Kahu	Labourer	Pita te Hau, Muriwai, Gisborne.
16/229	,,	Hohepa, Ahore te Koari	Farmer	Pera Hohepa, Puketapu.
16/275	,,	Kingi, John Henry	Agent	Wiranima Kingi, Hastings.
16/345	,,	Ngatai, Tame	Carpenter	Puka Ngapapa, Whakarewarewa.
16/107	,,	Puha, Waiheke	Farmer	Heromia Puha, Te Araroa.
16/62	,,	Rukingi, Waretini	Student	Pinenga Rukingi, Rotorua.
16/161	,,	Vercoe, Henry Rae	Surveyor's Assistant	Mrs. Aver Vercoe, Ohinemutu, Rotorua.
16/155	,,	Wi Hapi, Aritaku	Engineer	Wi Hapi Tekoata, Te Puke.
16/243	Corporal	Hawkins, Friday Patric	Carpenter	Robert N. Hawkins, 106 Victoria Street, Hastings.
16/147	,,	Kahukore, Charlie	Labourer	Heni Erwana, Owhata, Rotorua.
16/110	,,	Kohere, Tawhai	Farmer	Henarata Kohere, Te Araroa.
16/66	,,	Ngamoki, Paora Whareparoa	Compositor	Paora Ngamoki, Omaio, Opotiki.
16/28	,,	Paku, Akuhata	Painter	Mrs. Whare Carroll, care of Lady Carroll, Gisborne.
16/247	,,	Paraone, Wi	Farm Labourer	W. Paraone, Te Oreore, Masterton.

Reg. No.	Rank.	Name.	Occupation.	Next-of-kin.
\multicolumn{5}{c}{B COMPANY—continued.}				
16/154	Corporal	Poata, Tupu	None	Pipi Poata, Whakarewarewa.
16/184	,,	Raponi, Hone Tatarani	Chauffeur	Terangi Katukua, Whakarewarewa.
16/204	,,	Rimeni, Tipi	Labourer	Witinitara Rimeni, Te Oreore, Masterton.
16/224	Lance-Corpl.	Hakiwai, Hoani	None	Peni Hakiwai, Omahu, Fernhill.
16/517	,,	Hakopa, Kotuku Horima	Farmer	Tukino Hakopa, Moawhango, Taihape.
16/96	,,	Hale, Maku	Labourer	Sonny Richmond Hale, Tuparoa.
16/18	,,	McAndrew, Joseph	Law Clerk	J. I. McAndrew, Wairoa, Hawke's Bay.
16/86	,,	Merito, Topia	Saddler	Merito Hetaraka, Whakatane.
16/165	,,	O'Gallaghan, Tai	Labourer	Ngawara Tamihana, Te Puke.
16/32	,,	Pewhairangi, Pare	Student	Mangaone Pewhairangi, Waipiro Bay.
16/49	,,	Thompson, James	Labourer	Te Hereaikaha Teao, Tolaga Bay.
16/145	,,	Whareraupo, Tuakanakore	,,	T. Whareraupo, Rotoiti, Rotorua.
16/4	Bugler	Halbert, William	Shepherd	Thomas Halbert, Manutuke.
16/75	,,	Paenga, Remana	Sheep-farm Cadet	Hira Paenga, Whangara, Gisborne.
16/246	,,	Pineaha, Watarawi	Farm Hand	Pineaha Mokihi, Fernhill, Hawke's Bay.
16/130	,,	Rotohiko, Amahia Kingi	Tailor	Te Rinui Rangiriri, Ohinemutu.
16/156	Private	Ahomiro, Arapeta	Farmer	Ahomiro Ngakuku, Te Puke.
16/562	,,	Ahuriri, Etera	Mechanic	Rukeruke Ahuriri, Wairoa, Hawke's Bay.
16/128	,,	Akapita, Mekiora	Labourer.	Ngamihi Mekiora, Akapita, Ohinemutu.
16/195	,,	Akuhata, Orihau	,,	Hikowera Akuhata, Hastings.
16/210	,,	Anaru, Hiko	,,	Wetini Anaru, Tangoio, Napier.
16/87	,,	Aramakutu, Herewini	,,	Mrs. Anderson, Omaio, Opotiki.
16/512	,,	te Awarau, Hori Karaka	Student	Emma Matehe, Waipiro Bay.
16/142	,,	te Awekotuku, Kiri	Labourer	H. K. te Kiri, Te Ngae, Rotorua.
16/524	,,	Baker, Whare	,,	Jack Baker, Waipiro Bay.
16/69	,,	Bristowe, Edward	,,	Kiri Bristowe, Karetu.
16/111	,,	Bristowe, Joe	,,	Mr. D. Bristowe, Hicks Bay.
16/572	,,	Carroll, Tuahae	,,	Mo Pohatu, Gisborne.
16/567	,,	Christie, Hapi	,,	William Christie, Te Karaka.
16/509	,,	Delaney, Roy	Station Hand	Beatrice Delaney, Te Karaka.
16/143	,,	Devon, Roy	Labourer	Charles Devon, Maketu.
16/508	,,	Downes, Albert	Station Hand	Henry Downes, sen., Kohukohu.
16/206	,,	Elers, Rangi	Jockey	Eti Elers, Masterton.
16/519	,,	Ferris, Donald	Sheep-farmer	C. W. Ferris, Gisborne.
16/173	,,	Franks, Samuel Osman	Labourer	William Franks, Rotorua.
16/138	,,	Fraser, John	Farmer	Atareta Tihini Fraser, Te Ngae, Rotorua.
16/120	,,	Gerrard, Harry	Labourer	C. Gerrard, Tuparoa.
16/65	,,	Grace, Abraham Turei	,,	Hamiora Grace, Tuparoa.
16/2	,,	Grant, Rawiri	,,	Jim Grant, Port Awanui.
16/168	,,	Haerehuka, Tiare	,,	Ani te Paerakau Tamairangi, Rotoiti, Rotorua.
16/134	,,	Haira, Kapu	,,	Haira Himiona, Whakarewarewa.
16/570	,,	Halbert, Thomas Tawera	Bushman	Matehaere Ripeka Halbert, Manutuke.
16/5	,,	Hale, Richard	Labourer	Mrs. A. G. Hale, Mangatuna, Tolaga Bay.
16/6	,,	Hamana, Kingi	,,	Pine Hamana, Wairoa, Hawke's Bay.
16/536	,,	Hape, Hona	,,	Hera Inumia, Opoutama, Hawke's Bay.
16/59	,,	Haraki, Wiremu	Carpenter	Wiremu Haraki, Wairoa, Hawke's Bay.
16/7	,,	Haronga, Tamahou	Labourer	Paora Haronga, Nuhaka, Hawke's Bay.
16/560	,,	Hauiti, Hani	,,	Rawinia Hauiti, Te Araroa.
16/574	,,	Heany, Walter	Station Hand	Mrs. Donald Gordon, Toheroa Station, Gisborne.
16/132	,,	Hemapo, Pari	Gardener	Tiamu Hemapo, Oruanui, Taupo.
16/176	,,	Herewini, Hohepa	Labourer	Ruahuihui Herewini, Ngapuna, Rotorua.
16/116	,,	Hirini, Haimona	,,	Repora, Poroporo, Whakatane.
16/190	,,	Hirini, Mohi	,,	Repora Whango, Whakatane.
16/182	,,	Hoani, Pita	,,	Petera Haereiteao Tu, Ngapuna, Rotorua.
16/510	,,	Honeycomb, Charles	Station Hand	Charles Honeycomb, Mamaku, Rotorua.
16/8	,,	Kainga, Tamihana	Labourer	Tamihana Kainga, Wairoa, Hawke's Bay.
16/148	,,	Kaipara, Hori	Farmer	P. T. K. Mokonuiarangi, Waiotapu.
16/9	,,	Kani, Tero	Labourer	Hohepa Pirima, Nuhaka, Hawke's Bay.
16/11	,,	Karaitiana, Tiaki	,,	Raiha Karaitiana, Wairoa, Hawke's Bay.
16/129	,,	Karaka, Hori Urukohu	,,	Mrs. U. Karaka, Te Puke.
16/121	,,	Karehana, Wiremu	Farmer	John Karehana, Raukokore, Bay of Plenty.
16/95	,,	Kawhia, Eruera	,,	Raniera Tuhoro Kawhia, Kahukura, Port Awanui.
16/12	,,	Keeti, Rangi	Labourer	Rota Keeti, Omaio, Bay of Plenty.
16/13	,,	Keneti, Hekiera Kupara	,,	Miria Teomerenhi, Tokomaru Bay.
16/114	,,	Kere, Paro	,,	Kere Rangi, Opotiki.
16/504	,,	te Kihi, Peniha	,,	Te Kihi Hone, Wairoa, Hawke's Bay.
16/528	,,	Kingi, Karauria	,,	Tuteari Kingi, Te Karaka.
16/573	,,	Kingi, Paul	,,	Tu te Ari, Te Karaka.
16/152	,,	Kingi, Raiona	,,	Tauhu Kingi, Te Puke.
16/172	,,	Kingi, Raniera	,,	William Kingi, Ohinemutu.
16/500	,,	Kingi, Wiremu	,,	Elizabeth Kingi, Sand Spit, Whakatiri.
16/537	,,	Kinita, Paki	,,	Rangi Karutua, Muripara, Rotorua.
16/551	,,	te Kiri, Abraham	Farm Labourer	Te Ngahoa te Kiri, Te Ngae, Rotorua.
16/167	,,	Kiri, Albert	Blacksmith	Meropaea Paratomeo, Matata.
16/14	,,	Kirimana, Rewiri	Farmer	Taare Kirimana, Tolaga Bay.
16/552	,,	Konuko, Pat	Farm Labourer	Annie Konuke, Wairoa, Hawke's Bay.
16/64	,,	Kopae, Tamihana	Labourer	Kopae Ikara, Poroporo, Bay of Plenty.
16/15	,,	Kouka, Wiremu	,,	Te Kaumarua Kainuku, Manutuke.
16/16	,,	Lambert, Thomas	,,	Fenton Lambert, Frasertown, Hawke's Bay.
16/88	,,	McClutchie, Joseph William	,,	Henry George McClutchie, Tuparoa.
16/507	,,	Manuera, Pukupuku	,,	Jim Lewis, Hastings.
16/117	,,	Maraki, Tautuhi	,,	Maraki Tautuhi, Waipiro Bay.

Reg. No.	Rank.	Name.	Occupation.	Next-of-kin.
		B COMPANY—*continued.*		
16/139	Private	Marino, Hohepa	Labourer	Hura Marino, Tolaga Bay.
16/146	,,	Matain, Hataraka	,,	Te Rauparaha Matain, Rotorua.
16/207	,,	Mihaere, Taiamai	,,	Charley Pompey, Tangoio, Hawke's Bay.
16/21	,,	Mihaere, Toko	Chauffeur	Katiana Whakahewa, Wairoa, Hawke's Bay.
16/99	,,	Mikaere, Rawiri	Labourer	Mihaere Apanui, Opotiki.
16/22	,,	Mills, Whare	Bushman	Kereawa Tihema, Te Kapa, Port Awanui.
16/194	,,	Mita, Matene	Labourer	Te Ohau Mita, Tangoio, Hawke's Bay.
16/84	,,	Mitai, Wharepapa	,,	Mitai Hoera, Opotiki.
16/181	,,	te Moni, Matehaere	,,	Te Moni Ngarewa, Te Puke.
16/23	,,	Morete, Hone Henry	,,	J. H. Morris, Te Karaka.
16/24	,,	Morgan, John	,,	Materitewai Honatana, Opotiki.
16/25	,,	Morris, William	,,	William Morris, Te Karaka.
16/248	,,	te Muera, Wetini	,,	Row Tokoaitua te Muera, Otaki.
16/26	,,	Namana, Rata	,,	Namana Takawhenua, Mohaka, Hawke's Bay.
16/239	,,	Nelson, David	Chauffeur	Mary Mohi, Waimamara, Hawke's Bay.
16/568	,,	Nepia, Hone	Labourer	Wheku Nepia, Manutuke.
16/27	,,	Neri, Uorata	,,	Uorata Neri, Nuhaka, Hawke's Bay.
16/42	,,	te Ngaio, Wharekete	,,	Materua te Ngaio, Opoutama, Hawke's Bay.
16/160	,,	Ngaki, Awatapu	Farmer	Te Ari Turuturu, Te Puke.
16/185	,,	Ngamu, Hoani	,,	Tamihana Tikitere, Pukehina, Ohinepanea.
16/534	,,	Ngarangioue, Huki	Labourer	Roha Matutaera, Opoutama, Mahia, Hawke's Bay.
16/163	,,	Ngatipohi, Umanui	Sailor	Te Mamaeroa Ngatipohi, Ohinemutu.
16/245	,,	Ngatuere, Phillip Kingi	Labourer	Raukura Phillip Kingi, Carterton.
16/244	,,	Nia Nia, Ereatara	Shearer	Hipora Nia Nia, Te Reinga, Wairoa.
16/242	,,	Nia Nia, Matiu Ereatara	,,	Hori Nia Nia, Te Reinga, Wairoa.
16/164	,,	Nicholls, Thompson William	Sailor	Ngakoura Tamihana, Te Puke.
16/183	,,	te Otimi, Pitonga	Farmer	Te Otimi Marupo, Maketu.
16/108	,,	Pahina, Whare	Labourer	Penetana Pahina, Te Araroa.
16/159	,,	Pakana, Nikorina	,,	Te Pakana te Awaawa, Te Puke.
16/177	,,	Paora, Manu	,,	Paora Paruhi, Okere, Rotorua.
16/201	,,	Paora, Paetaha	Farmer	Paora Kohatu, Taupo.
16/493	,,	Papuni, Kurei	Labourer	Tapeka Papuni, Omarumutu, Opotiki.
16/29	,,	Paputene, Tiara	,,	Mrs. J. R. Hale, Tokomaru Bay.
16/74	,,	Paraone, Marama	,,	Whakahara Paraone, Raukokore, Opotiki.
16/126	,,	Paraone, Tame	,,	Kauamo Paraone, Maraenui, Opotiki.
16/76	,,	Paraone, Tapauri	,,	Paraone Heremia, Te Kaha.
16/309	,,	Pararaki, Puruma	,,	Raraki Wikiriwhi, Maketu.
16/566	,,	Parata, Paul	,,	Iritana Aria, Waipiro Bay.
16/162	,,	Pari, Ropiha	Farm Labourer	Amoroa Arama Karaka, Te Puke.
16/30	,,	Peka, Hohepa	Labourer	Maaka Peka, Raukokore, Opotiki.
16/92	,,	Penetito, Hori	,,	Penetito Hawea, Te Teko.
16/559	,,	Pera, Pani	,,	Pera Karaur, Waerengaahika.
16/33	,,	Pera, Piana	,,	Kararehe Pera, Waerengaahika.
16/105	,,	Pereto, Pono	Farmer	Henare Pereto, Te Araroa.
16/31	,,	Pereto, Rua	Labourer	Ema Pereto, Te Araroa.
16/82	,,	Petiha, Hone	Farrier	Makahuri Petiha, Hastings.
16/149	,,	Pikikotuku, Tame	Carpenter	Thomas Curtis, Rotoiti, Rotorua.
16/166	,,	Piti, Warihi	Labourer	Piti Pene, Matata.
16/34	,,	Pohatu, Renata	Shearer	Eru Pohatu, Muriwai, Gisborne.
16/122	,,	Poi, Te Rere	Labourer	Henare Poi, Kahukura, Port Awanui.
16/218	,,	Poihipi, Rakataha	,,	Tearuhau Poihipi, Carterton.
16/513	,,	Poi Poi, Pita	,,	Ripeka Poi Poi, Opoutama, Hawke's Bay.
16/81	,,	Potae, Enoka	Farmer	Pani Potae, Te Araroa.
16/63	,,	Poutu, Komene	Labourer	Wi Poutu, Te Araroa.
16/198	,,	Power, Hone Manahi	Shepherd	Henry R. Power, Aohanga.
16/205	,,	Power, William Edwin	Labourer	Fanny Power, Aohanga.
16/35	,,	Puhipuhi, Karu	,,	Karauria Puhipuhi, Tolaga Bay.
16/233	,,	Pullen, Ernest	Farmer	James Pullen, Motueka.
16/219	,,	Puna, Houiana	Labourer	Matewai Puna, Tangoio, Napier.
16/41	,,	te Pani, Tihema	Farm Hand	Rua Kirikiri, Hiruharama, Waipiro Bay.
16/36	,,	Puru, Epiha	Labourer	Mere Tutapu, Waikari, Mohaka.
16/104	,,	Puru Mika	Farm Labourer	Mihi Mere Tutapu, Te Arai, Gisborne.
16/83	,,	te Raihi, Pukerimu	Labourer	Te Raihi Pukerimu, Otamarakau.
16/158	,,	Raimona, Rangi	,,	Raimona Piripi Ngaki, Matata.
16/37	,,	Rangi, Hapi	,,	Iriheke Rangi, Wairoa, Hawke's Bay.
16/38	,,	Rangi, Wiremu Haeta	Farmer	Mrs. Pekeiha, Gisborne.
16/234	,,	Rangitakawaho, Rawhiti	Labourer	Miriana Rangitakawaho, Greytown.
16/525	,,	Rapona, Kiri	,,	Pita Rapona, Mangatu, Gisborne.
16/91	,,	Ratima, Nepia	,,	Mrs. Wharekohuru Romana, Poroporo, Whakatane.
16/94	,,	Ratima, Romana	Farmer	Mrs. Wharekohuru Romana, Poroporo, Whakatane.
16/521	,,	Rauawa, Matiu	Painter	Rangiwhata Rauawa, Rotorua.
16/530	,,	Rawhiti, Huki	Labourer	Rangikuio Hapeta, Tokomaru Bay.
16/73	,,	Rawiri, Whai	,,	Mate Ruru Puha, Gisborne.
16/89	,,	Reihana, Rutene	,,	Raiha Reihana, Rangitukia, Gisborne.
16/529	,,	Renata, Re	,,	Tuhirapa Renata, Muriwai, Gisborne.
16/115	,,	Rewa, George Rangitikei	,,	Hori Rewa, Motiti Island, Tauranga.
16/102	,,	Richmond, Tom	,,	T. Rihimona, Torere, Opotiki.
16/39	,,	Rotoatara, Charlie	,,	Kingi Rotoatara, Wairoa, Hawke's Bay.
16/326	,,	Rotoatara, Kipa	Bushfeller	Kingi Rotoatara, Wairoa, Hawke's Bay.
16/457	,,	Rotoatara, Tupara	Labourer	Kingi Rotoatara, Wairoa.
16/40	,,	Rua, Rangi	Blacksmith	Hone te Rua, Te Arai, Gisborne.
16/531	,,	Savage, James	Labourer	Hirim Savage, Pariokara or Hawaii.

Reg. No.	Rank.	Name.	Occupation.	Next-of-kin.
		B COMPANY—*continued*.		
16/506	Private	Simpson, George	Seaman	Kerara Rewiri Patara, Whakatane.
16/569	,,	Sullivan, Jury	Shearer	Haeta Wiremu, Manutuke.
16/68	,,	Taewa, Rawiri	Labourer	Erueti Kopa Taewa, Tuparoa.
16/44	,,	Tahu, Hau	,,	Raniera Tahu, Frasertown, Hawke's Bay.
16/101	,,	Taia, Hori	,,	Paora Taia, Opotiki.
16/113	,,	Tairua, Joseph	,,	Tairua Apanui, Waiaua, Opotiki.
16/179	,,	Tamihana, Tame	Seaman	Tamihana Putoko, Te Puke.
16/43	,,	Tamihana, Tipene	Farmer	Rewi Tamihana, Wairoa, Hawke's Bay.
16/535	,,	Tamihana, Wi	Labourer	Raki Tamihana, Muriwai, Gisborne.
16/175	,,	Tapihana, Kouma	Farmer	Kouma Tapsell, Maketu.
16/153	,,	Tapihana, Pita	Labourer	Ngatai Tapihana, Maketu.
16/133	,,	Tapihana, Rewi	,,	Ngatai Retireti, Maketu.
16/71	,,	Tapine, Ruru	Butcher	Hone Taahiawa, Tokomaru Bay.
16/135	,,	Tapsell, Winiata	Drainer	Ira Tapsell, Maketu.
16/78	,,	Taumaunu, Hare	Labourer	Hapi Taumaunu, Reporua, Port Awanui.
16/557	,,	Tauranga, Mark	,,	Kereama Tauranga, Hicks Bay.
16/561	,,	Tautuhi, Hiki	,,	Mrs. Maggie Tautuhi, 201 Childer's Road, Gisborne.
16/144	,,	Tawa, Hori	Surveyor's Chainman	Tawa Ropiha, Otamarakau.
16/571	,,	Tawera, Barney	Labourer	Barney Tawera, Nuhaka, Hawke's Bay.
16/215	,,	Tawhai, Pa	Farmer	Jack Tawhai, Dannevirke.
16/48	,,	Teito, Eru	,,	Poata Teito, Opoutama, Hawke's Bay.
16/236	,,	Thompson, Edward	Labourer	Rakai Thompson, Gisborne.
16/119	,,	Tioke, Timutimu	,,	Tioke Hakaiparu, Waimana.
16/131	,,	te Toa, Hona	,,	Whakahiki te Toa, Whakarewarewa.
16/103	,,	Toka, Taane	Engineer	Atareta Herewini, Torere, Opotiki.
16/80	,,	Tokara, Hirini	Labourer	Eru Tokara, Waipiro Bay.
16/235	,,	Toki, Noho	,,	Ngoingoi Toki, Greytown.
16/123	,,	Tuati, Pareiha	,,	Emere Tuati, Thames.
16/100	,,	Tuati, Tuhituhi	Engineer	C. Stewart, Whakatane.
16/200	,,	Tuhana, Davie	Shearer	Rewiri Tuhana, Wairoa, Hawke's Bay.
16/46	,,	Tuhiwai, Wiremu	Labourer	Mereana Tuhiwai, Tolaga Bay.
16/125	,,	Tunoa, Hamiora	,,	Tunoa Lawson, Whakatane.
16/127	,,	Tunui, Ihaka	Farmer	Wirinia Tunui, Poroporo, Whakatane.
16/225	,,	Tunuiarangi, James Carroll	Labourer	Major H. P. Tunuiarangi, Carterton.
16/45	,,	Turi, Rena	,,	Mihaka Turi, Hicks Bay.
16/47	,,	te Urupu, Paora Rerepu	Farmer	Remuera te Urupu, Mohaka, Hawke's Bay.
16/77	,,	Utauta, Rotohiko	Labourer	Paretai Utauta, Motiti, Tauranga.
16/565	,,	Waaka, Toro	,,	Ani Waaka, Mohaka, Hawke's Bay.
16/52	,,	Waara, Piripi	,,	Tanara Waara, Te Araroa.
16/55	,,	Waihape, Puke	,,	Renata Waihape, Mohaka, Hawke's Bay.
16/54	,,	Wainohu, Hemi	Sheep-farmer	Paea Wainohu, Mohaka, Hawke's Bay.
16/203	,,	Wainohu, Whitu	Labourer	Hiromina Wainohu, Landsdown, Masterton.
16/51	,,	Waipara, Rota	Blacksmith	Rota Waipara, Gisborne.
16/53	,,	Wairau, Ra	Labourer	Wahati Wairau, Mahia, Hawke's Bay.
16/549	,,	Waiti, Hauraki	,,	Apikara Mangaone, Hiruharama, Waipiro Bay.
16/563	,,	Warakihi, Eruera	,,	Taare Warakihi, Ormond, Gisborne.
16/564	,,	Warakihi, Poihipi	,,	Puku Warakihi, Ormond, Gisborne.
16/57	,,	Whatuira, Poni	,,	Rameka Kainga, Wairoa, Hawke's Bay.
16/174	,,	Wi Hapi, Arama Karaka	,,	Te Amu Wi Hapi, Te Puke.
16/112	,,	Williams, Joe	,,	Wiremu Rori, Hokianga.
16/60	,,	Winterburn, Albert	,,	Alfred Winterburn, Otaki.
16/237	,,	Wiremu, Rupi	Chauffeur	Tauwhitu Wiremu, Waikaremoana.
16/109	,,	Wi Repa, Tuhitaare	Labourer	Dr. Tutere Wi Repa, Te Araroa.
16/208	,,	Wirihana, Ihaia	,,	Hone Kereama, Greytown.
16/136	,,	Wirikake, Hare	Surveyor's Chainman	Ruiha Pinenga Rukingi, Rotorua.

The Nominal Rolls of the Maori Contingents and Reinforcements 1914–1918

ROLL OF THE SECOND MAORI CONTINGENT

Number	Rank	Name	Next-of-Kin
OFFICERS			
16/1026	Lieutenant	Ashton, Lionel George	Mrs K. Ashton (mother), Great North Road, Epsom, AUCKLAND.
16/977	2nd Lieutenant	Bush, George Arthur	Mrs A.M. Bush (wife), Victoria Street, PAEROA.
16/1017	2nd Lieutenant	Dansey, Harry Delamere	R.D. Dansey (father), ROTORUA.
16/999	Captain	Duncan, John Donald Campbell	Mrs C. Duncan (wife), C/- NZ High Commissioner, LONDON.
16/872	2nd Lieutenant	Ehau, Kepa Hamuera Auaha	Mrs Wikitoria N. Ehau (wife), ROTORUA.
16/590	2nd Lieutenant	Hall, John Henry	Mrs Hilda Hall (wife), Parnell, AUCKLAND.
16/1021	Chap-Major	Hawkins, Hector Alfred	Mrs M.A. Hawkins (wife), Remuera, AUCKLAND.
16/620	2nd Lieutenant	Kaa, Pekama	Panikena Kaa (father), Rangitukia, via GISBORNE.
16/1018	2nd Lieutnant	Kohere, Henare Mokena	Rev P.M. Kohere (trustee), RANGITIKEI.
16/651	2nd Lieutenant	McGregor, Hori	Mrs K.M. McGregor (wife), Mount Stuart, Glenmore near MILTON.
16/689	2nd Lieutenant	O'Neill, John Irvine	Mrs Chas Cowan (aunt), 19 Russell Street, Devonport, AUCKLAND.
16/1023	Captain	Rice, Stanley	Mrs S. Rice (wife), 6 Sims Street, Maori Hill, DUNEDIN.
NON COMMISSIONED OFFICERS			
16/561	Corporal	Apanui, Apiati	Renata Pohatu (uncle), KAHUKURA.
16/878	Sergeant	Bryers, Charles Sedborough	Mrs M.A. Bryers (mother), Hokianga Heads, OMAPERE.
16/568	Q.M. Sergeant	Clark, Henry William	Mrs H. Clark (wife), 17 Voelas Road, LYTTLETON.
16/883	Corporal	Cross, Thomas Henry, Louis	Joseph Cross (father), Kaka Point, Port Molyneux, OTAGO.
16/576	Sergeant	David, Robin	Hepa David (brother), AHIPARA.
16/578	Sergeant	Dufaur, David	Percy Dufaur (uncle), C/- Dufaur and Biss, AUCKLAND.
16/579	Lance Corporal	Ellison, Thomas	D. Ellison (father), Te Aute, HAWKES BAY.
16/876	Corporal	Ferris, Jack Sydney	C.W. Ferris (brother), GISBORNE.
16/972	Corporal	French, Thomas	John French (father), Te Rauamoa, via TE AWAMUTU.
16/971	Corporal	Geary, James Henry	William Geary (father), Portobello, DUNEDIN.
16/582	Corporal	Goldsmith, Charles	Edward Goldsmith (father), Rangitukia, GISBORNE.
16/797	Sergeant	Heta, Warepuni	Mrs Heta (mother), DANNEVIRKE.
16/935	Lance Corporal	Hina, Paparua	Tua Hina, Kauangaroa, WANGANUI.
16/887	Sergeant	Hodge, Samuel Ngaru	Mrs S. Hodge (mother), Ohinemutu, ROTORUA.
16/606	Lance Corporal	Houia, Wiremu Peha	Rota Houia (father), Reporua, TEWERA.
16/616	Sergeant	Jones, Francis Moncur	Mrs Terna Jones (mother), Pirongia, via TE AWAMUTU.
16/628	Corporal	Kaipo, George Cecil	Rev. W.H. Kaipo (father), Waitara, TARANAKI.
16/608	Corporal	Kaipo, William Walter	Rev. W.H. Kaipo (father), Waitara, TARANAKI.
16/809	Q.M. - Sergeant	McNichol, Duncan Bannatyne	Mrs E.F. McNichol (mother), Ohaeawai, BAY OF ISLANDS.
16/656	Sergeant	Manuel, Josiah	W. Manuel (father), Te Kao, NORTH AUCKLAND.
16/673	Corporal	Merito, David	Heteraka Merito (father), WHAKATANE.
16/882	Corporal	Paki, John	R. Paki (father), Wangaehu, WANGANUI.
16/870	Sergeant	Paora-Chamberlain, Paui	Mrs Rimi Paora-Chamberlain (wife), Khandallah, WELLINGTON.
16/823	Lance Corporal	Paul, James	Mrs A. Hohepa (mother), Kaeo, MATAURI BAY.
16/826	Corporal	Peters, Clement	Mrs Daisy Peters (wife), Blacktown, SYDNEY NSW.
16/704	Sergeant	Petihai, Ngahiwi	Makahuri Peitha (brother), HASTINGS.
16/831	Corporal	Pohatu Turoa	Mrs Raiha Petiha (wife), Awapuni, GISBORNE.
16/567A	Corporal	Pokure Ruakirikiri	Mrs Hariata Tangira (mother), Ruakokore, BAY OF PLENTY.
16/732	Corporal	Saunders, Thomas Victor	Delac Te Whaiti, Pirinoa, FEATHERSTON.
16/888	Sergeant	Savage, Charles	Miss Delia Savage (sister), Kopu, THAMES.
16/733	Lance Corporal	Shepherd, Thomas	Tau Shepherd (father), Saies, WHANGAROA.
16/1025	Sergeant-Major	Singleton, John William Massey	Mrs S.L. Singleton (mother), London, Cottage Yeovil, ENGLAND.
16/925	Corporal	Spencer, Robert Edmond Bruce	Mrs R.V. Spencer (wife), Moeraki House, BLUFF.
16/743	Sergeant	Tamepo, Taiwahi	R. Tamepo (father), WAIPIRO BAY.
16/926	Sergeant	Tamou, Rangiore	Whakapae Tamou (brother), Kai Iwi, WANGANUI.
16/894	Corporal	Tareha, Kapi	Kurupo Tareha, Jnr (son), TARADALE.
16/843	Lance Corporal	Te Kiri, Korokaihau	Te Ngahoa Te Kiri (father), Te Ngae, ROTORUA.
16/171	Sergeant	Te Kiri, Rake	Te Ngahoa Te Kiri (father), Te Ngae, ROTORUA.
16/761	Sergeant	Te Tau, Wiremu	Pukera Te Tau (father), MASTERTON.
16/771	Corporal	Turei, Peta	Mrs K. Turei (mother), Rangitukia, GISBORNE.
16/855	Sergeant	Wahipeihana, Whetu	Rohana Wehipeihana (father), OHAU.
16/856	Corporal	Werohia, Whetu	Henare Werohia (father), Papamoa, TAURANGA.
16/858	Sergeant	Wickham, Menia	Mrs Rangimatakite Mawhatura (aunt), WAITARA.
16/1001	Sergeant-Major	Winiki, Thomas Merlin	Rangi Taura (adopted father), Waitara, TARANAKI.
PRIVATES			
16/596	Private	Abraham, John	Poihipe Te Kume (father), Owaahui, LAKE TAUPO.
16/1007	Private	Adam, Kiro Luke	Manuel Luke (step brother), Avarua, Rarotonga, COOK ISLANDS.
16/578	Private	Akena, Rakapa	Paho Akena, Kahukura, TOKOMARU.
16/599	Private	Anderson, George	John Anderson (father), Kopu, THAMES.
16/924	Private	Anderson, Wiremu	Jack Anderson (uncle), Kopu, THAMES.
16/1020	Private	Antony, Samuel James	Mrs Thomas Woods (sister), Puketeraki, OTAGO.
16/563	Private	Berghan, Edward Louis	Mrs Elizabeth Berghan, AHIPARA.
16/564	Private	Brown, James	Mrs Mere Brown (aunt), Mahia, OPOUTAMA.
16/1005	Private	Cameron, Rewai	Mrs Turihiara Cameron (mother), PUKEPOTO.
16/566	Private	Campbell, Thomas Robert	Mrs T.R. Campbell (wife), Opoutama, HAWKES BAY.
16/567A	Private	Christie, Tuke	Niwha Christie, Wairoa, HAWKES BAY.
16/569	Private	Clendon, Henry Pou	Mrs Kiritapu Clendon (mother), Rawhiti, BAY OF ISLANDS.
16/570	Private	Clune, James	Miss Daisy Clune (sister), C/- Mrs F. Cleaver, 5 Cross Street, Newton, AUCKLAND.
16/572	Private	Cook, Samuel, L.	Samuel Cook (father), OTAKI.
16/573	Private	Cooper, Johnny	Mrs Tripeti Cooper (mother), POUKAWA.
16/947	Private	Crawford, Henry	Wi Crawford (father), TE ARAROA.

Number	Rank	Name	Next-of-Kin
16/575	Private	Danger, James	Mrs Eria Te Whaiti (aunt), GREYTOWN.
16/577	Private	Davis, Robert	Miss H. Davis (sister), 44 Brighton Road, Parnell, AUCKLAND.
16/884	Private	Davis, Waka	Mrs Miriama Rameka (mother), Takaka, NELSON.
16/580	Private	Eruera, White	E. Harawira (father), Raukokore, via Opotiki, BAY OF PLENTY.
16/982	Private	Fairlie, Godfrey Alexander	Herbert H. Fairlie (father), TOKOMARU BAY.
16/983	Private	Forrester, Albert	Mrs Maud Pipier (mother), TOKOMARU BAY.
16/581	Private	Fox, Henry	Hurunui Apanui, WHAKATANE.
16/583	Private	Governor, Joe William	Mrs Olive Governor (mother), MASTERTON.
16/584	Private	Grace, Ben	S. Grace (father), TUPAROA.
16/586	Private	Grant, James	Dan Grant (brother), TOKOMARU BAY.
16/587	Private	Greaves, Henry	Mrs Lina Tipa Greaves (mother), KAITAIA.
16/588	Private	Haenga, Parekura	Mrs M. Haenga (mother), PORT AWANUI.
16/589	Private	Haenga, Urikore	Miss Materoa Haenga (sister), TIKAPA.
16/892	Private	Hancy, Micheal	Stephen Hancy (father), Rotukaraka, HOKIANGA.
16/949	Private	Hape, Tere	Tangiora Hape (father), Mahia, GISBORNE.
16/750	Private	Happy, Dick	Bill Happy (brother), ROTORUA.
16/592	Private	Harawira, Heta	Taki Harawira (brother), Te Kao, NORTH AUCKLAND.
16/796	Private	Harema, Heta	Mrs Miho Harema (mother), Omanaia, via RAWENE.
16/950	Private	Hauiti, Henry	Pira Hauiti (father), TE ARAROA.
16/593	Private	Hawkins, Henry	Mrs M. Hawkins (grandmother), Corner Ellison and Sylvia Roads, HASTINGS.
16/594	Private	Hawkins, Ned Tom	Karauia Eriha (uncle), MOHAKA.
16/650*	Private	Herberley, Cyril Llewelyn	Mrs Sarah Herberley (mother), 124 Dixon Street, WELLINGTON.
16/595	Private	Heremaia, Rewi Hari	Rewi Heremaia (father), RAETIHI.
16/798	Private	Heta, William	Thomas, Heta (father), Poroti, via WHANGAREI.
16/597	Private	Hillman, Charlie	Miss Ka Korohine (sister), Te Araroa, via GISBORNE.
16/600	Private	Hohepa, Huaki	Eparima Pehitia (uncle), PORANGAHAU.
16/601	Private	Hohepa, Rore	Miss Ngahiraka Hohepa (sister), TUPAROA BAY.
16/603	Private	Hori, Mita	Mrs Kaimataia Hori (mother), OTAKI.
16/941	Private	Horomona, Waka	Taruna Horomona (father), Whakaki, HAWKES BAY.
16/929	Private	Huatiki, Piripi	Miss Haine Moerua (daughter), Hiruharama, Tuperoa via GISBORNE.
16/607	Private	Hui, George	Miss Roka, Hui (sister), Waitakaruru, THAMES.
16/951	Private	Huihui, Tipene	Mrs Marae Wakapu (grandmother), Tikitiki, KAHUKURA.
16/610	Private	Hura, George	Mrs Mere Hura (mother), Wairoa, HAWKES BAY.
16/614	Private	Ihia, Heke	Miss Marata Ihia (sister), MATATA.
16/865	Private	Ihaka, Dan	Mrs Rihi Ihaka (mother), Poherau, DANNEVIRKE.
16/965	Private	Iraia, David	David W. Moetara (uncle), Aronga via KAIHU.
16/617	Private	Josephs, Rore John	P. Josephs (brother), TE KUITI.
16/618	Private	Jury, Hori Iaare	T.A. Jury (uncle), WANGANUI.
16/625	Private	Kahaki, Anaru Nganaia	Hoani Kahaki (father), Rangitukia via GISBORNE.
16/799	Private	Kahui, Papara	Mrs Whakapo Kahui (mother), Waiwhaata, OTOROHANGA.
16/626	Private	Kahukiwa, Momi	Te Kahukiwa (father), Waiohau, KOPURIKI.
16/627	Private	Kahukura, Herewira	Mrs Hohepa Kahukura (wife), Wairoa, HAWKES BAY.
16/800	Private	Kainuku, Rua	Miss Langi Kainuku (sister), Manutuke, GISBORNE.
16/629	Private	Kaiwai, Rewiti	Rutu Tawahiora (cousin), TUPAROA.
16/663	Private	Kana, Hume	Hori Kana (father), Te Horo, PORT AWANUI.
16/634	Private	Kanapu, Horomana	Haerehuka Kanapu, Springvale, WANGANUI.
16/637	Private	Kanika, Toi Wiremu	Wiremu Kanika (father), KAIMANUKA.
16/937	Private	Kara, Ioha	Henri Kara (father), Muriwai, GISBORNE.
16/936	Private	Kara, Rimu	Henri Kara, Muriwai, GISBORNE.
16/630	Private	Karaitiana, Rutene	Rangi Karaitiana (brother), HASTINGS.
16/632	Private	Karaka, Reihana	Miss Atareta Mateterangi (sister) Kahukura, EAST COAST.
16/631	Private	Karina, Rarere	Kariai Muhu (father), Koparanui, EAST COAST.
16/988	Private	Katau, Wilson	Wi Katau (father), Te Naihi, HAWKES BAY.
16/792	Private	Katene, Frederick B. William	Wi Katene (father), Lyall Bay, WELLINGTON.
16/636	Private	Katene, Rangi Wi	Wi Katene (father), Lyall Bay, WELLINGTON.
16/635	Private	Katene, Taku	Wi Katene (father), Lyall Bay, WELLINGTON.
16/622	Private	Keepa, Matenga	Miss Kuranga Taeri (sister), PIPIRIKI.
16/624	Private	Kerehi, Rewi	George, Hale (nephew), TOKOMARU BAY.
16/802	Private	King, Kohi	King Temate (father), OTOROHANGA.
16/805	Private	Kingi, Pianau	— Kingi (father), OTOROHANGA.
16/621	Private	Kingi, Tauiti	Tu Wiremu (uncle), MANIA COROMANDEL.
16/639	Private	Kirikiri, Henare	Mrs K. Lockwood (sister), TOLAGA BAY.
16/952	Private	Kiwara, Rongo	Mrs Harangi Kiwara (mother), TE ARAROA.
16/641	Private	Koia, Metehaere	Davis Green (brother-in-law), Kahakura, PORT AWANUI.
16/873	Private	Kopua, Hore	Mrs Hohepera Kopua (mother), TOKOMARU BAY.
16/643	Private	Kopua, Whetuki	Nihe Kopua (brother), TOKOMARU BAY.
16/968	Private	Koruarua, John	Mrs Kerland (mother), 55 Elizabeth Street, TIMARU.
16/647	Private	Kotua, William Koraka	Mrs Mattier Kotua (mother), TURAKINA.
16/645	Private	Kuturo, Tane	Heta Kain (cousin), Potangahau, HAWKES BAY.
16/649	Private	Lewis, Mana	Friday, Lewis Wairoa, HAWKES BAY.
16/806	Private	Luke, Maurice	W. Luke (father), Whakapara, WHANGAREI.
16/807	Private	Luke, Peter	W. Luke (father), Whakapara, WHANGAREI.
16/974	Private	McDonald, Murdock	Mrs E. McDonald (mother), HELENSVILLE.
16/899	Private	McDonell, Deed	Miss Haumiki (sister), Putiki, WANGANUI.
16/867	Private	MacKey, Kirihona	Jack Kerehana, 11 Crawford Road, Kaiti, GISBORNE.
16/654	Private	Maehe, Wi	Heremia Maehe (father), Wairoa, HAWKES BAY.
16/652	Private	Maere, Horomona	Mrs H. Maere (wife), HASTINGS.
16/653	Private	Mahanga, Ben	Sam Mahanga (father), PARUA BAY.
16/899	Private	Maka, Henry	James Maka (father), KAIHU.
16/655	Private	Mangapu, Henare	Wi Kenare (father), Northcote, AUCKLAND.
16/657	Private	Manuel, Tiweka	Aparina Manuera (father), Waihuka, Kahukura, PORT AWANUI.

* Main Body and Second Maori

Number	Rank	Name	Next-of-Kin
16/658	Private	Maopo, William Kaehau	Aterea Maopo, Taumutu, Southbridge, CANTERBURY.
16/939	Private	Mare, Renata	Tupeke Renata (father), Muriwai, GISBORNE.
16/660	Private	Marsh Jack	— Marsh (father), Frasertown, HAWKES BAY.
16/661	Private	Marunui, Pipi	Riwiri Marunui (father), Galatea, Kopuriki, via ROTORUA.
16/662	Private	Mason, Dick	Wi Duncan (uncle), Opoutama, HAWKES BAY.
16/663	Private	Matana, Karawira	Mrs Te Matana (mother), DANNEVIRKE.
16/810	Private	Matenga, Tuehe	Mrs Matire Matenga (mother), Muriwai, GISBORNE.
16/811	Private	Matia, Korua	Mrs Harete Matia (mother), TE PUKE.
16/813	Private	Matthews, Bushby William	Huirama Tukariri (father), Manganui, BAY OF ISLANDS.
16/669	Private	Matthews, Joseph	John Matthews (father), Kapuka, SOUTHLAND.
16/668	Private	Matthews, Joseph	Pehi Matthews (father), CARTERTON.
16/667	Private	Matui Tauranga	David Matthews (brother), THAMES.
16/670	Private	Maurirere, Mahu	Mrs Riria Pouaka (mother), Tuparoa, via GISBORNE.
16/671	Private	Maxwell, George	Mrs Hera Maxwell (mother), PORT AWANUI.
16/674	Private	Merriman, Makiwi	Tata Merriman (brother), Parawai, THAMES.
16/67	Private	Merrimana, Te Huku	Mrs Roma Merrimana (wife), Parawai, THAMES.
16/676	Private	Mihaere, Pura	Mrs Ketiana Mihaere (mother), Wairoa, HAWKES BAY.
16/900	Private	Mikaera, Wairua	— Mikaera (father), TOKOMARU BAY.
16/677	Private	Miller, David Mamaru	Mrs E Miller (mother), Post Office, PURAKANUI.
16/678	Private	Miromiro, Pani	Mrs Katarania Miromiro (mother), Kaunanga, Tuparoa, via GISBORNE.
16/679	Private	Mita Arapata	Mrs Tawhiwa Rekehana, OTAKI.
16/680	Private	Morehu, Hakopa	Mrs Hanitia Martin (mother), KAIKOURA.
16/681	Private	Morris, Richard	John Morris (father), Te Karaka, GISBORNE.
16/814	Private	Mua, Peta	Pari Mua (father), TOKOMARU BAY.
16/685	Private	Nepia, Wi	Miss Martha Nepia (sister), Hukarera School, NAPIER.
16/686	Private	Newton, James	Ihaia Katana, WAIPAWA.
16/958	Private	Ngatoro, Renata	Peter Ngatoro (father), TE ARAROA.
16/688	Private	Ngeru Kirikiri	Ngeru (father), HAWERA.
16/690	Private	Ormsby, Walter	Mrs Albert Ormsby (mother), OTOROHANGA.
16/817	Private	Owen, George William	Mrs Amelia Owen (mother), Poroti, WHANGAREI.
16/693	Private	Paipeta, Wiremu	Mrs W. Crane (sister), Woodend, NORTHER CANTERBURY.
16/694	Private	Panete, Wi	Mrs Pani Panete (mother), Kaikoura, MARLBOROUGH.
16/819	Private	Panoho, Bill Edwards	Paitere (grandfather), Paroti, WHANGAREI.
16/820	Private	Panaho, Henry Charles	Paitere (grandfather), Paroti, WHANGAREI.
16/821	Private	Panaho, Jack	Henry Panaho, Paroti, WHANGAREI.
16/697	Private	Parae, Hona	Whio Parae, Tuparoa, via GISBORNE.
16/699	Private	Paranaki, Winiata	Wiki Tua, MARTON.
16/959	Private	Parapora, Tuakaua	Mrs Hoana Papapapa (mother), TE ARAROA.
16/700	Private	Parata, Renata	Mrs Iritana Aria (mother), Waipiro Bay, GISBORNE.
16/931	Private	Patara, Hiroki Rere	Mrs Pukamire Patara (mother), PORT OWEN.
16/881	Private	Paul, George William Walton	Mrs S.J. Paul (mother), 19 Crummer Road, Grey Lynn, AUCKLAND.
16/824	Private	Paul, Willie	Henry Paul (father), OTOROHANGA.
16/825	Private	Pawhau, Henare	Hura Pawhau (father), PERIA.
16/703	Private	Pera, Hue	Mrs Rangi Hutata (mother), Puha, GISBORNE.
16/690	Private	Peri, Hoani	Hapu Peri (father), Te Araroa, GISBORNE.
16/960	Private	Piri, Hoani	Hapie Piri (father), TE ARAROA.
16/828	Private	Pohatu, Mahurangi	Mrs Aggie Walker (mother), Wairoa, HAWKES BAY.
16/829	Private	Pohatu, Mita	Mrs Ngaekihia Waeke (mother), Muriwai, GISBORNE.
16/830	Private	Pohatu, Pine Arnine	Papa Maru, C/- Ngakei Maru, Opoutama, HAWKES BAY.
16/706	Private	Pohatu, Tohana	Pera Abraham (grandfather), Opapa, HAWKES BAY.
16/707	Private	Pohio, Iraia Tehau	Mrs Hilda Tainui, Tuahane, KAIAPOI.
16/962	Private	Pohutu, Kingi	Mrs Anni Waitoa (aunt), TE ARAROA.
16/708	Private	Pokai, Tautuhi	Mrs Teoarani Pokai (wife), Kahakura, PORT AWANUI.
16/832	Private	Pomana, Hori	Siria Pomana, Manatuke, GISBORNE.
16/709	Private	Popata, Charles Henry	Mrs Maramai Hohepa Hoani (sister), Kaitaia, AWANUI NORTH.
16/938	Private	Porou, Billy	Mrs Bartlett Matire (mother), Muriwai, GISBORNE.
16/1003	Private	Povey, Pai	H. Povey (father), Peria, MANGONUI. Mrs Ivy Povey (wife), Post Office, WAIHOPO.
16/986	Private	Price, George	Mrs Mary Tomlins (sister), Pakipaki, HAWKES BAY.
16/833	Private	Priestley, Wi Kepa	William Priestley, Caretaker, Park Racecourse, GISBORNE.
16/835	Private	Puru, Tame	Rangi Puru (uncle), Whatatutu, GISBORNE.
16/710	Private	Rangiao, Wirihana Hori	Pukunui Rangiao (uncle), Kauangaroa, FORDELL.
16/711	Private	Ransfield, Robert Taru	S. Ransfield (father), OHAU.
16/712	Private	Rapatini, Teoti	Mrs M. Rapatini (mother), Little River, CANTERBURY.
16/713	Private	Raroa, Te Ata	Para Raroa (brother), Tekapa, AUCKLAND.
16/989	Private	Ratana, Toko	William Ratana, TURAKINA.
16/714	Private	Ratana, Wiremu	Tamaho Ratana, WHANGAPE.
16/715	Private	Rawiri, Horomona	Rawiri Amopo, Taradale, HAWKES BAY.
16/716	Private	Ray, John Te Reito	Naaka Te Toroa, Tupuna, Normanby, TARANAKI.
16/717	Private	Reedy, William	Thomas Reedy (father), TUPAROA.
16/836	Private	Reha, Philip	Mrs Kurawha Terewa (mother), Waimana, BAY OF PLENTY.
16/718	Private	Rei, Waari	Mrs Haana Rei (wife), Waikawa, PICTON.
16/719	Private	Reihana, Te Kareti	Mrs Reiha Reihana (mother), Rangitukia, PORT AWANUI.
16/720	Private	Reiroa, Martin Wesley	John Wesley Reiroa, WAIKUKU.
16/939	Private	Renata, Mare	Tupeka Renata (father), Muriwai, GISBORNE.
16/723	Private	Rickus, Thomas Samuel	Mrs Tainui (sister), KAIAPOI.
16/895	Private	Rini, Peri	Te Whau Rini (father), LOWER WAIHOU.
16/725	Private	Robson, Jesse	Hokianga William Robson (father), Pukepoto, via, MANGONUI.
16/726	Private	Roha, Tau	— Roha (father), OHAU.
16/727	Private	Royal, Hape	James Royal (father), OHAU.
16/728	Private	Royal, Huke	Turoa Royal (father), THAMES.
16/729	Private	Royal, Willie	Mrs Makareta Reora (mother), OHAU.
16/730	Private	Rupeen, Hoani	Sam Rupeen (father), KAIAPOI.

Number	Rank	Name	Next-of-Kin
16/630	Private	Rutene, Karaitiana	Rangi Karaitiana (brother), Petane, HAWKES BAY.
16/731	Private	Sainsbury, Etu	Mrs Hudson (aunt), Hikuai, TAIRUA.
16/734	Private	Simeon, Robin	Ripene Te Pa, Rikapoto, KAITAIA.
16/838	Private	Skelton, George Daniel	George Nepia (father), Motonui, WAIHI.
16/869	Private	Skelton, Harold George Nepia	Mrs Augusta Rahera (sister), Smart Road, Fitzroy, NEW PLYMOUTH.
16/1027	Private	Smith, D'Arcy Reginald	Mrs M.L. Smith (mother), 'Tirohia', Ascot Avenue, Remuera, AUCKLAND.
16/735	Private	Smith, Frank	Billy Smith (brother), Levuka, FIJI.
16/736	Private	Smith, Harold	Waikare Mela (cousin), Wairoa, HAWKES BAY.
16/737	Private	Smith, Joseph	P. Smith (father), Nuhaka, HAWKES BAY.
16/738	Private	Smith, Robert	George Smith (father), TOLAGA BAY.
16/998	Private	Snowdon, Henare	Mrs Mary Snowdon (mother), Seaview Terrace, Mt Albert, AUCKLAND.
16/739	Private	Sparks, Alfred	Mrs Sparks (mother), Waikowa, PICTON.
16/742	Private	Taiapa, Tamati	Tamati Taiapa Snr (father), Tikitiki, KAHUKURA.
16/744	Private	Taiaroa, Huruwhenua	Te Haku Rupine (aunt), Gonville Avenue, WANGANUI.
16/928	Private	Taiaroa, Mick	Hoani Taiaroa (father), WANGAEHU.
16/990	Private	Taipana, Charles	Mrs Hana Taipana (mother), Tuatapere, Maori Pa, TEMUKA.
16/991	Private	Taipari, Thomas	John Taipari (father), AHIPARA.
16/992	Private	Taitu, Taite	Pongi Tutaki, Porangahau, via WAIPUKURAU.
16/993	Private	Taiwhanga, Hirini	Nepa Taiwhanga (step brother), Tairua, THAMES.
16/995	Private	Takina, Hana	Rutene Takina (brother), Kaiti, GISBORNE.
16/740	Private	Takoko, Hori	Wi Takoko (father), Tikitiki, KAHUKURA.
16/891	Private	Takuao, Paul	Mehaere Takuao, Omahu, THAMES.
16/605	Private	Tamahau, Wiremu	Mrs Mauhau Te Tuihi (mother), TE WHAITI.
16/963	Private	Tamauaki, Papera	Piniha Tamauaki (father), Pakihiroa, WAIPIRO BAY.
16/842	Private	Tapine, Hotene	Mrs Maria Tapine, GISBORNE.
16/746	Private	Tapine, Mick	Mrs Heremia Tapopo (mother), Wairoa, HAWKES BAY.
16/840	Private	Tapsell, Robert	Mrs Ngati Tapsell (mother), Maketu, BAY OF PLENTY.
16/841	Private	Tauhou, Henare	Mrs Puiti Muiti Hapimana (mother), Te Ngae, ROTORUA.
16/874	Private	Teare, Whanoke	Mrs Whanaki Paore, RUATOKI.
16/964	Private	Te Hau, Pera	Pita Te Hau (father), Muriwai, GISBORNE.
16/751	Private	Te Kootu, Hohepa Paramu	Rangitua Paramana Te Kootu, OHAU.
16/752	Private	Te Kuru, Hoani	Hoani Te Kuru (father), Porangahau, HAWKES BAY.
16/754	Private	Te Maru, Hemi Pene	Robert Te Maru, Whananaki, WHANGAREI.
16/755	Private	Te Okeroa, Joe	Joe Ruihi, Mohaka, HAWKES BAY.
16/922	Private	Te Pene, James	Te Hau Tapene (uncle), THAMES.
16/758	Private	Te Purei, Mohi	Paratene Parinui (grandfather), Kahukura, PORT AWANUI.
16/759	Private	Te Rauna, Eruera	Heneriata Te Piri, Tuparoa, GISBORNE.
16/844	Private	Terekia, Manu	Rangi Te Kawri Pere (nephew), Fox Street, Whataupoko, GISBORNE.
16/760	Private	Te Rore, Jehu	Ra Te Rore (father), KAIHU.
16/846	Private	Te Ua, Te Miere	Hapi Porourangi (uncle), Ohiwa, WHAKATANE.
16/847	Private	Tewai, Paratawa	Paratawa Tewi (father), TOKOMARU BAY.
16/762	Private	Te Whau, Henry	John Te Whau (brother), Honikiwi, via OTOROHANGA.
16/764	Private	Tipuna, Wharau	Hekiera Te Tuna,, HICKS BAY.
16/765	Private	Tirikatene, Eruera Tihema	J.D. Tirikatene (father), Tawhakitiriki, KAIAPOI.
16/956	Private	Toa, Tom	Mrs T. Toa (mother), Otorohanga, KING COUNTRY.
16/850	Private	Tooke, Te Reinga	William Tooke, Munutuke, GISBORNE.
16/768	Private	Tuhaka, Maaka	Turei Tuhaka (father), PORT AWANUI.
16769	Private	Tuhora, Potene	Ramiera Tuhora (father), RONGATUHEA.
16/770	Private	Tukareoho, Matenga	Nurse Mataira (sister), Nuhaka, HAWKES BAY.
16/851	Private	Tukemata, Ingoa	Miss Honahu Tukemata (sister), OTOROHANGA.
16/772	Private	Turi, Mihaka	Tiwina Turi (brother), HICKS BAY.
16/773	Private	Tutaki, Tiaki	Mrs Emma Ngarino (mother), TAURANGA.
16/815	Private	Tutaki, Pakipaki	Mrs Emma Ngarino (mother), TAURANGA.
16/1004	Private	Tutt, Thomas Kene	— Maru (brother), KAIWHIA.
16/941	Private	Waaha, Horomana	Horomana Taruna (father), Whakaki, HAWKES BAY.
16/781	Private	Waaka, Waitohi	Mrs Waitohi Waaka (wife), Muriwai, GISBORNE.
16/774	Private	Waerea, Jimmy	Pango Ware, Beach Road, HASTINGS.
16/927	Private	Waerea, Pura	Riki, Waerea (brother), Pakipaki, HAWKES BAY.
16/852	Private	Waikare, Pene	Mrs Mereana Takataka (aunt), Te Arai, Manutuke, GISBORNE.
16/777	Private	Waipapa, Rahau	Miss Kate Waipapa (sister), WAIPIRO BAY.
16/779	Private	Wairau, Ramera	Miss Wahatu Wirau (sister), Niania, HAWKES BAY.
16/782	Private	Waldron, George	Mrs Pare Hipirini (mother), P.O. Box 17, MAKIRIKIRI.
16/853	Private	Walker, Wirimu	Mrs Mary Walker (mother), TOLAGA BAY.
16/966	Private	Wanoa, Tahanga	Whanaku Parakau (stepfather), HICKS BAY.
16/755	Private	Warehu, Rutene	Mrs Hera Hamera (sister), Kahukura, GISBORNE.
16/741	Private	Warema, Takana	Ngahuia Koe,, Te Kauangaroa, WANGANUI.
16/854	Private	Wehipeihana, Heke	Rohana Wehipeihana (father), OHAU.
16/967	Private	Weko, Wi	Hohepa, Weko (father), Nuhaka, HAWKES BAY.
16/783	Private	Wereta, Mack	Mrs Raina Rangiare (wife), WAITOTARA.
16/785	Private	Wereta, Poi	W.H. Wareta, P.O. 17, WAITOTARA.
16/786	Private	Whaanga, Tuati	Ihana Whaanga (father), Nuhaka, HAWKES BAY.
16/787	Private	Wharehinga, Kereopa	Raana Wharehinga (father), Rangitukia, via, GISBORNE.
16/788	Private	Wharekura, Joe	Wharekura, Nuhaka, GISBORNE.
16/857	Private	Whenuanui, Roki	Mrs Mokomatatua (mother), Waikaremoana, via Wairoa, HAWKES BAY.
16/789	Private	Whitau, Arapata Koti P.	Hiria Parete, "Teruapu", TEMUKA.
16/859	Private	Wilkinson, Thomas	Oneroa (brother-in-law), OTOROHANGA.
16/790	Private	Williams, Thomas	Mrs John Hall, Ohinemutu, ROTORUA.
16/791	Private	Wilson, Henry	Te Kai Wilson, OTAKI.
16/860	Private	Wineti, Dick	Mrs Waikawa (mother), Wairoa, TAURANGA.
16/861	Private	Winterburn, Richard	Alfred Winterburn (father), OTAKI.
16/863	Private	Wipa, Tangi	Mrs Raumiriu Purangi (sister), OTOROHANGA.
16/793	Private	Wirimu, Teu	Mrs Moiraka Stone (sister), Ahipara, NORTH AUCKLAND.

3RD MAORI CONTINGENT.

LEFT NEW ZEALAND, 5TH FEBRUARY, 1916.

Reg. No.	Rank.	Name.	Occupation.	Name and Address of Next-of-kin.
		A COMPANY.		
16/1327	Lieutenant	Sutherland, Frank Emanuel	Clerk	Mrs. C. J. Schnauer (sister), Arthur Street, Onehunga.
16/1326	2nd Lieut.	Goodwin, Erdington		Mrs. A. V. Goodwin (wife), O'Neil Street, Hamilton.
16/1310	,,	Karauria, Rii	Farmer	Ruma Karauria (wife), Dannevirke.
16/1329	,,	Moore, Stanley	Physical Instructor, Education	Mrs. S. Moore, 17 College Hill, Auckland.
16/897	Sergt.-Major	Moko, Peter Thomas	Agent	Mrs. Roka Waiaria Moko (wife), 16 Murphy Street, Wellington.
16/1380	Q.M. Sergt.	Mason, Hawea	Farmer	Mrs. Reremoana Meihana (wife), Carterton.
16/981	Sergeant	Bannister, David		J. W. Bannister (father), Bruce Bay, South Westland.
16/1279	,,	Cook, Harry	Bushman	J. B. Cook (father), Rangiahua Post-office, Hokianga.
16/1254	,,	Emia, William	Builder	Mrs. K. Emia (wife), Gonville, Wanganui.
16/803	,,	Kingi, Ihaia	Clerk	Tuteari Kingi (father), Te Karaka, Gisborne.
16/894	,,	Te Heu Heu, Matene	Law	Mrs. Martin (grandmother), Fyfield House, Oxfordshire, England.
16/640	Corporal	Kiri, Ben	Labourer	Mrs. T. Karepa (mother), Victoria Valley, Mongonui.
16/705	,,	Pine, John	Farmer	Mrs. Mataroa Pine (wife), Manaia, Taranaki.
16/1251	,,	Rewa, Waaka Simon	School-teacher	Mrs. Pare Rewa (mother), Te Kopuru.
16/1284	,,	Rupene, Aperahoma	Farmer	Mrs. E. M. Reuben (wife), Pipiriki, Wanganui.
16/954	,,	Taupaki, Rameka	Labourer	Mrs. Raiha Iri Kowhai (mother), Paeroa.
16/1232	,,	Wilkinson, Henry Te Haeta	Cadet	Mrs. G. W. Wilkinson (mother), Otorohanga.
16/1233	Lance-Corpl.	Butt, Edgar	Clerk	W. A. Butt (father), Rotorua.
16/1013	,,	Kaimoana, Piripi	Labourer	Papakaura Kaimoana (father), Wairoa, Hawke's Bay.
16/1260	,,	McGregor, Arona	Flax-mill Hand	Miss Rangitaiki McGregor (sister), Foxton.
16/1239	,,	McPherson, Hugh	Farmer	Mrs. J. McPherson (mother), Rotorua.
16/1244	,,	Stanley, George Rangihiroa	Carpenter	James Stanley (grandfather), Rotorua.
16/1252	Private	Anderson, Andrew	Seaman	Mrs. Anderson (mother), Pipiriki, Wanganui.
16/1318	,,	Clark, Tohu Adam	Mill Hand	Mrs. Clark (mother), Kohukohu, Hokianga.
16/1317	,,	Coffey, George	Seaman	Mrs. Jane Coffey (wife), Poutu, Kaipara.
16/1299	,,	Cook, George Gray	Clerk	Samuel Cook (father), Otaki.
16/1296	,,	Cotton, Simon	Bushman	Mrs. B. S. Cotton (mother), Te Ahuahu, Ohinewai.
16/1282	,,	Cross, Napier Charles	Farmer	Henry Cross (father), Opua, Bay of Islands.
16/1255	,,	Edwards, Henry	Clerk	Parekarewa, Manakau, Wellington.
16/1277	,,	Edwards, Taylor	Labourer	John Edwards (father), Pukehou, Hawke's Bay.
16/1234	,,	Gray, Albert	Surveyor's Cadet	Wilson Gray (brother), Te Puke.
16/1235	,,	Hall, Tukua	Farmer	Rangimakehu Hall, Rotorua.
16/1268	,,	Hamahona, Hastings	Labourer	Haretama Hamahona (father), Petane, Hawke's Bay.
16/1351	,,	Harrison, Henry	Shearer	Mrs. F. Harrison (mother), Waipiro Bay.
16/1302	,,	Hawira, Rangi Louis	Shepherd	T. Hawira (brother), Karioi, Main Trunk.
16/1320	,,	Hemi, Skipper Pou	Labourer	Pou Whiro Hemi (father), Canvastown, Havelock.
16/1257	,,	Hina, Pera	Farm Labourer	Tua Hina, Kauangaroa, Fordell.
16/1338	,,	Hodges, John Henry	Labourer	Henry Hodges (father), Mohaka, Hawke's Bay.
16/1376	,,	Honeycombe, Norman	Farmer	Mrs. Mary Honecombe (mother), Porirua.
16/1256	,,	Horipuha, Rota	Labourer	Mrs. Te Irikau (mother), Otaki.
16/1298	,,	Hura, Teo	,,	Mere Hura, Wairoa, Hawke's Bay.
16/1238	,,	Huriwaha, George	Farm Labourer	Mrs. K. Kingi (aunt), Omaha Street, Rotorua.
16/1334	,,	Jackson, Henry Wilkinson	Seaman	Mrs. E. Jackson (mother), Kingston, Norfolk Island.
16/1340	,,	Joe, Charlie	Labourer	Hanna Blake (sister), Wairoa, Hawke's Bay.
16/1293	,,	Kake, Jack	Bushman	Mrs. Katherine Kake (mother), Kiripaka, Whangarei.
16/1311	,,	Kaneri, Tupoto	Farmer	W. Kaneri, Northcote, Auckland.
16/1269	,,	Karena, Wiremu	Motor-driver	Rua Tutapa Karena (father), Te Arai, Gisborne.
16/1236	,,	Katene, Matete	Labourer	Hiria Katene (wife), Ohinemutu, Rotorua.
16/1316	,,	Kena, Roa	Seaman	Kawhi Kena (uncle), Poutu, Kaipara, Helensville.
16/1290	,,	Keppa, William	Labourer	Mrs. Pia Keppa (mother), Tukahiwai, Marsden Point, Whangarei.
16/114	,,	Kere, Pare		Rangi Kere (father), Opotiki.
16/1237	,,	Kereti, Tuhimata	Gardener	Mrs. Erenoia Tuhimata (wife), Ohinemutu, Rotorua.
16/1324	,,	King, Peter	Farm Labourer	Mrs. Te Wha King (mother), Manakau.
16/1128	,,	Kohimoka, George	Bushman	Warori Kohimoka (father), Motukaraka, Hokianga.
16/1292	,,	Luke, William		Mrs. Tita Luke (mother), Whakapara, Whangarei.
16/1259	,,	McDonald, Thomas	Flax-mill Hand	Christina McDonald (cousin), Koputaroa.
16/1258	,,	McDonald, Tutepourangi	Farmer	Karaitana McDonald, Koputaroa.
16/1323	,,	McGregor, Poutu	Labourer	Mrs. Ruhia McGregor (wife), Koputaroa.
16/1306	,,	McManus, Charlie	Farmer	H. McManus (father), Waihopo, Bay of Islands.
16/1276	,,	Maatiaha, Raharuhi	Labourer	Raharuhi Hemi Te Whiti (nephew), Masterton.
16/648	,,	Macke, Kotua	Farmer	Taniora Keppa (father), Waipawa.
16/1294	,,	Mahanga, George	,,	Mrs. Ngamohio Mahanga (mother), Parua Bay, Whangarei.
16/1295	,,	Mahanga, James	Bushman	Mrs. Ngamohio Mahanga (mother), Parua Bay, Whangarei.
16/890	,,	Maka, Peehinui	Labourer	Tarapipi Tupu (niece), Morrinsville.

Reg. No.	Rank.	Name.	Occupation.	Name and Address of Next-of-kin.
		A COMPANY—*continued*.		
16/1374	Private	Matene, Rameka	Farm Hand	M. Rongohira Tautoro (father), Kaikohe, Bay of Islands.
16/1285	,,	Matia, Tuhe Rini	Gum-digger	Mrs. Meynell (mother), Waikarara.
16/812	,,	Matiu, Tamati	Labourer	Ngawai Waana (aunt), Gisborne.
16/1283	,,	Mikaire, George	Gum-digger	Kato Mikaire (father), Komiti Estate, Northern Wairoa.
16/1370	,,	Morgan, Thomas Tutawake	Labourer	Tutawake Morgan (father), Kawhia.
16/1300	,,	Ngakai, Tainui	Driver	Ripikoi Ngakai (brother), Pipiroa.
16/1093	,,	Ormsby, William	Farmer	Mrs. W. Ormsby (wife), Otorohanga.
16/1241	,,	Paki, Reweti	Labourer	Lily Reweti (daughter), Waihou, Opotiki.
16/1242	,,	Paki, Wi	,,	Lily Reweti (sister), Waihou, Opotiki.
16/1281	,,	Parata, Reihana	,,	Riu Pai Parata (sister), Mangere, Auckland.
16/1347	,,	Peciman, William Hiakia	Farmer	Rupeke Peciman (sister), Kawhia, Auckland.
16/1271	,,	Perenara, Bob	Labourer	Makere Paraihi (mother), Poukawa, Hastings.
16/1332	,,	Phillips, Morgan Harold	Clerk	J. G. Phillips (father), Matapu, Taranaki.
16/1341	,,	Pitama, Tiaki	Labourer	George Beccham (father), Tarapatiti, Hawke's Bay.
16/1261	,,	Poni, Matarini	Farmer	Matarini Poni (father), Raorikia, Wanganui.
16/1363	,,	Rameka, Pereri	Surveyor's Asst.	Kere Rameka (father), Tauranga.
16/1243	,,	Rangitahi, Pita	Farmer	Wenarata Pirimi (aunt), Ohinemutu.
16/1272	,,	Ratema, Timarana	Labourer	Mrs. Ripirata Topia (mother), Teringa, Wairoa, Hawke's Bay.
16/1273	,,	Rawiri, August Wakaiti	,,	Te Ahu Rawiri (father), Te Harota.
16/1265	,,	Rawiri, Tai	,,	Heremaia Rawiri (father), Raetihi.
16/721	,,	Rewi, Petera	,,	Tanatiu Rewi (father), Whakatane.
16/1274	,,	Riki, Pi	,,	Mrs. Tipuna (mother), Hastings.
16/1342	,,	Rotoatara, Karena	,,	Karena Rotoatara (father), Wairoa, Hawke's Bay.
16/1015	,,	Ruru, Rangi Horawera	,,	Hemaina Ruru (grandmother), Waiari, Muriwai, Gisborne.
16/1245	,,	Taiaroa, Matenga Haeroa	Farmer	Mrs. Margaret Karetai (mother), Otakou, Dunedin.
16/1343	,,	Tamati, Waikare	Labourer	Waikare Mete (father), Wairoa, Hawke's Bay.
16/1014	,,	Tamihana, Wi	,,	Harata Tamihana (grandmother), Rutariwha, Wairoa, Hawke's Bay.
16/1275	,,	Tangatake, Whiri	,,	Rehia Tangatake (mother), Ngaruawahia.
16/1246	,,	Tapihana, Potikai Haereata	Survey Hand	Mrs. Hareata Kiharoa (mother), Ohinemutu, Rotorua.
16/1263	,,	Taputoro, Manu	Farmer	Mrs. Sarah Toro (mother), Opotiki.
16/1247	,,	Tawhai, Rua	Labourer	Mrs. Hera Tawhai (wife), Rotorua.
16/1344	,,	Te Aho, Albert Paul	,,	Paul Te Aho (father), Mohaka, Hawke's Bay.
16/1305	,,	Te Aniani, Hoani Pokaihaku	,,	Ranginohitihi Te Aniani (daughter), College Road, Northcote, Auckland.
16/1289	,,	Te Haara, Wi	Farmer	Rui Te Haara, Ngawha, Ohinewai.
16/1248	,,	Te Kohi, Matini	Labourer	Mrs. Te Ra Kohi (mother), Tarukenga, Rotorua.
16/757	,,	Te Patu, Tamati	Farmer	Tirepa Te Patu (father), Karioi.
16/845	,,	Te Rewa, Meihana	Labourer	Waimana Te Rewa (father), Bay of Plenty.
16/1266	,,	Te Wiata, Tauhia	Compositor	Tarako Te Wiata, Otaki.
16/1345	,,	Turetahi, Whare	Labourer	Ataria Turetahi (father), Waihua, Wairoa, Hawke's Bay.
16/1249	,,	Waata, Pene	,,	Peter Waata (father), Hokianga.
16/1319	,,	Waetford, Charles Berry	,,	C. A. Waetford (father), Kamo, Whangarei.
16/1297	,,	Waetford, Eugene	,,	Posey Waetford (son), Kamo, Whangarei.
16/780	,,	Waetford, James Walford	Driver	C. A. Waetford (father), Kamo, Whangarei.
16/1314	,,	Waipouri, Pirimoana	Sailor	Mrs. Porengi Pirimoana (mother), Omapero, Hokianga.
16/1264	,,	Wakefield, Wallie	Farmer	H. Wakefield (father), Sydenham, Christchurch.
16/996	,,	Wharekino, William	Labourer	J. Wharekino, Whangara, Gisborne.
16/1280	,,	White, David	,,	Mrs. D. White, Hitana, Picton.
16/1250	,,	Whititera, Te Rire	,,	Riwa Marino, Ohinemutu, Rotorua.
16/1287	,,	Wihongi, Wiremu Paki	,,	Mrs. Rangi Mumura Wi Paki (wife), care of W. Spence, Evans Corner, Northcote, Auckland.
16/1291	,,	Wiki, Whiro	,,	Hohana Wiki (mother), Karatu, Kawakawa, Bay of Islands.
16/1325	,,	Wilson, Puku	,,	Hori Wilson, Wararoa.

Reg. No.	Rank.	Name.	Occupation.	Name and Address of Next-of-kin.

RAROTONGANS.
Attached A Company.

Reg. No.	Rank.	Name.	Occupation.	Name and Address of Next-of-kin.
16/1200	Sergeant	Tepuretu, Raitia	Clerk	Mrs. Metua Tepuretu (wife), Avarua, Rarotonga.
16/1182	Corporal	Anthony	Labourer	Manuera (father), Avarua, Rarotonga.
16/1033	,,	Isaacs, Solomon	,,	Henry Isaacs, Tautu, Aitutaki.
16/1194	,,	Ropu, John	,,	Ropu (adopted father), Avarua, Rarotonga.
16/1222	,,	Tepuretu, Apu	,,	Tepuretu (father), Avarua, Rarotonga.
16/1333	Lance-Corpl.	Kaipati	Policeman	Mrs. Tainuna (mother), Manumea, Ellis Island.
16/1193	,,	Pita	Labourer	Mere Ke (sister), Mataure, Rarotonga.
16/1196	,,	Solomona	,,	Poki Poki (father), Mawihiki.
16/1183	Private	Ainia	,,	Kapi (cousin), Avarua, Rarotonga.
16/1205	,,	Angene	,,	Angene (father), Avarua, Rarotonga.
16/1321	,,	Apa, John Tuaine	Steward	John Apa (father), Aitutaki, Cook Islands.
16/1139	,,	Arii	Labourer	Pito Vaine (friend), Avarua, Rarotonga.
16/1206	,,	Ataataivi	,,	Arapoiti (father), Tamarua, Mangaia, Rarotonga.
16/1184	,,	Inga	,,	Ngau (father), Avarua, Rarotonga.
16/1185	,,	Kamati	,,	Mamanu (brother), Arorangi, Rarotonga.
16/1208	,,	Kavae	,,	Kavae (father), Aitutaki, Amuri, Cook Islands.
16/1207	,,	Kopungaiti, Tau	,,	Mirin (adopted father), Oneroa, Mangaia, Rarotonga.
16/1212	,,	Mahoa	,,	Piharoa (father), Parapara, Rarotonga.
16/1214	,,	Makaroa	,,	Tananira (father), Arorangi, Rarotonga.
16/1187	,,	Mataia	,,	Paitaim (father), Avarua, Rarotonga.
16/1211	,,	Mataira	,,	Tinirau (father), Makea, Avarua, Rarotonga.
16/1189	,,	Matau	,,	Manvaroa (father), Arorangi, Rarotonga.
16/1188	,,	Metua, Moeau	,,	Moeau (father), Arorangi, Rarotonga.
16/1210	,,	Metua, Samuela	,,	Upoko (mother), Avarua, Rarotonga.
16/1191	,,	Metua	,,	Tangata (uncle), Mauke, Rarotonga.
16/1190	,,	Moeau	,,	Taria (father), Arorangi, Rarotonga.
16/1209	,,	Mou	,,	Ina (brother), Avarua, Rarotonga.
16/1192	,,	Nena	,,	Noa (father), Arorangi, Rarotonga.
16/1227	,,	Ngapo, Bob	Cook	Kapatiau, Tautu, Avtuaki, Cook Islands.
16/1215	,,	Patu	Labourer	Moetana (brother), Avarua, Rarotonga.
16/1216	Private	Pori, Jim	Labourer	Pori (father), Avarua, Rarotonga.
16/1218	,,	Remuera	,,	Paiti (father), Arorangi, Rarotonga.
16/1217	,,	Rere	,,	Mrs. Vaine Maki (wife), Avarua, Rarotonga.
16/1195	,,	Rima	,,	Pa Nirau (father), Avarua, Rarotonga.
16/1198	,,	Takaroka	,,	Takaroka (adopted father), Matavera, Rarotonga.
16/1335	,,	Taliauli, John	Medical Student	Malkai (brother), Tukuafu, Nukualofa, Tonga.
16/1201	,,	Taneao	Labourer	Kiri (father), Matavera, Rarotonga.
16/1224	,,	Tanga	,,	Kautai Vaine (friend), Avarua, Rarotonga.
16/1228	,,	Tararo, Frank William	Gardener	Mrs. Tararo, Mauke, Cook Island.
16/1199	,,	Taringa	Labourer	Mateaenga (father), Atiu, Areora, Cook Island.
16/1223	,,	Tauarua	,,	Rangi, Tepuretu, Rarotonga.
16/1202	,,	Taura	,,	Tuakina (father), Atiu, Rarotonga.
16/1221	,,	Tipoki	,,	Vaevaeonga (father), Oneroa, Rarotonga.
16/1219	,,	Tivini Pai	,,	Mrs. Etetera (mother), Maraerenga, Avarua, Rarotonga.
16/1197	,,	Tupu	,,	Mrs. Ani (mother), Arutanga, Aitutaki, Rarotonga.
16/1220	,,	Tutavake	,,	Mrs. Raa Vaine (mother), Avarua, Rarotonga.
16/1203	,,	Vavia	,,	Williams (father), Makatea, Mauke, Rarotonga.

Attached B Company.

Reg. No.	Rank.	Name.	Occupation.	Name and Address of Next-of-kin.
16/1309	2nd Lieut.	Fromm, George August	Clerk	A. A. Fromm (father), Cheesemen Road, Gisborne.
16/1330	,,	McDonald, Archibald	Civil Servant	A. McDonald (father), Grace Street, Invercargill.
16/1303	,,	Melles, Alexander George	Dentist	W. Melles (father), Willis Street, Palmerston North.
16/1328	,,	Young, Charles Lefana	Student	J. Young (father), College Street West, Palmerston North.
16/1226	Sergt.-Major	Holmes, Frederick	Police Officer	Mrs. F. Ashley (aunt), care of Mrs. Hibbert, 1 Hornsby Rise Gardens, Crouch End, London.
16/1176	,,	Uea	Parson	Tione Kilifi (brother), Lalofetau, Niue Island.
16/1229	C.Q.M.S.	Westbrook, Edward	Wheelwright	G. E. L. Westbrook (father), Samoa.
16/1315	Sergeant	Leger, Baisley	Boatbuilder	J. Leger (father), Nukulofa, Tonga.
16/1052	,,	Hemu	Settler	Miss Tifuongo (sister), Hikutavake, Niue Island.
16/1107	,,	Pulu	,,	Vaiata (wife), Alofi, Niue Island.
16/1034	Corporal	Fasene	Teacher	Tosene (father), Avetele, Niue Island.
16/1053	,,	Hipa	Settler	Tifa (wife), Hikutavake, Niue Island.
16/1064	,,	Lapa		Tegiafuhi (father), Tamakautoga, Niue Island.
16/1068	,,	Latoa (2)	Settler	Ikinofo (father), Alofi, Niue Island.
16/1102	,,	Manatoa		Nuahemotu (wife), Luapa, Niue Island.
16/1104	,,	Nui, Aleo		Ligimataki (wife), Alofi, Niue Island.
16/1148	,,	Tefatumoana	Settler	Totau (wife), Liku, Niue Island.
16/1133	,,	Tionesini	,,	Maife (wife), Hakupu, Niue Island.
16/1091	,,	Tiulai	Schoolmaster	Hamoa (father), Alofi, Niue Island.
16/1030	Lance-Corpl.	Alotau	Settler	Folole (wife), Alofi, Niue Island.
16/1090	,,	Manuela	,,	Nafoagamata (wife), Omahi, Niue Island.
16/1089	,,	Moana		Mata (mother), Alofi, Niue Island.
16/1313	,,	Payne, Frank	Farmer	Amy Payne (sister), care of Mrs. Chamberlain, Waimarino.
16/1130	,,	Sisikefu	Settler	Mohematagi (father), Mutalau, Niue Island.
16/1143	,,	Tagimau		Niuloa (father), Alofi, Niue Island.
16/1131	,,	Tauliti	Settler	Logatupe (wife), Tamakautoga, Niue Island.
16/1142	,,	Tionehafa	,,	Maina (wife), Alofi, Niue Island.

Reg. No.	Rank.	Name.	Occupation.	Name and Address of Next-of-kin.
		RAROTANGAS—*continued*.		
		ATTACHED B COMPANY—*continued*.		
16/1032	Private	Elone	,,	Laka (father), Hakupu, Niue Island.
16/1035	,,	Fakahoa		Pose (father), Alofi, Niue Island.
16/1041	,,	Fakalagakai		Farani (father), Lakepa, Niue Island.
16/1040	,,	Fakauka		Muitoa (father), Lakepa, Niue Island.
16/1037	,,	Fakile	Settler	Tamahemata (wife), Mutalau, Niue Island.
16/1044	,,	Fahoa		Tosene (father), Avetele, Niue Island.
16/1038	,,	Faletogia	Settler	Uesi (father), Mutulau, Niue Island.
16/1036	,,	Fanatoa	,,	Mago (father), Tamakautoga, Niue Island.
16/1043	,,	Fanavai		Mareni (father), Lakepa, Niue Island.
16/1348	,,	Fata	Labourer	Line (mother), Tuapa, Niue Island.
16/1042	,,	Fatamaka	Settler	Taufitimoka (wife), Lakepa, Niue Island.
16/1039	,,	Fati		Togia (father), Mutulau, Niue Island.
16/1046	,,	Filitoua		Folevohetupe (wife), Makefu, Niue Island.
16/1047	,,	Finiki		Tavita (father), Alofi, Niue Island.
16/1045	,,	Fohetaha	Sailor	Liliola (wife), Alofi, Niue Island.
16/1048	,,	Gumaka	Settler	Tifaogo (wife), Hikutaveke, Niue Island.
16/1049	,,	Gutupuloga		Tagaloa (mother), Mutulau, Niue Island.
16/1371	,,	Harry, Purie Dave	Cook	Niutoga (father), Niue Island.
16/1051	,,	Hegatuki	Settler	Mele (wife), Alofi, Niue Island.
16/1055	,,	Ikitane		Kalopa (father), Hakupu, Niue Island.
16/1057	,,	Ikito	Settler	Ikinoi (father), Tuapa, Niue Island.
16/1054	,,	Imiu	,,	Fetolini (wife), Hakupu, Niue Island.
16/1062	,,	Kaimanu		Tapuga (wife), Hikutaveke, Niue Island.
16/1061	,,	Kalupa	Settler	Patoga (father), Hikutaveke, Niue Island.
16/1059	,,	Kamupeli	,,	Ahitau (wife), Hakupu, Niue Island.
16/1063	,,	Kanatau		Leno (wife), Makefu, Niue Island.
16/1058	,,	Ku		Totule (father), Tamakautoga, Niue Island.
16/1060	,,	Kuluia	Settler	Fineli (wife), Alofi, Niue Island.
16/1080	,,	Lagigie	,,	Tanesi (wife), Tuapa, Niue Island.
16/1081	,,	Latitu		Fakaaga (mother), Tuapa, Niue Island.
16/1066	,,	Latoa (1)		Finiata (wife), Hakupu, Niue Island.
16/1077	,,	Laufoli	Villager	Peau (brother), Liku, Niue Island.
16/1349	,,	Lauho	Wharf Labourer	Lueua (mother), Whenutu Niue Island.
16/1082	,,	Laupa	Settler	Fakalaga (father), Makefu, Niue Island.
16/1084	,,	Lautagata	,,	Nia (father), Makefu, Niue Island.
16/1071	,,	Lavaika		Tavita (father), Alofi, Niue Island.
16/1072	,,	Lavini		Taufitimamuke (wife), Hikutaveke, Niue Island.
16/1336	,,	Leger, Francis	Seaman	Kate Leger (aunt), 129 Wellington Street, Auckland.
16/1070	,,	Leini		Latika (father), Alofi, Niue Island.
16/1074	,,	Leotoga	,,	Pakitoa (father), Hikutaveke, Niue Island.
16/1076	,,	Likatau	Settler	Taumanogi (mother), Alofi, Niue Island.
16/1079	,,	Litioti		Tomumu (father), Avatele, Niue Island.
16/1073	Private	Litipa		Puketoa (wife), Hikutaveke, Niue Island.
16/1083	,,	Liu		Togialele (father), Tuapa, Niue Island.
16/1069	,,	Lui	Settler	Tiahi (wife), Alofi, Niue Island.
16/1065	,,	Luivae	,,	Hai (father), Hakupu, Niue Island.
16/1075	,,	Lukupa		Lino (wife), Liku, Niue Island.
16/1086	,,	Maka	Settler	Motutoa (father), Hakupu, Niue Island.
16/1094	,,	Makafitu	,,	Vavahe (father), Mutalau, Niue Island.
16/1092	,,	Malefitu		Tumaki (wife), Alofi, Niue Island.
16/1101	,,	Matiutama		Matiu (father), Makefu, Niue Island.
16/1085	,,	Meti		Ukufia (father), Tamakautoga, Niue Island.
16/1100	,,	Mitihepe		Lamatoa (father), Makefu, Niue Island.
16/1087	,,	Mitikele	Settler	Hegatagaloa (wife), Hakupu, Niue Island.
16/1097	,,	Mitikone		Togiatau (father), Mutalau, Niue Island.
16/1095	,,	Mitikoneua		Kalaina (mother), Mutalau, Niue Island.
16/1099	,,	Mitiloti		Mititala (father), Avatele, Niue Island.
16/1096	,,	Mitipauni	Settler	Tamatagi (father), Mutalau, Niue Island.
16/1088	,,	Moki	,,	Pokihega (father), Fatiau, Niue Island.
16/1103	,,	Motutoa		Fahisipi (father), Tuapa, Niue Island.
16/1098	,,	Muimatagi		Hega (mother), Mutalau, Niue Island.
16/1105	,,	None		Manamana (father), Avetele, Niue Island.
16/1106	,,	Otitoa		Tuleikafa (wife), Hakupu, Niue Island.
16/1112	,,	Pafalani		Pulegapule (father), Hikutaveke, Niue Island.
16/1119	,,	Pakitau	Settler	Pepe (wife), Mutalau, Niue Island.
16/1123	,,	Paleko		Lafu (father), Makefu, Niue Island.
16/1125	,,	Patuki	Settler	Fakato (mother), Alofi, Niue Island.
16/1307	,,	Pauhumoana (6)	Fruiterer	Nuitonga (father), Laku, Niue Island.
16/1115	,,	Peni	Settler	Puakafa (wife), Hikutaveke, Niue Island.
16/1122	,,	Pieti		Mareni (father), Lakepa, Niue Island.
16/1118	,,	Pimeleko	Settler	Matafotu (wife), Matafotu, Niue Island.
16/1126	,,	Piniki	,,	Takaheone (wife), Alofi, Niue Island.
16/1110	,,	Pinimaka		Mugaiki (father), Alofi, Niue Island.
16/1114	,,	Pita		Malama (father), Tagaloa, Hikutaveke, Niue Island.
16/1117	,,	Poihalagi	Settler	Kalika (brother), Liku, Niue Island.
16/1108	,,	Poimatagi	,,	Tiupeli (wife), Hakupu, Niue Island.
16/1120	,,	Puhotau		Togiatau (father), Mutalau, Niue Island.
16/1113	,,	Pulegamata		Kilipula (father), Hakapu, Niue Island.

Reg. No.	Rank.	Name.	Occupation.	Name and Address of Next-of-kin.

RAROTANGAS—continued.
ATTACHED B COMPANY—continued.

Reg. No.	Rank.	Name.	Occupation.	Name and Address of Next-of-kin.
16/1124	,,	Pulegatau		Puretekai (wife), Tuapa, Niue Island.
16/1127	,,	Pulekanamata		Maea (mother), Makefu, Niue Island.
16/1121	,,	Pulemoana		Falani (father), Lakepa, Niue Island.
16/1111	,,	Puleoti		Pulego (wife), Vailoa, Alofi, Niue Island.
16/1109	,,	Pulu (2)	Settler	Limaole (wife), Tamakautoga, Niue Island.
16/1159	,,	Tafale		Mrs. Fiatagaloa (wife), Mutalau, Niue Island.
16/1138	,,	Tafana	Settler	Tagasili (father), Hakapu, Niue Island.
16/1147	,,	Tafua		Tavaha (father), Hikutaveke, Niue Island.
16/1166	,,	Tagavaikuilu		Foufou (wife), Avatili, Niue Island.
16/1168	,,	Tahikona		Kapitiga (father), Avatele, Niue Island.
16/1162	,,	Talauta	Settler	Alise (wife), Mutalau, Niue Island.
16/1132	,,	Taleva	,,	Filitupe (wife), Tamakautoga, Niue Island.
16/1163	,,	Tamaheton	,,	Mokapala (mother), Lakepa, Niue Island.
16/1154	,,	Tamatafiti		Tupelima (wife), Niue Island.
16/1155	,,	Tauetuli		Hikiloka (wife), Liku, Niue Island.
16/1136	,,	Taukilo	Settler	Talomaka (wife), Hakapu, Niue Island.
16/1161	,,	Taulisi (1)		Faletiu (wife), Mutalau, Niue Island.
16/1165	,,	Taumataua	Settler	Laka (wife), Lakepa, Niue Island.
16/1167	,,	Taveli		Hakeagaiki (father), Avatele, Niue Island.
16/1150	,,	Tavili		Mokakolikoli (wife), Liku, Niue Island.
16/1156	,,	Tiafa		Malagahola (wife), Mutalau, Niue Island.
16/1178	,,	Tilimaka		Patutoa (father), Liku, Niue Island.
16/1153	,,	Tilo		Tialeone (wife), Liku, Niue Island.
16/1134	,,	Timoko	Settler	Kepuhega (father), Hakupu, Niue Island.
16/1164	,,	Tineatama		Luvea (father), Lakepa, Niue Island.
16/1141	,,	Tio	Settler	Tulua (father), Alofi, Niue Island.
16/1135	,,	Tionemale		Mika (father), Hakupu, Niue Island.
16/1149	,,	Tionemouga	Settler	Mokahulugia (wife), Liku, Niue Island.
16/1137	,,	Tionetali		Fanatau (father), Hakupu, Niue Island.
16/1146	,,	Tionetini	Settler	Tuhau (father), Tamakautoga, Niue Island.
16/1129	,,	Tipi		Punuatogia (father), Mutalau, Niue Island.
16/1169	,,	Toamio		Foeume (father), Avatele, Niue Island.
16/1157	,,	Togiahemetu	Settler	Motu (father), Mutalau, Niue Island.
16/1170	,,	Tohovaka		Palaone (father), Makefu, Niue Island.
16/1145	,,	Toi		Lumeka (mother), Makaheheko, Niue Island.
16/1158	,,	Tomati		Nogihau (mother), Mutalau, Niue Island.
16/1152	,,	Tukimata		Talagi (father), Liku, Niue Island.
16/1144	,,	Tukuaho		Tioti (father), Alofi, Niue Island.
16/1175	,,	Uku	Settler	Alama (wife), Tuapa, Niue Island.
16/1174	,,	Ulukita		Fatu (father), Lakepa, Niue Island.
16/1179	,,	Vaihola		Moleni (father), Avatele, Niue Island.
16/1180	,,	Vaiua	Settler	Meleteine (mother), Avatele, Niue Island.
16/1181	,,	Vakatama		Tiahi (wife), Makefu, Niue Island.
16/1177	,,	Vasau	Settler	Siline (mother), Alofi, Niue Island.

3RD MAORI CONTINGENT.—DETAIL.

Reg. No.	Rank.	Name.	Occupation.	Name and Address of Next-of-kin.
16/767	Private	Trood, Henry	Sailor	Mrs. Rosa Trood (wife), care of British Consul, Apia.

4TH MAORI CONTINGENT.

Reg. No.	Rank.	Name.	Occupation.	Name and Address of Next-of-kin.
16/1308	2nd Lieut.	Karauti, Hori	Farmer	Mrs. Wiripini Waiwera Karauti (wife), Ohau, Manawatu Line.
16/1350	,,	Overton, Thomas Richard	Electrical Engineer	Mrs. Eva Ross Overton (wife), care of J. Carson, Murray Street, Caversham, Dunedin.
16/1403	Sergeant	Fromm, Percy Thomas	Linotype Operator	A. A. Fromm (father), Peel Street, Gisborne.
16/1172	,,	Roberston, John	Lighthouse-keeper	Mrs. Edith Willoughby Robertson (wife), Otakou, Dunedin.
16/1404	Corporal	Barclay, Francis	Farmer	Mrs. F. Barclay (wife), care of W. Duncan, Tahoraiti, Dannevirke.
16/1369	,,	Rukingi, Pini	,,	Mrs. Pinenga Rukingi (mother), Ohinemutu, Rotorua.
16/985	,,	Williamson, William	Stockman	Mrs. T. H. Wilmhurst (grandmother), 213 Chapel Street, Masterton.
16/1374	Lance-Corpl.	Boyer, Charles William	Salesman	A. Rounds (friend), Nukualofa, Tonga.
16/456	,,	†Kipa, Hori	Butcher	Mrs. Mere Reweti (mother), Kopu, Thames.
16/1388	,,	Mika, Wharekaniwha	Clerk	Mrs. Maunike Mika (mother) (Ngapuna), Whakarewarewa, Rotorua.
16/1401	,,	Paora, Wiremu	Surveyor	Mrs. H. Paora (mother), Reweti, Waitemata.
16/246	,,	†Pineaha, Watarawi	Farm Hand	Pineaha Mokiha (brother), Fernhill, Hastings.
16/1470	,,	Saunders, Hirini Patrick	Shepherd	Mrs. Amiria Willis (aunt), Owetea, Tokomaru Bay.
16/170	,,	†Savage, Thomas	Labourer	Thomas Savage, care of R. G. M. Parke, Wanganui.
16/1430	,,	Wairoa, Henry Theodore	Farmer	Mrs. P. Johnson (mother), North Clive, Wairoa.

† Ex 1st Maori Contingent.

Reg. No.	Rank.	Name.	Occupation.	Name and Address of Next-of-kin.
		4TH MAORI CONTINGENT—*continued.*		
16/1405	Private	Ah Mu, Maloga	Engineer	Mrs. Aifai Ah Mu (wife), Apia, Samoa.
16/562	,,	†Ahuriri, Etera	Mechanic	Rukeruke Ahuriri, Wairoa.
16/1392	,,	Anaru, Albert Paul	Clerk	Te Wika Anaru (father), Rotorua.
16/1490	,,	Anderson, Andrew	Telegraph Lineman	A. Anderson (father), Awanui.
16/1365	,,	Apatari, Manu	Labourer	G. H. Walker (stepfather), Muriwai, Gisborne.
16/1406	,,	Broughton, John	Farmer	Miss J. Kelsall (stepsister), Peria.
16/1469	,,	Brown, Henry	Sailor	Mrs. Maud Hooker (mother), Post-office, Kaikohe.
16/1407	,,	Cross, Norman	Bridge-builder	H. Cross (father), Bay of Islands.
16/509	,,	†Delaney, Roy	Station Hand	Miss Beatrice Delaney (sister), Te Karaka, Gisborne.
16/1384	,,	Duffy, Edmund	Overseer	A. Duffy (brother), Apia, Samoa.
16/1408	,,	Dunn, Walter	Rafter	Mrs. W. Dunn (wife), Omapere, Hokianga.
16/265	,,	†Ellison, Piri	Driver	Mrs. Hera Ellison (wife), Waikanae.
16/1501	,,	Gemmell, Benjamin	Labourer	Henry Gemmell (brother), Wairoa.
16/1550	,,	Hawira, Joe	,,	Mrs. J. Hawira (wife), Halcombe.
16/1492	,,	‡Hayes, John	Sheep-farmer	Mrs. Caroline Green (wife), Brown Street, Ponsonby, Auckland.
16/444	,,	†Hemana, Kohi Tatana	Farmer	Tatana Hemana, Batley, Kaipara.
16/1424	,,	Heta, John	Bushman	Mrs. Para Heta (mother), Whangarei.
16/1339	,,	Hura, Raukawa	Labourer	Mrs. Mere Hura (mother), Ruataniwha, Hawke's Bay.
16/1231	,,	Jones, Thomas Edward	Farmer	Mrs. Tema Jones (mother), Pirongia, Waipawa.
16/1491	,,	Karapaina, Hakota	,,	Paratene Karapaina (brother), Te Kaha, Bay of Plenty.
16/1500	,,	Karehana, Martin	,,	M. Karehana (father), Awahuri, Feilding.
16/1367	,,	Karepa, Nohoroa	Labourer	Karepa Wahanui (father), Te Karaka, Gisborne.
16/1394	,,	King, Ned	,,	Mrs. Mihi Tewau (mother), Lower Waihou, Hokianga.
16/1391	,,	Kingi, Wiremu	Bushman	Mrs. Reremoana (mother), Te Kaha, Bay of Plenty.
16/1418	,,	Lazarus, Jack	Trader	Miss Anne Lazarus (sister), Suva, Fiji.
16/1396	,,	Mano, Hii	Labourer	Mano Makaraka (father), Taheke, Hokianga.
16/1376	,,	Meredith, Frank	Trader	Mrs. A. T. Meredith (mother), Leone, Pago Pago, Samoa.
16/1375	,,	Meredith, Oscar	,,	O. Meredith (father), Apia, Samoa.
16/1378	,,	Mitchell, Ernest	Overseer	E. H. Mitchell (father), Rarotonga.
16/682	,,	Mohi, Hori	Labourer	Mrs. Kaimatai Hori Mohi (wife), Otaki.
16/408	,,	†Paora, Tauri	Farmer	Paora Tokoahu, Taupo.
16/1366	,,	Para, Kohu	Labourer	Mo Pohatu (father), Manutuke, Gisborne.
16/1359	,,	Pencha, Tohu	,,	Pencha Kingi (father), Kaikohe.
16/1355	,,	Pera, Tote	,,	Pee March (brother-in-law), Kaikohe.
16/1362	,,	Rauahi, Taki	,,	Mrs. Iha Pera Rauahi (wife), Kaikohe.
16/1356	,,	Renata, Harry	,,	Ngapuhi Renata (father), Heiekeino, Mangonui County.
16/1382	,,	Roberts, Frank	Trader	Mrs. K. Roberts (wife), Faleasiu, Samoa.
16/1383	,,	Stowers, James	Carpenter	James Stowers (father), Apia, Samoa.
16/1416	,,	Stowers, Robert	,,	Mrs. Mary Stowers (mother), Apia, Samoa.
16/1494	,,	Subritzky, Robert	Clerk	Arthur William Thomas Subritzky (father), Awanui.
16/1419	,,	Swanney, James	Carpenter	Mrs. M. Swanney (mother), care of Mrs. Sanders, Apia, Samoa.
16/1381	,,	Sydney, Graham	Coal-miner	Hirini Enoka (father), Tauranga.
16/1393	,,	Tairua, Peter	Farmer	Tairua (father), Matata, Bay of Plenty.
16/1417	,,	Tangiora, Broughton	Labourer	Hape Tangiora (father), Mahia Peninsula.
16/1499	,,	§Te Au, James	Fisherman	Mrs. J. Winiata (mother), Colac Bay, Southland.
16/1390	,,	Tetuhi, Nikora	Labourer	Te Moki Tetuhi (father), Matata, Bay of Plenty.
16/1488	,,	Tini, John	,,	Mrs. Mary Tini (mother), Little River.
16/1482	,,	Trotter, Ronald	Shepherd	Mrs. J. Collier (mother), Waikanae.
16/1357	,,	Tuauru, Ewata	Labourer	Miss Kiwi Tuauru (sister), Kaikohe.
16/1421	,,	Tuauru, Mateora	,,	Kiri Tuauru (sister), Kaikohe.
16/1364	,,	Vuiyasawa, Tiale Bau Mara	Student	Mrs. Litiana Maapa (mother), Bau, Fiji.
16/427	,,	†Warahi, Rua	Labourer	Tamatewai Maria (niece), Manunui.
16/1354	,,	Warena, Kitohi	,,	Mrs. Arahia Warena (mother), Kaikohe.
16/1278	,,	Wharerau, Joseph	Mill Hand	Mrs. Te Haumahana (mother), Waima, Hokianga.
16/57	,,	†Whatuira, Poai	Labourer	Rameka Kainga (uncle), Wairoa.
16/1360	,,	Wihongi, Wiremu	,,	Hemi Wihongi (father), Kaikohe.
16/1398	,,	Wipani, John	,,	Dick Wipani (brother), Kohukohu.
16/109	,,	†Wi Repa, Tuhitaare	,,	Dr. Tutire Wi Repa (brother), Te Araroa.
16/1361	,,	Witute, Whira	,,	Mrs. Mere Witute (mother), Kaikohe.

† Ex 1st Maori Contingent.   ‡ Assumed name (Green, John Francis).   § Disembarked at Albany (hospital).

4TH MAORI CONTINGENT (No. 2 PLATOON).

Reg. No.	Rank.	Name.	Occupation.	Name and Address of Next-of-kin.
16/1377	2nd Lieut.	Little, William James	Sheep-farmer	Robert Little (father), Kaiti, Gisborne.
16/1493	Sergeant	Holden, John	Farmer	J. Holden (father), Tikokino, Hawke's Bay.
16/1472	,,	Swanson, Charles	Accountant	Mrs. M. E. Swanson (wife), Vauxhall Road, Devonport, Auckland.
16/1549	Corporal	Brooking, Jack	Farmer	Julian A. Brooking (father), Te Kaha, Opotiki.
16/1471	,,	Mapu, Waitaringa	Interpreter	Porokoru Mapu Moteo (father), Puketapu, Napier.
16/1474	Lance-Corpl.	Jones, Michael Rotohiko	Clerk	Pei Jones (brother), Ongarue, King-country.
16/1447	,,	Poutahi, Reuben	Shearer	Poutahi Hapimana (father), Frasertown, Wairoa, Hawke's Bay.
16/1448	,,	Te Hau, Huitau	,,	Wera Te Hau (brother), Mahia, Wairoa, Hawke's Bay.
16/1432	Private	Brown, Tono	Labourer	Tahu Brown (father), Waiomio, Bay of Islands.
16/1451	,,	Cooper, Ashley Kiwara	,,	William Henry Cooper (father), Gisborne.
20617	,,	Edwards, Henry	Shepherd	Pahu Edwards (father), Te Waiti, Opotiki.
16/1437	,,	Greaves, William	Fisherman	Walter Williams (cousin), Taipara, Mangonui.
16/1486	,,	Hale, Nathaniel	Farmer	Mrs. A. G. Hale (mother), Tolaga Bay, Gisborne.
16/1463	,,	Hapi, Ashton H.	Labourer	Hikamate Hapi (brother), Levin.
16/1446	,,	Harawira, Cyril	Farmer	Mrs. Matiria Harawira (mother), Mohaka, Wairoa, Hawke's Bay.
16/1466	,,	Herewini, Mahuika	Bushman	Piripi Herewini (father), Te Kaha, Bay of Plenty.
16/1478	,,	Hopa, Murphy	Labourer	Mrs. Cosgrove (mother), Tuahiwi, Kaiapoi.
16/1442	,,	Huki, Raymond	,,	Mrs. Raupapaika Rammond (wife), Fernhill, Hastings.
16/1438	,,	Johnson, Rome	Farmer	Mrs. Ida Vashter C. Johnson (wife), Karetu, Bay of Islands.
16/1453	,,	Jones, Charles	Station Hand	Mrs. Paku Maraea Goldsmith (mother), Manutuke, Gisborne.
16/1477	,,	Korako, Henry	Labourer	Miss Ema Korako (sister), Tuahiwi, Kaiapoi.
16/1435	,,	Latimer, Paul	,,	Mrs. Tahanga Latimer (wife), Rangitihi, North Auckland.
16/1454	,,	Lewis, Archibald	,,	Mrs. A. J. Lewis (mother), Wairoa, Hawke's Bay.
16/1484	,,	Lockwood, Joseph Spencer	Storeman	W. Lockwood (father), Tolaga Bay, Gisborne.
16/1485	,,	Lockwood, William Mason	,,	W. Lockwood (father), Tolaga Bay, Gisborne.
16/1441	,,	Mate, Te	Cabin Boy	Taputoi te Mate (father), Aitutaki, Cook Islands.
16/1455	,,	Mika, Rangi	Labourer	Tawho Mika (father), Ruatoki, Whakatane.
16/22	,,	†Mills, Whare	Bushman	Mrs. Kereama Tihema (mother), Te Kapa, Port Awanui, East Coast.
16/1548	,,	Momo, Honi	Labourer	Miss Erina Momo (sister), Tuahiwi, Woodend, Canterbury.
16/1487	,,	Moore, George Auckland	Shepherd	J. A. Moore (father), Tolaga Bay, Gisborne.
16/344	,,	†Morgan, Joseph Iraia	Labourer	Miss Iwingaro J. Morgan (daughter), Whirinaki, Hokianga.
16/1481	,,	Moses, Charles	Bushman	Mrs. Riwi Moses (mother), Whangaruru.
16/1456	,,	Nelson, George	Station Hand	John Nelson (father), East Coast.
16/1473	,,	Ormsby, Gilbert Richard	Driver	Miss Martha Ormsby (sister), Otorohanga.
16/1457	,,	Paku, Moronai	Labourer	Moronai Paku (father), Whakaki, Hawke's Bay.
16/1458	,,	Paku, Sonny	Farm-assistant	Mrs. Maggie Paku (wife), Wairoa, Hawke's Bay.
16/1467	,,	Pohatu, Matewai	Labourer	Henry Pohatu (father), Wairarapa.
16/1425	,,	Puru, Hemi	,,	Mrs. Mere Tutatu (mother), Gisborne.
16/1379	,,	Reweti, Wipahaka Paora	Farmer	Miss Mariana Roera (cousin), Te Pua, Helensville.
16/1459	,,	Ruru, Vivian	Station Hand	Henare Ruru (father), Te Karaka, Gisborne.
16/1464	,,	Skipworth, William	Bushfeller	William Skipworth (father), Kawakawa, Bay of Islands.
16/472	,,	†Smith, William	Labourer	Mrs. Helena Smith (wife), Poroti, Whangarei.
16/1468	,,	Tahau, Peter	Farm Hand	Ranginui Tahau (father), Taupo.
16/1460	,,	Tangiora, Rewi	Station Hand	Hapeta Tangiora (father), Mahia, Gisborne.
16/1479	,,	Tawhai, Hohepa Taupaki	Railway Guard	Hone Mohi (father), Waima, Hokianga.
16/1461	,,	Taylor, Mangu	Shearer	Fuki Taylo (f the), Manutuke, Gisborne.
16/1482	,,	Te Ohaere, Karaitiana	Labourer	Mrs. Hana te Ohaere (mother), Tokomaru Bay.
16/1436	,,	Te Paa, Pau	,,	Hihi te Paa (father), Okahu.
16/1483	,,	Te Whare, Pounara	,,	Miss Okeroa te Whare (sister), Maungatangi, Pokeno, Auckland.
16/1475	,,	Thompson, Charles	Farmer	Mrs. Kiri Whero (mother), Pirongia, King-country.
16/1449	,,	Tokotana, Tukotahi	Labourer	Tainui te Warihi (father), Tarata, New Plymouth.
16/1476	,,	Trikateni, Hone	Farmer	Miss Rau Trikateni (sister), North Road, Kaiapoi.
16/1444	,,	Tuatara, Charles	Bootmaker	Charles Tuatara (father), Tauhei, Morrinsville.
16/1427	,,	Watene, Eri	Labourer	Mrs. P. Watene (mother), Dargaville.
16/1429	,,	Wihongi, Matin Paki	,,	Philip Paki Wihongi (brother), Kaikohe, Bay of Islands.
16/1431	,,	Wiki, Joe	Bushman	Mrs. Susan Wiki (mother), Karetu, Bay of Islands.
16/1385	,,	Williams, Allan	Carpenter	Allan Williams (father), Apia, Samoa.
16/1462	,,	Winiana, Ponga	Station Hand	Charlie Wynyard (father), Karetu, Bay of Islands.

† Ex 1st Maori Contingent.

5TH MAORI CONTINGENT.

LEFT NEW ZEALAND 29TH JULY, 1916.

Reg. No.	Rank.	Name.	Occupation.	Name and Address of Next-of-kin.
16/1537	2nd Lieut.	Gardner, Peter Robertson	Brickmaker	Mrs. L. Gardner (mother), New Lynn, Auckland.
1/244	,,	†Woodward, Charles Burgess	Draper	Charles Woodward (father), 52 Ellice Avenue, Wellington.
16/1530	Sergeant	Miru, Mikaera	Farmer	Mrs. Kararaina Miru (wife), Batley, Kaipara.
16/1439	,,	Ruki Ruki, Te Ao	Sheep-farmer	Marianata Ruki Ruki (mother), Waipawa, Hawke's Bay.
16/1372	Corporal	Carroll, Whare	Farmer	Mrs. Mehira Carroll (wife), Gisborne.
16/1480	,,	‡French, Samuel James	Fitter	Mrs. Mary French (wife), Peel Street, Westport.
16/1440	,,	Heketa, Tarakitai	Clerk	Mrs. Rupina Helen Heketa (wife), 11 Naughton Terrace, Kilbirnie, Wellington.
16/1505	,,	Hooper, Edward	,,	E. D. Hooper (father), 9 Lowe Street, Gisborne.
16/1542	,,	Nathan, Louis	Surveyor	Mrs. Hiria Nathan (mother), Rewiti, Helensville.
16/1555	,,	Pineaha, Tutero Rumatiki	Labourer	Mohiki Pineaha (father), Fern Hill, Hastings.
16/1534	Lance-Corpl.	Herewini, William	,,	Tipene Herewini (father), Parenga, North Cape.
16/1545	,,	Hopkinson, James Daniel	,,	D. Hopkinson (father), Temuka.
20614	,,	Hotere, Joseph	Porter	Mane Hotere (father), Mitimiti, Hokianga.
16/1562	,,	Karetu, Timona	Station Hand	Sam Karetu (brother), Hastings.
16/1567	,,	Leach, Tom	,,	R. Leach (father), Whangara Native School, Poverty Bay.
16/1502	,,	Penfold, John Mason	Carter	Mrs. W. Penfold (mother), Tolaga Bay, Gisborne.
16/1584	,,	Tuhoe, Hani K.	Shearer	Tauau Tuhoe (father), Ruatoki North.
16/1497	Bugler	Heka, Warnock Pake	Labourer	Pake Heka (father), Te Kao, North Auckland.
20596	,,	King, George	Farmer	Mrs. Ngaronoa (mother), Waihou.
16/1397	Private	Abraham, Richard	Labourer	Mrs. Rameka Abraham (mother), Tutekehua, Hokianga.
16/1395	,,	Abraham, Robert	,,	Orikena Abraham (father), Lower Waihou, Hokianga.
16/1519	,,	Ahpene, Joseph	,,	John Ahpene (father), Kaihu, Dargaville.
16/1532	,,	Albert, Jack	Farmer	Mrs. Carroll (sister), Te Oreore, Masterton.
16/1535	,,	Anderson, Joseph	Labourer	Andrew Anderson (father), Awanui, North Auckland.
16/1515	,,	Dalton, Jack	,,	Solomon Tuari (father), Maraenui, Gisborne.
16/1509	,,	Epiha, Daniel	Farmer	Epiha (father), Matauri Bay, Whangaroa.
20607	,,	Eruini, Rangi	,,	Teaiatini Eruini (father), Okere Falls, Rotorua.
20711	,,	Graham, George	,,	Raika Graham (father), Awahuri, Palmerston North.
16/1399	,,	Greaves, Rameka	Labourer	Eriha Kiriwi (uncle), Parapara, Mangonui.
16/1558	,,	Hakaraia, John	Farmer	George Hakaraia (father), Rawhiti, Russell.
16/1527	,,	Heke, Charles	Labourer	Turei Heke (father), Mangamuka, Hokianga.
16/1512	,,	Hokai, Andrew	,,	Hokai (father), Whangape.
16/1514	,,	Joel, Taha	,,	Mrs. Peni Marsh (mother), Waiharara.
16/1452	,,	John, David	,,	Mrs. Oreti Pamana (mother), Nuhaka, Hawke's Bay.
16/1540	,,	Jury, Guy Robert	Farmer	Mrs. Jury (mother), Nukualofa, Tonga.
16/1533	,,	Karaitiana, Hohua	,,	K. Karaitiana (father), Akura, Masterton.
16/1583	,,	Karaitiana, James	,,	Mrs. Paara Kenrick (mother), Te Oreore, Masterton.
16/1565	,,	Katete, Pene	Labourer	Mrs. Maggie Cassidy (wife), Peria, Mangonui.
16/1489	,,	Kerehoma, Thomas	,,	Rev. Rewiti Kerehoma (father), Ahipara Bay, Mangonui.
20595	,,	Koha, Kahiti	Farmer	Koha (father), Herekino, North Auckland.
16/1566	,,	Lardelli, William	,,	Mrs. B. S. Lardelli (mother), Whangara, Gisborne.
16/1524	,,	Mark, Ned	Station Hand	Erueti Terewai (father), Tuparoa, Gisborne.
20602	,,	Mason, Luigi	Sawmill Hand	Mrs. L. Mason (mother), Arahura.
16/1557	,,	Mathew, Wetini	,,	Miss Puti Mathew (sister), Waipuna.
16/1556	,,	Moananui, Hawea	Labourer	Mrs. Matarita Ruri (mother), Pakipaki, North Auckland.
16/1523	,,	Moari, Tame	Farmer	Mrs. Te Keringa Moari (mother), Taumarunui.
16/1575	,,	Mokaraka, Rawiri	Bushman	Rawiri Mokaraka (father), Kaikohe.
16/1529	,,	Mounsell, Raumanga	Farmer	William Mounsell (brother), Whananaki, Whangarei.
16/1538	,,	Muller, Adolph	,,	Miki Muller (brother), Nukualofa, Tonga.
20605	,,	Netana, Arthur	,,	Rata Netana (brother), Matapihi, Tauranga.
20606	,,	Ngatai, Bon Swainson	,,	Wetini Ngatai (father), Otumotai, Tauranga.
16/1522	,,	Paeroa, Nehe	Labourer	Ratawera Paeroa (father), Tuparoa, Gisborne.
16/1536	,,	Paki, Rimi	,,	Taurau Paki (father), Mangapai, Whangarei.
20599	,,	Paku, Hemi	,,	Tame Paku (father), Whakaki, Wairoa.
16/1564	,,	Panapa, Mari	Shearer	King, Panapa (brother), Waipata, Hastings.
16/1577	,,	Paraone, Joe Hokaia	Bushman	Materua Paraone (brother), Kaikohe.
16/1552	,,	Phillips, William	Labourer	Henry Phillips (brother), Lake Ohia, Mangonui.
16/1510	,,	Pomana, Mita	Farmer	Mrs. Pomana (mother), Matangirau, Whangaroa.
16/1581	,,	Pomare, Tautoro	Tunnelling	Mrs. Paki Pomare (wife), Kaikohe, Bay of Islands.
16/1573	,,	Pou, Reihana Eru	Bushman	Mrs. Mere Erupou (mother), Kaikohe.
16/1516	,,	Puha, Charlie	Labourer	Puha (father), Te Araroa, East Cape.
16/1434	,,	Rameka, George	,,	Kere Rameka (father), Tauranga.
16/1574	,,	Rameka, Percy	Blacksmith	Waikerepuru Rameka (father), Ohaeawai, Bay of Islands.
16/1531	,,	Ranui, William	Farmer	W. Ranui (father), Okaiawa, Taranaki.
16/1551	,,	Rapata, Eri	Gum-digger	Richard Robert (brother), Waipapakauri, North Auckland.
16/1570	,,	Rewha, Joe	Farmer	Te Rewha (father), Russell, Bay of Islands.
20597	,,	Rewiri, Rata	Labourer	Terekia Rewiri (uncle), Te Hapua, Parenga.
16/1543	,,	Rickus, Thomas Percival	Clerk	Mrs. H. Rickus (mother), 17 Wilkin Street, Temuka.

† Ex Samoan Advance.   ‡ Died at sea, 7th August, 1916.

Reg. No.	Rank.	Name.	Occupation.	Name and Address of Next-of-kin.
16/1520	Private	Ruatara, James Henare	Labourer	Mrs. Annie Ruatara (mother), Aranga, Kaihu.
16/1563	,,	Runga, Kingi Teokoro	Farmer	Mrs. Herbert Kiel (mother), Opoutama, Hawke's Bay.
16/1541	,,	Silva, James	Carpenter	Mrs. Silva (wife), Nukualofa, Tonga.
16/1539	,,	Skeen, Parker	,,	Mrs. W. Tarr (sister), Nukualofa, Tonga.
16/1517	,,	Stephens, Wilfred	,,	Henry J. Stephens (brother), Suva, Fiji.
20600	,,	Tainguru, Kepa	Labourer	Mrs. Mairiana Pahawaiki (mother), Whakakai, Wairoa.
16/1495	,,	Taite, Piter	Bushman	Piter Taite (father), Ruatahuna, Rotorua.
16/1506	,,	Takei, Rangi	Station Hand	Mrs. Moengaroa (mother), Nuhaka, Wairoa, Hawke's Bay.
16/1504	,,	Tangaoro, Hori	Labourer	Mrs. Runaha Wairaku (mother), Tokomaru Bay.
16/1496	,,	Tangohau, Teau Kopa	Shearer	Mrs. Rama Tangohau (mother), Ruatoki North, Bay of Plenty.
16/557	,,	†Tauranga, Mark	Labourer	Kereama Tauranga (father), Hicks Bay.
16/1513	,,	Taylor, Joe	,,	—. Taylor (father), Whangape.
20604	,,	Te Hore, Amokawa	Farm Hand	Mrs. Pare Te Hore (mother), Paranui, Wanganui River.
16/1503	,,	Te Runa, Wi Paku	Labourer	Mrs. Puti Puti Te Pere (mother), Tokomaru Bay.
16/1507	,,	Thompson, Alf	Bushman	Mrs. Hukatai Thompson (mother), Whangaruru, North Auckland.
16/1528	,,	Toki, Meto	Drainer	Pangari Toki (father), Kohukohu, Hokianga.
20613	,,	Topi, Patu	Bushman	Raharuhi Puru (brother), Rotorua.
16/1569	,,	Toroaiwhiti, Taka	Labourer	Mrs. Ani Waaka (mother), Mohaka, Wairoa, Hawke's Bay.
16/1450	,,	Tume, William	Farm Hand	Tutanuku Tume (father), Purangi, New Plymouth.
16/1576	,,	Turner, Robert	Engineer	Miss Raumake Hemipapa (sister), Kaikohe.
16/1525	,,	Walker, Taylor	Labourer	Mrs. Marela Walker (mother), Pamapuria, North Auckland.

† Ex 1st Maori Contingent.

MAORI CONTINGENT.

7TH REINFORCEMENTS.

Reg. No.	Rank.	Name.	Occupation.	Name and Address of Next-of-kin.
30139	2nd Lieut.	Quane, William Vincent	Ironmonger	P. Quane (father), Ngarua.
20668	Sergeant	Hopa, Tano	Labourer	Mrs. O. L. Cosgrove (mother), Tuahiwi, Kaiapoi.
20673	,,	Hori, Kereapa	,,	Mrs. Tuhi Hori (wife), Whakarewarewa, Rotorua.
20615	Corporal	Kawhareu, John Mokau	Sheep-farmer	Mokau Kawhareu (father), Awahohonu, Pelorus Sound.
20644	,,	Kohi, William	Farmer	Takoro Kohi (father), Huntly.
30137	,,	Pihema, Tautuhi	Labourer	Wi Pihema (grandfather), Pouto, Kaipara Heads.
20656	,,	Tamati, Poururu	Carpenter	Mrs. Bella Poururu (wife), Rotorua.
30133	Lance-Corpl.	Brown, Tommy	Shepherd	Mrs. Mary Ann Rakiroa (sister), Te Rerenga, Gisborne.
20684	,,	Epiha, Tame	Shearer	Epiha te Ahu (father), Opapa, Hawke's Bay.
30134	,,	George, Abraham	Labourer	Mrs. Parekairewa Kinomoerua (wife), Manakau, Manawatu Line.
20643	,,	Smith, Tommy	Taxi-driver	Tommy Smith (father), Nuhaka, Wairoa.
20649	Private	Agassiz, Louis	Farmer	Mrs. Arounpapuni (mother), Opotiki.
20610	,,	Apanui, Paroa	,,	Mrs. Raria Apanui (mother), Otara, Bay of Plenty.
20666	,,	Barrett, Henry	Factory Assistant	Robert Barrett (father), Aria, Te Kuiti.
20648	,,	Brown, William	Labourer	Mrs. Ethel Brown (mother), 21 Kaiti Esplanade, Gisborne.
20633	,,	Cook, Richard	Bushman	Thomas Cook (father), Ivydale, Hokianga.
20640	,,	Edwards, Willie	Labourer	James Edwards (brother), Matakohe, Kaipara.
20634	,,	Eruera, Tu	Bushman	Taupuhi Eruera (brother), Utakura, Hokianga.
20632	,,	Eru Toe, Fred	,,	Mrs. Isabelle Toe (mother), Kohukohu, Hokianga.
30136	,,	Gardyne, James	Steward	Mrs. Amy Gardyne (mother), Hampden Street, Hokitika.
20647	,,	Haora, John	Farmer	Mrs. Caroline Haora (mother), Tamatarau, Whangarei Heads.
20618	,,	Harper, John	Storekeeper	Mrs. Emily Harper (mother), Nukualofa, Tonga.
20658	,,	Harris, Arapeta	Settler	Miss Kate Harris (sister), Motukaraka, Hokianga.
20657	,,	Harris, Kiri	,,	Frank Harris (father), Motukaraka, Hokianga.
20663	,,	Harris, Reti	Bushman	Miss Jane Harris and Miss Kate Harris (sisters), Motukaraka, Hokianga.

Reg. No.	Rank.	Name.	Occupation.	Name and Address of Next-of-kin.
20662	,,	Harris, Tihi	Settler	James Harris (father), Motukaraka, Hokianga.
20623	,,	Heperi, Richard	Mill Hand	Joe Heperi (father), Waihou, Hokianga.
30135	,,	Hetaraka, Onepu	Labourer	Taniora Herataka (father), Mangakahia, Kaikohe.
20650	,,	Hiraka, Ruteni	,,	Jim Hiraka (father), Puketapu.
20655	,,	Hitu, Keith	Bushfeller	Hana Whakataka (father), Tokomaru Bay.
20642	,,	Horomona, Rewi	Ploughman	Puru Horomona (father), Whakaki, Hawke's Bay.
30138	,,	Jackson, Charles	Labourer	Mrs. Evelyn Jackson (mother), Norfolk Island.
20680	,,	Karini, Toi	,,	Hana Karini (father), Mangatuna, Tolaga Bay.
20682	,,	Keepa, Hami	Jackman	Mrs. Meta Keepa (mother), Otoroa, Whangaroa, Bay of Islands.
20638	,,	Kelly, Harry	Horse-breaker	Frank Kelly (father), Gumtown, Mercury Bay.
20678	,,	Kemp, Kawenata	Labourer	Taiporutu Kemp (father), Okauia, Matamata, Tauranga.
20646	,,	Kopa, Pera	,,	Mrs. Paki (mother), Kaiwai, Marsden Point, near Whangarei.
20620	,,	King, William	Mill Hand	Mrs. Ngaronoa King (mother), Lower Waihou, Hokianga.
20669	,,	Loma, David	Assistant Harbourmaster	Mafu (father), Nukualofa, Tonga.
20631	,,	Mangai, Donald	Shearer	Mrs. Hemaima Mangai (mother), Te Hauke, Hawke's Bay.
20611	,,	Matehaere, Tu Hawaiki	Labourer	Matehaere (father), Rotorua.
20641	,,	Munro, Raki	,,	Mrs. Mena Munro (mother), Whakaki, Hawke's Bay.
20622	,,	Ngapera, John	Mill Hand	Thomas Ngapera (father), Taheke, Hokianga.
20625	,,	Padlio, David	Carpenter	Mrs. Julia Padlio (mother), Kaikohe, North Auckland.
20676	,,	Rameka, George	Farmer	Rameka Kere (father), Matakana, Tauranga.
20612	,,	Rangiaho, George Mihaka	Labourer	Jack M. Rangiaho (brother), Opotiki.
20639	,,	Raureti, Tommy	,,	Pararika Raureti (father), Whakaki, Wairoa.
20664	,,	Rewi, Perenara	Settler	Mrs. Homo Rewi (mother), Mangonui, North Auckland.
20675	,,	Rogan, Richard	Farmer	Wi Rogan (father), Matakohe, Kaipara.
20630	,,	Ruha, John	Shearer	Pera Ruha (father), Kiwikiwi Station, Te Araroa.
20637	,,	Rukamiromiro, John	Labourer	Mrs. Karterina Rukamiromiro (mother), Hokianga.
20626	,,	Smith, William Seon	Bushman	Richard Smith (father), Kohukohu.
20653	,,	Stephen, James	Farm Hand	Steve Tawhata (father), Kohukohu.
20674	,,	Tawhara, Manuera	Farmer	Mrs. Tarere (mother), Waioeka, Opotiki, Bay of Plenty.
20702	,,	Taylor, David	Bush Contractor	William Taylor (father), near Rawene, Hokianga.
20679	,,	Taylor, Waaka	Labourer	Paki Taylor (father), Te Aroha.
20629	,,	Teki, Turei	Farmer	Aimana Teki (father), Turakina, Wanganui.
20621	,,	Te Whata, Peter	Mill Hand	John te Whata (brother), Horeke, Hokianga.
20677	,,	Toitoi, Hautu	Farmer	Toitoi Maki (father), Matakana, Tauranga.
20636	,,	Toki, Rangi	Farm Labourer	Toki (father), Hokianga.
20616	,,	Tuki, Manu	Telegraphist	Mrs. M. Brett (mother), Manawahe, Matata.
20659	,,	Waata, Henare	Bushman	Waata Hohepa (father), Motukaraka, Hokianga.
20652	,,	Walker, Robert	Labourer	Mrs. Mary Walker (mother), Tolaga Bay.
20681	,,	Wharehinga, Penetana	,,	Rana Wharehinga (father), Awanui, North Auckland.
20667	,,	Wharekura, Pera	Shepherd	Mrs. Hikihiki Wharekura (mother), Nuhaka, Hawke's Bay.
20687	,,	Wi, Heta	Navvy	Mrs. Hariata Waru (mother), Te Kao, North Auckland.
20665	,,	Wiki, Frank	Sawmill Hand	Mrs. Harata Wiki (mother), Herekino, Kaitaia.
20654	,,	Williams, Moa	Farmer	Wi Williams (father), Kohukohu.
20670	,,	Williams, Tuki	Driver	Miss Mary Williams (sister), Tauranga, Bay of Plenty.
20624	,,	Williams, Willie	Barman	Wi Williams (father), Kohukohu, Hokianga.
20635	,,	Wiperi, Boxer	Bushman	Boxer Wiperi (father), Oriki, Hokianga.
20686	,,	Wright, Barney	Labourer	Mrs. Emily Wright (mother), Herekino, North Auckland.

8TH REINFORCEMENTS.

Reg. No.	Rank	Name.	Occupation.	Name and Address of Next-of-kin.
16/518	2nd Lieut.	†Broughton, Edward Renata Muhunga	Landbroker	Mrs. Atiria Broughton (mother), Fernhill, Hawke's Bay.
20699	Sergeant	Adlam, John	Fireman	Mrs. Ramari Adlam (mother), Waitara, Taranaki.
16/1547	Corporal	Mulligan, Tori	Farmer	Mrs. Celia Mulligan (wife), Tokomaru Bay.
20754	,,	Te Tau, Reki	,,	Puhara te Tau (father), Masterton.
20704	,,	Wynyard, John	Sugar-works	John Lewis Leonard (friend), Chelsea, Auckland.
20741	Lance-Corpl.	Hawaikirangi, Puhera	Clerk	Puhera Hawaikirangi (father), Hastings.
20752	,,	Hughes, Edwin	Carpenter	Peckham Hughes (father), Fiji.
20714	,,	Waiomio, Niho	Bushman	Wiki Waiomio (father), Towai, Bay of Islands.
20755	,,	Nathan, Alick	Farmer	Wi Nathan (father), Taita, Northern Wairoa.
20698	,,	Pirimi, Toma	,,	Mrs. Terehina (mother), Maketu, Bay of Plenty.
20710	,,	Kemara, Robert	Clerk	Mrs. Katene (aunt), 60 Wanganui Avenue, Ponsonby Auckland.
20690	Private	Akuhata, Rau Herewini	Bushman	Erika Akuhata (brother), Kaikohe, Bay of Islands.
20708	,,	Akurangi, Hira	Labourer	Wi Akurangi (father), Opotiki.
20718	,,	Akurangi, Mohi	,,	Wi Akurangi (father), Opotiki.
20750	,,	Albert, Peter	,,	Ehe Albert (brother), Makarau, North Auckland
20740	,,	Bell, Turner	Farmer	Mrs. Ngarima Bell (mother), Te Kuiti.
20712	,,	Birch, Tau	,,	Mrs. Celia Birch (mother), Punaruku, Whangaruru.
20688	,,	Cotton, William	Bushman	Mrs. Fanny Cotton (mother), Paihia, Russell.
20731	,,	Enoka, Mita	Roadman	Wharengaro (father), Rotorua.
20742	,,	Erimana, Wi	Farm Hand	Hirini Erimana (father), Mohaka, Hawke's Bay.
20729	,,	Farrell, Peter	,,	Mrs. Putiputi Hapimana (mother), Hinemoa Point, Te Ngae, Rotorua.
20692	,,	Harris, Frank	Bushman	Miss Jane Harris (sister), Motukaraka, Hokianga.
20762	,,	Hautapu, Pera	Labourer	Hare Hare Hautapu (father), Tokomaru Bay.
20693	,,	Hoani, Billy	Bushman	Mrs. Ellen Hoani (mother), Motukaraka, Hokianga.
20744	,,	Hotu, Ta	Driver	Harry Hotu (father), Hangatiki.
20745	,,	Hunt, John	Labourer	Charles Hunt (father), Hawera, Taranaki.
20733	,,	Jones, Jimmy	,,	Mrs. Mary Jones (mother), Manutuke, Gisborne.
20707	,,	Kere, Hiki	Engineer	Rangi Kere (father), Opotiki.
20760	,,	Kopua, Nehe	Labourer	Rota Kopua (father), Tokomaru Bay.
20724	,,	Leach, John	Farmer	James Leach (father), Whangara, Gisborne.
20700	,,	Leef, Edward Tai	Bushman	Tai Leef (father), Whirinaki, Hokianga.
20715	,,	Leef, George	Labourer	Wario Leef (brother), Waipuna, Kawakawa.
20751	,,	Leef, Ruki	Bushman	Tai Leef (father), Whirinaki, Hokianga.
20756	,,	Maitai, Hata	Driver	Miss Ema Maitai (sister), Tolaga Bay.
20619	,,	Marsh, Jack Thomas	Bushman	Tommy Marsh (father), Whangape, Hokianga.
20689	,,	Moller, Henry	Farmer	Kipa te Whatanui (grandfather), Otaki.
20753	,,	Moore, William Robert	Carpenter	Thomas Moore (father), Tonga.
20713	,,	Moses, David	Farmer	Charles Moses (father), Whangaruru, Bay of Islands.
16/26	,,	†Namana, Rata	Labourer	Mrs. Hunga Hunga (sister), Lower Mohaka.
20738	,,	Ngatai, Hautonga	,,	Wiremu Ngatai (father), Waiapu, Rangitukia.
20695	,,	Nicholls, George	Driver	Amohanga Nicholls (father), Hangatiki.
20761	,,	Northover, William	Labourer	Joe Northover (father), Tokomaru Bay.
20719	,,	Park, Wi	,,	Mrs. Ka Porangi (mother), Gisborne.
20691	,,	Poihipi, Nick	Shepherd	Nikorima Poihipi (father), Maranui, Opotiki.
20743	,,	Poutawera, James	Quarryman	Thomas Hira Poutawera (brother), Te Kuiti.
20726	,,	Raharuhi, Patu	Farmer	Pururu Raharuhi (father), Rotoiti, Rotorua.
20709	,,	Rangi, Jerry	Labourer	Rangitaiwira (father), Ohinemutu, Rotorua.
20736	,,	Raroa, William	,,	Riwai Raroa (father), Waiapu, Rangitukia.
20727	,,	Ratete, Whakarongotai	Sawmilling	Charles Rogers (father), Maketu, Bay of Plenty.
20722	,,	Rawhira, Hakopa	Taxi-driver	Rawhira (father), Manutuke, Gisborne.
20757	,,	Runga Runga, Nuia	Labourer	Wiremu Runga Runga (father), Tokomaru Bay.
20725	,,	Smith, Matthew	Farmer	George Smith (father), Nuhaka, Hawke's Bay.
20734	,,	Smith, William	Labourer	Matawhaua Smith (father), Te Arai, Gisborne.
20672	,,	Tarau, Puru	,,	Mrs. Ada Harding (cousin), Waikaria, Bay of Islands.
20697	,,	Te Hini, Ateremu	,,	Aperahama te Hini (father), Te Puke, Bay of Plenty.
20728	,,	Te Keepa, Wharekaramu	,,	Keepa Taiporutu (father), Matamata.
16/362	,,	†Te Paa, Neri	Bushman	Neri te Paa (nephew), care of Hemi te Paa, Post-office, Ripia.
20737	,,	Thompson, Saul	Farmer	Hirini Thompson (father), Whangaruru.
20735	,,	Toheriri, Moetu	Labourer	Enoka Toheriri (father), Waipiro, Tokomaru Bay.
20730	,,	Ua, George	Timber-worker	Uahori (father), Te Ngae, Rotorua.
20696	,,	Waipuka, Fred	Shepherd	Mrs. Waimatao Waipuka (mother), Dannevirke.
20758	,,	Wawatai, Heta	Labourer	Mrs. Rawinia Terapu (mother), Hicks Bay.
20759	,,	Whakataka, Hori	,,	Haua Whakataka (father), Tokomaru Bay.
20720	,,	Williams, Hiwa	Farmer	Tu Williams (father), Manutuke, Gisborne.

† Ex First Maori Contingent.

9TH REINFORCEMENTS.

Reg. No.	Rank.	Name.	Occupation.	Name and Address of Next-of-kin.
26/1549	2nd Lieut.	Hair, Harold Gilbert	Bank Officer	James Hair (father), A.M.P., Nelson.
16/1226	Sergt.-Major	†Holmes, Frederick	Police Officer	Mrs. F. Ashley (aunt), care of Mrs. Hibbert, 1 Hornsey Rise Gardens, Crouch End, London N.
16/1229	Q.M.-Sergt.	†Westbrook, Edward	Wheelwright	G. E. S. Westbrook (father), Samoa.
16/1315	Sergeant	†Leger, Baisley	Boatbuilder	J. Leger (father), Nukualofa, Tonga.
20795	,,	Tepene, James William	Somes Isl'd Guard	John William Tepene (father), Otago Heads, Dunedin.
20779	,,	Wharepapa, Turi	Railway Employee	Mrs. Auatea Wharepapa (mother), Tokaanu, near Lake Taupo.
20774	Corporal	Reid, Samuel	Shepherd	Edward Reid (father), Whangara, via Gisborne.
20706	,,	Smith, Joseph Richard	Bushman	Rihari Mite (father), Kohukohu.
20694	,,	Tahana, Kepa	Student	Rewi Tahana (father), Te Kowhai, via Frankton Junction.
20799	Lance-Corpl.	Faletau, Sateki	Medical Student	John Faletau (father), Niua-fu, Tonga.
20801	,,	Florian, Gaston	Storeman	Mrs. Filiata Florian (wife), Apia, Samoa.
20796	,,	Jackson, Egbert Brooks	Boatman	Mrs. Evlyn Jackson (mother), Norfolk Island.
20808	,,	Moana, Riwai	Labourer	Wi Moana (father), Tuparoa Bay.
20782	,,	Tehata, John Winiata	Mechanic	Hoeta Tehata (father), Fernhill, Hastings.
20775	Private	Albert, Sam	Labourer	Mrs. Heri Patuwai (mother), Wairoa.
20798	,,	Andrews, Phillip	Blacksmith	William Andrews (father), Kasaru, Fiji.
20804	,,	Andrews, William	Farmer	Mrs. Paerangi (sister), Raetihi.
20763	,,	Babbington, Tipi	Labourer	John Babbington (father), Tokomaru Bay.
20835	,,	Barnett, Tui	Sawmilling	Miss Paerakau Barnett (sister), Waiotapu, via Rotorua.
20813	,,	Brass, Tahu	Gum-digger	Mrs. Ngari Brass (wife), Ahipara.
20825	,,	Brott, Abraham	Labourer	George Brott (father), Parua Bay, Whangarei.
20787	,,	Conred, Paki	Gum-digger	Mrs. Ripine Conred (mother), Awanui North.
20781	,,	Dickey, Howard	Seaman	Andrew Dickey (father), Roetahi, Whangarei.
20786	,,	Hadfield, Matthew Petewiki	Labourer	Wiki Hadfield (father), Awanui North.
20794	,,	Hanita, Wae	,,	Hanita Temaero (father), Takapau, Hawke's Bay.
20769	,,	Harding, Whetu	Farmer	Mrs. Alick Harding (mother), Whirinaki, Hokianga.
20764	,,	Heta, William	Labourer	Putahi Heta (father), Pakotai, North Auckland.
20770	,,	Kaio, Hone	Farmer	George Kaio (father), Whirinaki, Hokianga.
20831	,,	Karipa, Edward	Driver	Mrs. Emily Karipa (mother), Kaikohe.
20771	,,	Kereama, Hori	Labourer	Peter Kereama (brother), Te Whaiti.
20797	,,	Leef, Henry Tai	Bushman	Tai Leef (father), Whirinaki, Hokianga.
16/1336	,,	†Leger, Francis	Seaman	Mrs. Kate Leger (aunt), 129 Wellington Street, Auckland.
20824	,,	McGregor, John Henry	Labourer	Mr. McGregor (father), Vincent Street, Auckland.
20766	,,	Maitai, William		Miss Ema Maitai (sister), Tolaga Bay.
20833	,,	Makene, Tom	Bushman	Mrs. Pikake Makene (mother), Mangamuka, via Kohukohu.
20815	,,	Matiu, Kauri	Engine-driver	Mrs. Rihi Matiu (mother), Opotiki.
20820	,,	Mete, Rihari	Labourer	Keepa Mete (father), Te Kao, North Cape.
20776	,,	Ngapo, Robert	Farmer	Hohepa Ngapo (father), Kennedy's Bay, Coromandel.
20777	,,	Ngapo, Samuel	,,	Pine Ngapo (father), Kennedy's Bay, Coromandel.
20821	,,	Nopera, Honere	Labourer	Nopera Mumu (father), Houhora, North Auckland.
20783	,,	Paris, David Gordon	,,	Charles Paris (father), Wairoa, Hawke's Bay.
20812	,,	Pene, Paki	Farm Hand	Mrs. Hemoata Pene (mother), Ahipara, North Auckland.
20789	,,	Pohi, Tu	Farmer	Pohi (father), Parawera, Kihikihi.
20793	,,	Poihipi, Riki	Bushman	Hoani (father), Waiomio, Thames.
20792	,,	Rahipere, James	,,	Mrs. Tipare Ngaripini (mother), Hikutaia, via Thames.
20768	,,	Rawiri, Thompson Pariki	Shearer	Parakiri Rawiri (father), Muripara, Rotorua.
20819	,,	Retimana, Pari	Labourer	Mrs. Eliza Retimana (wife), Waihopo, North Auckland.
20814	,,	Reweti, Harawe H.	Gum-digger	Mrs. Janie Marsh (wife), Ahipara, North Auckland.
20818	,,	Tahitahi, Tamati	Farm Hand	Tahitahi (father), Houhora, North Cape.
20791	,,	Taputoro, Taurerewa	Farmer	Mrs. Hera Chadwick (mother), Wanganui.
20716	,,	Tawhai, Hone Mohi	Flax-miller	Mohi Tawhai (father), Waima, Hokianga.
20784	,,	Thompson, John	Labourer	Kahu Thompson (brother), Wairoa, Hawke's Bay.
20807	,,	Toheriri, Tangiwai	,,	Mrs. Waara Toheriri (mother), Tuparoa.
20823	,,	Waaka, Hapi	Gum-digger	Hapi Waaka (father), Te Kao, North Cape.
20816	,,	Waaka, Hohepa	Farmer	Sam Waaka (father), Houhora, North Cape.
20767	,,	Waaka, Pera Hemi		Mrs. Rina Waaka (wife), Muriwai, Gisborne.
20832	,,	Waiomio, Wati	Bushman	Mrs. Rewhia Whatarau (mother), Hukerenui.
20723	,,	Westrupp, Charlie	Farmer	Charlie Westrupp (father), Manutuke, Gisborne.
20802	,,	Williams, John David	Storeman	Mrs. Maria Williams (wife), Levuka, Fiji.
20765	,,	Wilson, Rawira H.	Labourer	Mrs. Hannah Martha Wairoa (cousin), Wairoa, Hawke's Bay.
20803	,,	Wise, Benjamin	Carpenter	George Wise (father), Levuka, Fiji.
20778	,,	Witana, Abraham	Farmer	Witana (father), Lower Waihou, Hokianga.

† Ex 3rd Maori Contingent.

10TH REINFORCEMENTS.

Reg. No.	Rank.	Name.	Occupation.	Name and Address of Next-of-kin.
22539	2nd Lieut.	Hickson, Theodore Ernest	Agent	Mrs. E. G. Hickson (mother), Arthur Street, Ellerslie, Auckland.
20873	Sergeant	Dehamere, Hiki	Farmer	Mrs. Polly Black (sister), Otara, Opotiki.
20865	,,	Te Whetu, Tame	,,	Mrs. Ruihi Tehike Whetu (mother), Ruatoki, via Rotorua.
20883	Corporal	Horopapera, Tame		Mrs. Hauraki Horopapera (wife), Whakatane.
20846	,,	Murray, Raika Whakarongatai	Labourer	Wikitoria Tengahue (mother), Kopu, Thames.
20868	,,	Paora, Rangi	Farmer	Mrs. Matehuirua Paora (mother), Ruatoki, via Rotorua.
20843	,,	Ryland, Matiaha	Labourer	Charley Ryland (brother), Tokomaru Bay.
20848	Lance-Corpl.	Hawira, Matene	Flax-cutter	Mrs. Ngahaka Hawira (mother), Maketu, via Rotorua.
16/359	,,	†Tamihana, Rapi	Clerk	Miss Hetty Hetherington (friend), care of Rendell's Place, Eden Terrace, Auckland.
20847	,,	Tapihana, Tamupo	Farmer	Rewi Tapihana (father). Maketu, via Rotorua.
20817	Private	Anaru, Wi	Labourer	Henry Davis (stepfather), Ahipara, North Auckland.
20876	,,	Aramakutu, Wiki	,,	Mrs. Ema Aramakutu (mother), Tauranga, Kawau, Waitemata.
20874	,,	Arapeta, Paora	,,	Mrs. Awhirakau Arapeta (mother), Omaio, Opotiki.
20892	,,	Barrett, James	Farm Hand	Mrs. Huia Barrett (mother), Waitomo Caves.
19360	,,	Bragg, John	Fisherman	John Bragg (father), Half-moon Bay, Stewart Island.
20891	,,	Davies, Henry Marshall	Farmer	Roland Charles Davies (father), care of R. Davies, Te Kuiti.
20849	,,	Evans, Charles	,,	Leonard Christian (uncle), 4 Roslyn Terrace, Devonport, Auckland.
20854	,,	Faithfull, Lloyd Richard	Driver	Mrs. Kathereen Faithfull (mother), Dargaville.
20850	,,	Haore, Harry	Labourer	Mrs. Matiria Haore (mother), Whangaroa North.
19351	,,	Hapuku, Manukea K.	Fencer	Kara Hapuku (father), Opapa, Hawke's Bay.
20872	,,	Hare, Tawhio	Labourer	Mrs. Whitinira Hare (mother), Waiohau, Galatea, via Rotorua.
20829	,,	Hau, Hami	,,	Hone Hau (father), Waimate North.
20875	,,	Hill, Hemi	Bushman	Miss Elen Hill (sister), Raukokini, Bay of Plenty.
20859	,,	Hohua, Mita Hori	Farmer	Mrs. Ihipera Hohua (mother), Ruatoki, via Rotorua.
20888	,,	Hori, Maki	,,	Mrs. Katie Hori (mother), Tokaanu, Lake Taupo.
20866	,,	Hunia, Te Ruawai	,,	Mrs. Mere Ihaia Tairua (mother), Matata, Bay of Plenty.
19355	,,	Hunter, Jack	Labourer	— Hunter (father), Takapau.
20732	,,	Ihaia, Joseph	,,	Mrs. Murphy (mother), Sophia Street, Rotorua.
20851	,,	Jones, Henry	,,	Rev. T. Paerata (uncle), Awanui, North Auckland.
20844	,,	Kihi, Pua	Farmer	Mrs. Mihi Kihi (wife), Kaikohe.
20863	,,	Kopae, Tarewa	,,	Mrs. Mihi Kopae (mother), Poroporo, Whakatane.
20878	,,	Koopu, Rawiri	,,	Mrs. Matekino Koopu (mother), Maraenui, Opotiki.
20877	,,	Maaka, Tu	Bushman	Mrs. Ana Tehui Maaka (mother), Hawera.
20869	,,	Mamaku, Taiporutu	Labourer	Mrs. Temihi Mamaku (mother), Otimarakau, Matata.
20842	,,	Manuel, Apirana	Bushman	Mrs. Heni Manuel (wife), Tokomaru Bay.
19361	,,	Mason, Harry	Sawmiller	Mrs. Tipara Mason (mother), Arahura, Hokitika.
20881	,,	Mitai, Wharai	Bushman	Mrs. Teao Mitai (mother), Komate, Bay of Plenty.
20886	,,	Naera, Tame	Labourer	Mrs. Paho Naera (mother), Ohinomutu, Rotorua.
20885	,,	Nikorima, Fred	,,	Nikorima te Haunga (father). Waotu, via Pataruru.
16/76	,,	†Paraone, Tapauri	,,	Paraone Heremia (father). Te Kaha, Opotiki.
19406	,,	Paris, Fred Alonzo	Theatrical Artist	Charles William Paris (father), Post-office, Wairoa, Hawke's Bay.
20836	,,	Pohe, Taitare Tewhiri	Farmer	Pohe Homi (father), Pakipaki, Hawke's Bay.
20856	,,	Rakena, Rori	Police Constable	John R. Rakena (son). Kaitaia, North Auckland.
16/94	,,	†Ratima, Romana	Farmer	Mrs. Wharekohuru Romana (mother), Poroporo, Whakatane.
20810	,,	Reihana, Tukawhena	Station Hand	Mrs. Raiha Reihana (mother), Rangitukia, via Gisborne.
20852	,,	Smith, John	Farmer	Mrs. Elen Smith (mother), Awanui, North Auckland.
19354	,,	Smith, Toru	,,	Mrs. Hahata Harata Smith (mother), Puha, Gisborne.
20853	,,	Smith, William	,,	Mrs. Elen Smith (mother), Awanui, North Auckland.
19356	,,	Snee, Leonard Rupena	,,	Miss Beatresse Snee (sister), Takapau.
20839	,,	Strongman, Peter	,,	Mrs. Birch (mother), Whakapara, Whangarei.
19357	,,	Taipana, Wi Hapi	Labourer	Mrs. Hana Taipana (mother), Temuka.
20870	,,	Takao, Karaka	Farmer	Mrs. Pine Takao (mother), Ruatoki, via Rotorua.
20837	,,	Tamarapa, Wiremu	,,	Matehaukere Tamarapa (father), Meremere, Hawera.
20862	,,	Tamehana, Puia	Farmer	Mrs. Rerokai Tamehana (mother), Ruatoki, via Rotorua.
20871	,,	Tawa, Hawea	,,	Mrs. Mihikau Hawea (mother), Ohinepane, Tauranga.
20860	,,	Te Amo, Pa	Bushfeller	Mrs. Rehia te Amo (mother), Ruatoki, via Rotorua.
20838	,,	Te Huatahi, Toi	Labourer	Mrs. Takahuri (mother), Raetihi.
20864	,,	Te Pairi, Wirihana	Farmer	Mrs. Make te Pairi (mother), Waimana, Bay of Plenty.
20857	,,	Te Rangi, Mannie	Labourer	Mrs. Puru King (sister), Papawai, Greytown.
20890	,,	Timothy, Francis Ernest	,,	Mrs. Evelyn Lethart (aunt), Graham Street, Green Lane, Remuera, Auckland.
20882	,,	Topi, Rutene	,,	Te Aroha Topi (father), Maraenui, Opotiki.
20879	,,	Waititi, Hirini	Farmer	Matemoana Runi (sister), Whakatane.
19353	,,	Webb, James	Blacksmith	Mrs. Sarah Rose (mother), Clarendown, Franklin Field, Jamaica.
20895	,,	Whaanga, Ihaka	Labourer	Ihaka Whaanga (father), Nuhaka, Wairoa.
20845	,,	Whyte, Walter	Flax-cutter	Peter Whyte (father), Whangamata, Thames.
20861	,,	Wimutu, Hini	Bushman	Mrs. Hina te Whare Mutu (mother), Waimana, Bay of Plenty.
20867	,,	Wineti, Hoani T.	Labourer	Mrs. Mene Tahei Wineti (mother), Whakatane.
20889	,,	Wipa, Tira	,,	Wipa Wharaunga (father), Waitotara, Taranaki.
20880	,,	Witeria, Awhe Kaike	Farmer	Riria Awhe Kaike Witeria (daughter), Omaio, Bay of Plenty.
19359	,,	Wixon, Arthur Emanuel	Independent	James Henry Wixon (father), Tisbury, Southland.
20840	,,	Yorke, Ernest	Farmer	James Yorke (father), Waitangi Falls, Russell.

† Ex 1st Maori Contingent.

(11th REINFORCEMENTS—RAROTONGANS).

SAILED, "MANUKA," 16th NOVEMBER, 1916.

Reg. No.	Rank.	Name.	Occupation.	Name and Address of Next-of-kin.
16/977	2nd Lieut.	*Bush, George Arthur	Accountant	Mrs. A. M. Bush (wife), "Tiroa," Mangahao Road, Pahiatua.
22541	,,	Coull, John	Auctioneer	George Coull (father), St. John's Hill, Wanganui.
16/1309	,,	†Fromm, George August	Clerk	Alfred Antoine Fromm (father), Cheeseman Road, Gisborne.
19236	Sergeant	Banaba, Beni	Labourer	Mrs. Api Banaba (wife), Marairenga, Rarotonga.
19243	,,	Iorangi, Pitian	Butcher	Mrs. Iorangi (wife), Awaroa, Rarotonga.
19237	,,	Marsters, Carl	Store Assistant	Mrs. Tehiwa Marsters (wife), Awaroa, Rarotonga.
19270	,,	Mataio, Kea Rongomatane	Labourer	Mrs. Kea Mataio (wife), Atiu.
19289	Corporal	Karika, Pa George	Tally Clerk	Mrs. Pa George Karika (wife), Rarotonga.
19257	,,	Kopaki	Labourer	Maori (mother), Tainui, Atiu.
19249	,,	Kuo, Metua Mate	,,	Metua Mate (father), Awaroa, Rarotonga.
19265	,,	Ma, Kainana	Planter	Mrs. Meri Tepurutu (wife), Rarotonga.
19276	,,	Ngoroio, Makea Pori	Labourer	Pori (father), Rarotonga.
19264	Lance-Corpl.	Angene, Mata	,,	Angene (father), Rarotonga.
19247	,,	Kopu, Pakari	,,	Mrs. Pakari Wahine (mother), Awaroa, Rarotonga.
19269	,,	Meau, Tearai Vaine	,,	Mrs. Akatuko (mother), Atiu.
19281	,,	Ngaia, Kapao	,,	Kapao (father), Atiu.
19282	,,	Ngarea, Tukaroa	,,	Amaru (father), Rarotonga.
19293	,,	Raki, Punoua	,,	Mrs. Ani (mother), Aitutaki.
19240	,,	Roi, Charlie	Hospital Attendt.	Charlie Roi (father), Amuni, Aitutaki.
19275	,,	Taiki, Nio	Labourer	Pito Tamara (father), Rarotonga.
19339	,,	Tangitoru, Tekaratai	,,	Tangitoru (father), Mangaia.
19335	,,	Tiria, Taraia	,,	Mrs. Tiria (mother), Mangaia.
19233	Private	Ah Kew, Apongi	Baker	Ah Kew (brother), Awaroa, Rarotonga.
19322	,,	Akatauina, Tu	Labourer	Akatauina (father), Atiu.
19232	,,	Aki	,,	Etiki Teawa (father), Avarua, Rarotonga.
19246	,,	Aperau, Jam	,,	Mrs. Aperau (mother), Matauwera, Rarotonga.
19231	,,	Aupini	,,	Kairenga Tama (father), Rakahanga.
19244	,,	Iaveta, Karika	,,	Mrs. Iaveta (wife), Umaroa, Rarotonga.
19254	,,	Kakepare, Tariu	,,	Tariu (father), Areora, Atiu.
19258	,,	Kapi, Paiorua	Planter	Mrs. Maruia (wife), Rarotonga.
19350	,,	Karotana, Toariki	,,	Tekiiono (father), Rarotonga.
19299	,,	Kaurevai, Rima	Labourer	Mrs. Motuanga (mother), Rarotonga.
19251	,,	Ke, Ivitu	,,	Mrs. Rongomaki (wife), Rarotonga.
19253	,,	Kirikiri, Naero	,,	Mrs. Naero (mother), Atiu.
19248	,,	Koria, Manu	,,	Miss Manu (sister), Awaroa, Rarotonga.
19252	,,	Kuraia, Tapapa	,,	Tapapa (father), Areora, Atiu.
19261	,,	Makiru, Ongariti	,,	Ongokoreiti (father), Rarotonga.
19267	,,	Mamanu, Vaimutu	Planter	Miss Vaimutu (sister), Rarotonga.
19266	,,	Mana, Samuel	Labourer	Samuel (father), Mauke.
19262	,,	Mani, Piautu Marama	,,	Marama (father), Rarotonga.
19271	,,	Mania	,,	Teaea (father), Rarotonga.
19250	,,	Maitaiti, Kai	,,	Mrs. Te Pai Rua Mata (mother), Oneroa, Mangaia.
19343	,,	Maratai, Ua	Planter	Maratai (father), Rarotonga.
19268	,,	Mata, Takoto	Labourer	Takoto (brother), Atiu.
19277	,,	Mateora, Ngarua	,,	Mateora (father), Mangaia.
19272	,,	Moriaiti, Mate	,,	Moriaiti (father), Mangaia.

* Ex 2nd Maori Contingent.   † Ex 3rd Maori Contingent.

Reg. No.	Rank	Name	Occupation	Name and Address of Next-of-kin
19295	Private	Muiti, Pipiki	Planter	Mrs. Tangi (wife), Rarotonga.
19297	,,	Muiti, Ra	Labourer	Rimaura (mother), Mangaia.
19278	,,	Naka	,,	Taimau (father), Mangaia.
19292	,,	Nati, Pi	,,	Nati (father), Atiu.
19280	,,	Ngaata, Terepai	,,	Tauturu (father), Atiu, Rarotonga.
19242	,,	Ngavaarua, Ioteva	,,	Ngararua (father), Amuri, Aitutaki.
19283	,,	Nio	Planter	William Kelly (father), Rarotonga.
19286	,,	Okore	Labourer	Tarru (father), Atiu.
19259	,,	Paitai, Metua	,,	Paitai (father), Rarotonga.
19260	,,	Paora, Mate	,,	Paora (father), Atiu.
19321	,,	Paua, Tai	,,	Paua (father), Atiu.
19291	,,	Pepe	,,	Ngariki, Bishop (guardian), Avarua.
19348	,,	Piapo	,,	Taputu (father), Atiu.
19290	,,	Pio	,,	Apo (brother), Mauke.
19347	,,	Pita, Enoa	,,	Enoa (father), Rarotonga.
19287	,,	Po, Potaru	,,	Putaura (father), Rarotonga.
19288	,,	Puati	,,	Ngatama (father), Mangaia.
19300	,,	Rae, Taokete	,,	Taokete (brother), Atiu.
19298	,,	Rigot, J.	Musician	Mrs. Metuaone (wife), Rarotonga.
19263	,,	Ruaporo, Ma	Labourer	Uavaiute (wife), Avarua, Rarotonga.
19274	,,	Ruavai, Mare	,,	Ruavai (father), Mangaia.
19303	,,	Ruka, Willie	,,	Ikara (mother), Puka Puka.
19305	,,	Simeona, Piau	,,	Piau (father), Atiu.
19325	,,	Taianu, Makike	,,	Makike (father), Atiu.
19313	,,	Takake, Taiki	Planter	Taiki Henry (father), Rarotonga.
19301	,,	Takoto, Roo	Labourer	Takoto (father), Atiu.
19332	,,	Tangata	,,	Teava (father), Rarotonga.
19302	,,	Taori, Rere	,,	Taoi (father), Rarotonga.
19331	,,	Taote	,,	Ravea (mother), Atiu.
19239	,,	Tapapa, Akava	,,	Mrs. Tapapa (mother), Areora, Atiu.
19314	,,	Tarai, Tuira	Planter	Tarai (father), Mangaia.
19336	,,	Tau, Iti	,,	Rata (mother), Rarotonga.
19317	,,	Tautahana, Teataupuru	Labourer	Teata Tautipa (wife), Rarotonga.
19318	,,	Tavaka, Ken	,,	Taringa Maki (mother), Rarotonga.
19320	,,	Teapai, Parua	,,	Parua (father), Atiu.
19311	,,	Teariki, Paku	,,	Ratapu (mother), Atiu.
19309	,,	Tei, Enoa	,,	Enuangaro (father), Rarotonga.
19304	,,	Tekia, Rataro	Planter	Enua Tikia (father), Rarotonga.
19319	,,	Tekiri, Motu	Labourer	Tarerea (wife), Rarotonga.
19307	,,	Temaru	,,	Ngaau (father), Mauke.
19344	,,	Tepuretu, Vaine	,,	Mrs. Ina Vaine Tepuretu (wife), Rarotonga.
19315	,,	Terepii	Planter	Upokoroa (brother), Rarotonga.
19284	,,	Teto, Nikau	,,	John Mokoenga (father), Aitutaki.
19323	,,	Tetua, Nakura Mata	Labourer	Nakura (father), Atiu.
19312	,,	Tiputa, Uma	,,	Uma (father), Atiu.
19329	,,	Toroa, Iona Teipo	,,	Taungata (grandfather), Atiu.
19330	,,	Toroma, Tupou	,,	Komera (grandfather), Manihiki.
19234	,,	Totoroaere, Aria	,,	Totoroaere (father), Oneroa, Mangaia.
19337	,,	Tu, Paia	,,	Paia (father), Tahiti.
20841	,,	Tuaine, Tere	Cook	Metua (mother), Tautu, Aitutaki.
19327	,,	Tuakeo, Terongo	Labourer	Terongo (father), Atiu.
19285	,,	Tuikaa, Ngametua	,,	Tuika (father), Mangaia.
19245	,,	Tumu, Ito J.	,,	Akapi (father), Awaroa, Rarotonga.
19308	,,	Tungane, Ngamutu	,,	Vaine Tararo (sister), Mangaia.
19316	,,	Tuoe, Tearapo	,,	Karoke (mother), Atiu.
19310	,,	Tupa, Vaitoti	Planter	Epi (father-in-law), Rarotonga.
19306	,,	Turua, Pani	Labourer	Pani (father), Penrhyn.
19326	,,	Tutai, Pora	,,	Ua (wife), Atiu.
19273	,,	Tutara, Manu	,,	Piki Piki (sister), Rarotonga.
19341	,,	Upokokeu	,,	Ngaotu (wife), Atiu.
19340	,,	Uri	Planter	Taoivaini (mother), Rarotonga.
19338	,,	Urikapu, Teariki	Labourer	Rapea (mother), Rarotonga.
19342	,,	Uu, Turakina	,,	Turakina (father), Rarotonga.
19294	,,	Vakatini, Puti	Planter	Maka (mother), Rarotonga.
19345	,,	Vavia, Tuoro	Labourer	Tuorio, Vavia (father), Mitiaro.
19346	,,	Vavia, Puatuitui	,,	Puatuitui (brother), Tehenui, Atiu.
19328	,,	Varovaro, Tau	,,	Varovaro (father), Penrhyn.

12TH REINFORCEMENTS.

Reg. No.	Rank	Name.	Occupation.	Name and Address of Next-of-kin.
16/10	2nd Lieut.	†Kaipara, Autini Pitara	Interpreter	Mrs. Celia Kathrine Kaipara (wife), C.P.O., Auckland.
16/1025	Sergt.-Major	‡Singleton, John William Massey	Contractor	Mrs. S. L. Singleton (mother), London Cottage, Yeovil, England.
19408	Sergeant	Coe, Henry Caple	Civil Servant	Mrs. Elizabeth Coe (wife), Brighton Road, Parnell, Auckland.
19449	Corporal	Ormsby, Anthony	Interpreter	Mrs. Laura Marie Ormsby (wife). Otorohanga.
19427	,,	Pirini, Egbert	Surveyor's Assist.	Miss Wenarata Pirini (aunt), Ohinemutu, Rotorua.
16/1335	,,	§Taliauli, Jione	Medical Student	Malkai Tukuafu (brother), Nukualofa, Tonga.
19381	,,	Te Hatu, Tati	Labourer	Te Hatu Pirihi (father), Whakarewarewa, Rotorua.
19388	Lance-Corpl.	Hikamate, Maihi	Caretaker	Mrs. Kakume Hikamate (wife). Rotorua.
19385	,,	Hohepa, Kipa	Labourer	Mrs. Tatai Haea (mother), Rotorua.
19451	,,	Hunt, Thomas	,,	Miss Ellen Hunt (sister), Whakarewarewa, Rotorua.
19376	,,	Ririnui, Hekemaru	,,	Mrs. Manuariki Hikurangi (mother). Whakarewarewa, Rotorua.
19460	Private	Andrews, William Wilson	Planter	Lot Andrews (father), Kasavu, Fiji.
19444	,,	Asher, George Ngakiore	Hairdresser	David Asher (father), Tauranga, Bay of Plenty.
19432	,,	Barber, Puru	Bushman	Mrs. Tangiwai Pakia (mother), Mangamuka, Hokianga.
19372	,,	Brady, Joseph	Labourer	Mrs. Tauehe Brady (mother), Ohinemutu, Rotorua.
19433	,,	Chapman, Wira	Farmer	Pohonui Chapman (father), Matata, Bay of Plenty.
19423	,,	Clark, Clark	Dairyman	Jack Clark (father), Pamapuria, Kaitaia.
19463	,,	Clark, Ernest	Labourer	Mrs. Tuti Piri (friend), Chatham Islands.
19412	,,	Clark, John George	Farmer	Mrs. Mary Clark (mother), Kohukohu.
19387	,,	Galvin, Darkey	Labourer	Willie Galvin (father), Owhata, Rotorua.
19458	,,	Grant, Eric Lewis	Cinema Operator	Peter Grant (father), Suva, Fiji.
20811	,,	Haenga, Heremia Tawhero	Labourer	Ruka Haenga (father), Tuparoa Bay.
20894	,,	Haku, Tame	,,	Mrs. Hemo Wati (mother), Kaimaumau, North Auckland.
19415	,,	Heke, Tom	Bushman	Mrs. Mingi Heke (mother), Mangamuka, Hokianga.
19363	,,	Herewini, William	,,	Hohera Herewini (father), Opotiki.
19418	,,	Hetet, Wetene	Farmer	John Te Hetet (father), Te Kuiti.
19428	,,	Hoani, Atutahi	Labourer	Mrs. Heni Rukahina (wife), Te Ngae, Rotorua.
19378	,,	Hori, Monita	,,	Mrs. Taitimu Kitua (mother), Owhata, Rotorua.
20893	,,	Kanara, Rapata Wi	,,	Mrs. Ripine Wi Kanara (mother), Awanui North.
19422	,,	Karipa, George	,,	Mrs. Marama (mother), Victoria Valley, via Mangonui.
19384	,,	Keepa, Huna	,,	Mrs. Ngaroata Katene (mother), Whakarewarewa, Rotorua.
16/533	,,	Kereopa, John	Driver	Mrs. W. Winiata (guardian), Utiku.
20806	,,	Kiwara, Niha	Fencer	Tame Kiwara (father), Te Araroa.
19430	,,	Kokiri, Hapimana Reri	Labourer	Mrs. Rangitarahae Kokiri (mother), Te Ngae, Rotorua.
19368	,,	Marriner, George Michael	Cheesemaker	Mrs. Jean Marriner (mother), 2 Duppa Street, Wellington.
19455	,,	Matetu, Tame	Labourer	Mrs. Rangi Matetu (wife), Muriwai, via Gisborne.
19431	,,	Maxwell, Nicholas	,,	Hema Hakupa (uncle), Awaho, Rotorua.
19409	,,	Mei, Ripi	Bushman	Mei Otene (father), Mangamuka, Hokianga.
19383	,,	Mohi, Kena	Labourer	Mrs. Hariata Mohi (wife), Rotorua.
19425	,,	Mohi, Rangi	Bushman	Mrs. Hikairo Mohi (mother), Awahou, Rotorua.
19403	,,	Morgan, Pery	Carter	Mrs. Thompson (aunt), Mangawhare, Dargaville.
19447	,,	Morrison, Thomas Remi	Labourer	James Morrison (father), Ohinemutu, Rotorua.
19443	,,	Nathan, Richard Dick	Farmer	Eddie Nathan (brother), Peria, Mangonui, North Auckland.
19371	,,	Nicholls, Fredrick	Labourer	Humphrey Nicholls (father), Thames.
19407	,,	Norton, James Patrick	Carpenter	James Norton (father), Kaikoura.
19413	,,	Oneroa, Laurence	Bushman	Oneroa Mahima (father), Kohukohu, Hokianga.
19375	,,	Papara, George	Labourer	Mrs. Papara (mother), Te Waotu, Putaruru.
19386	,,	Petane, Tame	,,	Mrs. Pipi Haerehuka (mother), Ohinemutu, Rotorua.
19446	,,	Pirika, Nireaha	Cordialmaker	Pirika Hohepa (father), Ohinemutu, Rotorua.
19438	,,	Pitman, Warren	Farmer	Mrs. Hoana Pitman (mother), Whakapara, Whangarei.
19445	,,	Rangi, Edward	Blacksmith	Mrs. Te Matoha Rangitaira (mother), Ohinemutu, Rotorua.
19411	,,	Rata, Jerry	Farmer	Rata Herewaka (father), Mangamuka, Hokianga.
19391	,,	Reweti, Hami	Labourer	Waitai Reweti (father), Ahipara, North Auckland.
19379	,,	Rikihana, Hare	,,	Rikihana Aporo (father), Rotorua.
19369	,,	Rio, Rereti	Farmer	Rio Maaka (father), Waitotara, near Wanganui.
19421	,,	Ru, Hami	Bushman	Mrs. Rihi Ru (mother), Whatuwhiwhi, Mangonui.
19426	,,	Simon, Rameka	Labourer	Koki Paora (father), Awahou, Rotorua.
19429	,,	Slade, Joseph	,,	Mrs. Rangata Slade (mother), Whangamata, Thames.
19419	,,	Simpson, Samuel	Engineer	William Simpson (cousin), Levuka, Fiji.
19417	,,	Smith, Haka	Bushman	Mete Smith (father), Kohukohu, Hokianga.
20887	,,	Te Huaki, Matene	Labourer	Mrs. Rangi Tainui (sister), Rotorua.
19367	,,	Teka, Mana	Farmer	Mrs. Ngainuna Teka (wife), Maxwelltown, near Wanganui.
19398	,,	Te Kauru, John	Shepherd	Te Kauru (father), Nuhaka, Hawke's Bay.
19435	,,	Tepiihi, Teteira	Labourer	Mrs. Potehiku Tepiihi (wife), Taneatua.
19434	,,	Trau, Puhi	Dairy-farmer	Mrs. Maria Trau (mother), Te Puna, Tauranga.
19382	,,	Tumatahi, William	Photographer	Tumatahi Manahi (father), Rotorua.
19461	,,	Underwood, Gilbert	Labourer	Louis Underwood (brother), Post-office, Suva.
19400	,,	Walker, Jimmie	Farmer	Mrs. Kara Whaanga (mother), Nuhaka.
19374	,,	Walter, Tommy	Labourer	Waata Ngahana (father), Ohinemutu, Rotorua.
19464	,,	Whaitiri, Tahatu	Fisherman	Tesare Whaitiri (cousin), Chatham Islands.
19366	,,	Wiremu, Hiru	Farm Hand	Miss Miria Wiremu (sister), Taiporohenui, Hawera.

† Ex 1st Maori Contingent.　　‡ Ex 2nd Maori Contingent.　　§ Ex 3rd Maori Contingent.

13TH REINFORCEMENTS.

Reg. No.	Rank.	Name.	Occupation.	Name and Address of Next-of-kin.
33003	2nd Lieut.	Gannon, Arthur Te Waata	Clerk	Mrs. Edna Hiria Gannon (wife), Islington Street, Ponsonby, Auckland.
20773	Sergeant	Ferris, Kani	,,	Mrs. C. W. Ferris (mother), Wainui, Gisborne.
19468	Corporal	Graham, George	Labourer	Mrs. Ngarama Graham (mother), Te Hauke, Opapa.
19514	,,	Heberley, Walter	Slaughterman	Mrs May Heberley (wife), Picton
16/150	,,	Hunt, William	Bushman	Mrs. Susan Hunt (mother), Whakarewarewa, Rotorua.
19405	,,	Poutawera, Kerei	Labourer	Mrs. Gason (friend), Johnsonville, Wellington.
19515	Lance-Corpl	Etana, Rikihana	Gum-digger	Etana Heka (father), Te Kao, North Auckland
19509	,,	Haira, Eru	Flax-mill Hand	Haira Himiona (father), Whakarewarewa, Rotorua.
19493	,,	Peta, Timu Timu	Farmer	Mrs. Pitara Marewa (mother), Te Kaha, via Thames.
19516	,,	Takimoana, Puhi	Gum-digger	Takimoana Harawira (father), Te Kao, North Auckland.
19524	,,	Taurere, Tepana	Mill Hand	Mrs. Rawinia Taurere (mother), Kaikohe, Bay of Islands.
19525	,,	Wihapi, Tata	Labourer	Mrs. Pinia Wihapi (mother), Waitangi, Te Puke.
19495	Private	Allen, Jack Noble	Blacksmith	Mrs. Mary Noble Allen (mother), Ahipara, North Cape.
19484	,,	Amotawa, Moke	Labourer	Henare Amotawa (brother), Whakarewarewa, Rotorua.
20834	,,	Barlow, Wiremu Paitaki	,,	Mrs. Raukura Ngapuhoro (mother), Kawhia.
19496	,,	Beazley, Fredrick Thomas	,,	George Beazley (father), Omanaia, Hokianga.
19480	,,	Brown, Harry	Farmer	Mrs. Wehe Brown (mother), Tauranga, Bay of Plenty.
19453	,,	Cassidy, Perry	Labourer	Robert Cassidy (father), Kaihu, Northern Wairoa.
19364	,,	Fluety, John	Farmer	Mrs. Mary George Tauwhare (mother), Arahura, via Hokitika.
19489	,,	Flutey, Arthur George	Labourer	Mrs. Miria Flutey (mother), Woodend, Kaiapoi.
20717	,,	Haller, Mick	Cook	John Haller (father), Niue.
19520	,,	Harehuru, Karena	Labourer	Mrs. Ngareta Harehuru (mother), Herekino, North Auckland.
19487	,,	Harris, Arthur	Farm Hand	Mrs. Awe Harris (mother), Rangiahua, Hokianga.
19507	,,	Heke, George	Bushman	Mrs. Ani Kiro (mother), Mangamuka, Hokianga.
19448	,,	Heuheu, Tommy	Farmer	Mrs. Pingao Heuheu (mother), Porootarao, Te Kuiti.
19498	,,	Hohaia, Iwi	Bushman	Ipu Hohaia (father), Mangamuka, Hokianga.
19472	,,	Hona, Petera	Labourer	Mrs. Irihapeti Petera (wife), Tapuaekura, Rotoiti, Rotorua.
19490	,,	Huria, George Arthur	,,	Joseph Puniki Huria (brother), North Road, Kaiapoi.
19416	,,	Kakere, Paku	,,	Jimmy Kakere (brother), Tokomaru Bay.
19393	,,	Karauria, Tewa	Farmer	K. Rarauwha (friend), Waitotara.
19519	,,	Karena, Awarua	Gum-digger	Mrs. Ngataua Karena (mother), Te Kao, North Auckland.
19321	,,	Kingi, Heremaia	Labourer	Mrs. Huhana Kingi (wife), Herekino, via Kaitaia.
19370	,,	Koeti, Teoti	Bushman	Mrs. Sarah Lawry (sister), Arahura, via Hokitika.
19465	,,	McDonald, Hugh	Labourer	Mrs. Annie Sulbery (sister), Otaki.
19452	,,	Macki, Honi	Bushman	Maria Paniwaka (cousin), Ohinemutu, Rotorua.
19475	,,	Martin, William	Farmer	Mrs. Davis Ormsby (mother), Otorohanga.
19402	,,	Mataira, Sonny	Farm Hand	Karepa Mataira (father), Nuhaka.
19395	,,	Mete, Hoani	Farmer	Jimmy Smith (father), Nuhaka.
19503	,,	Moko, Horo	Labourer	Te Moko Haroto (father), Te Teko, Bay of Plenty.
19399	,,	Morris, Benjamin	,,	William Morris (father), Gisborne.
19518	,,	Pako, Taumaiti	Gum-digger	Mrs. Uneiki Pako (mother), Te Kao, North Auckland.
19500	,,	Phillips, Douglas Kaupaka	Farmer	Mrs. Polly Phillips (wife), Punaruku, via Whakapara.
19450	,,	Pita, Jimmy	Labourer	Mrs. Pani Pita (mother), Peria, Mangonui.
19462	,,	Piwari, Pahia	Farmer	Mrs. Kupa Piwari (mother), Chatham Islands.
19469	,,	Pori, Wi	Labourer	Rani Ruahuihui (father), Te Puke, Bay of Plenty.
19510	,,	Rangi, Harry	Farmer	Tanu Pakihiwi (father), Tapuaeharuru, Rotoiti, Rotorua.
19396	,,	Smith, George	Labourer	Hone Smith (father), Nuhaka.
19394	,,	Smith, Hoani	,,	Mrs. Heni Smith (mother), Nuhaka.
19404	,,	Smoke, John	,,	Tame Smoke (father), Manutuke, Gisborne.
20826	,,	Taki, Rauahi	Bushman	Mrs. Iha Pera (mother), Kaikohe.
19478	,,	Te Moananui, Stuart	Farmer	Mrs. Merina Moananui (mother), Parakiwai, Paeroa.
19401	,,	Te Ngaio, Hemi	Labourer	Hemi Te Ngaio (father), Mahia, Opoutama.
20683	,,	Te Ohu, Hare	Mill Hand	Mrs. Raiha Te Ohu (wife), Mangonui, North Auckland.
19479	,,	Tuahine, Tu	Labourer	Te Maraki Tuahine (brother), Te Kuiti.
19502	,,	Werohia, Waro	Farmer	Henare Werohia (father), Papamoa, Tauranga.
19470	,,	Wharetamatera, Puata	Labourer	Wharetamatera (father), Whangamata, Waihi.
19474	,,	Wi, Henry Wi Waka	Farmer	Wi Kio (father), Te Kuiti.
19508	,,	Wipani, Dick	Bushman	Hemi Wipani (uncle), Hawera, Taranaki.
19499	,,	Wipani, Peter	,,	Mrs. Te Paea Wipani (mother), Mangamuka, Hokianga.
19497	,,	Williams, Adam	Farmer	Wiremu Arama Wiremu (father), Mangamuka, Hokianga.
19476	,,	Williams, Thomas	Farm Hand	Remana Wiremu (brother), Okere, Rotorua.

14TH REINFORCEMENTS.

Reg. No.	Rank.	Name.	Occupation.	Name and Address of Next-of-kin.
33004	2nd Lieut.	Dansey, George Robert	Telegraphist	Roger Delamere Dansey (father), Rotorua.
20788	Sergeant	Mitchell, Zealand Niramona	Surveyor	Mrs. Nataria Mitchell (wife), Ohinemutu, Rotorua.
19506	Corporal	Pakuku, Peta	Farmer	Peta Pakuku (father), Wairoa, Hawke's Bay.
16/38	,,	†Rangi, Wiremu Hacata	,,	Mrs. Maraea Keiha (aunt), Gisborne.
19546	,,	Wi, Henry Teko	Labourer	Wi Kio (father), Te Kuiti.
19545	Lance-Corpl.	Anaru, Harry Pahira	Shearer	Mrs. Okeroa Anaru (wife), Masterton.
19552	,,	Babbington, Morgan Romeo	Labourer	Mrs. Hunia Taumutu (aunt), Tokomaru Bay.
19573	,,	Ereatara, Kouru	Clerk	Ereatara Toheriri (father), Te Puke.
19578	,,	Hetet, Charles William	Farmer	Mrs. Violet Hetet (wife), care of Mrs. Hugh Glover, Sussex Street, off Newton Road, Auckland.
19530	Private	Ahomiro, Aronia	Labourer	Ahomiro Ngakuku (father), Waitangi, Te Puke.
19551	,,	Babbington, Prince Wilson	,,	Mrs. Mira Wirihana Babbington (mother), Tokomaru Bay.
19564	,,	Cootes, Taipua Skipwith	Student	Mrs. Grace Irene Cootes (wife), 10 Wright Street, Wellington.
19547	,,	Creeke, George	Labourer	Mrs. Whai Creeke (wife), Matata, Bay of Plenty.
19585	,,	Dunn, Hiki	Bushman	Mrs. Hiria H. Dunn (wife), Opononi, via Rawene.
19529	,,	Graham, William	Driver	Graham Hapi (father), Ohinepanea, Thames.
19537	,,	Gray, Tata Paddie	Labourer	Paddie Gray (father), Te Puke.
19587	,,	Hahunga, Thomas	Bushfeller	Sam Hahunga (brother), Ngongotaha.
19568	,,	Hobson, Jeremiah William	Farmer	Patrick Hobson (father), Waipapakauri, via Mangonui.
19494	,,	Hohepa, Mea	Farm Labourer	Mrs. Mary Hohepa (wife), Muripara, via Rotorua.
19560	,,	Hokai, Tua	Farmer	Hokai Puku (father), Whangape, via Hokianga.
19586	,,	Honiana, Raka	,,	Mrs. Anamaria Honiana (mother), Papamoa, via Tauranga.
16/1284	,,	Hunter, Sidney James	,,	Mrs. Emily Hunter (wife), Waipapakauri, via Mangonui.
19556	,,	Jumbo, Henry	Labourer	Mrs. Ngahoari Hirini (mother), Matata, Bay of Plenty.
19420	,,	Kaio, William	Milker	Mrs. Kaio (mother), Awanui, via Mangonui.
19541	,,	Karaka, Ngamaunu	Labourer	Edward Clark (father), Te Puke, Bay of Plenty.
19583	,,	Karangaroa, Rewai	,,	Mrs. Ani Karangaroa (mother), Nuhaka, Hawke's Bay.
19543	,,	Katau, Augustus	,,	Te Nae Katau (father), Bruce Bay, South Westland.
19539	,,	Kirikau, Hihi	,,	Kirikau Raimona (father), Tauranga.
19439	,,	Manene, Billy Tarau	,,	Mrs. Kake Trau Manene (mother), Waihah, via Opua.
19584	,,	Marino, Herbert	Bushman	Mrs. Anamaraea Marino (mother), Te Ahuahu, via Kawakawa.
19477	,,	Mauhe, Hori	Farmer	Nurse Murphy (mother), "Wallace," Waipukurau.
19536	,,	Ngahana, Reggie Walter	Blacksmith	Waata Ngahana (father), Ohinemutu, Rotorua.
19550	,,	Ngapo, Fred	Farmer	Maaka Ngapo (father), Kennedy's Bay, via Coromandel.
19558	,,	Ngawaka, Tom	Farm Hand	Parore Ngawaka (father), Whangape, via Hokianga.
19491	,,	Osborne, Andrew	Farmer	Nguha Huirama (father), Mokai, Taupo.
19567	,,	Paki, David	,,	Rapana Paki (father), Wangaehu, via Wanganui.
19538	,,	Papa, Tauwhitu	Bushman	Papa Titore (father), Waiotemarama, via Hokianga.
19534	,,	Patene, John Hona	Labourer	Hona Patene (father), "Te Takapou," Rotoiti, via Rotorua.
19531	,,	Pinker, Alfred	Farm Hand	Ben Pinker (father), Paengaroa, via Rotorua.
19582	,,	Pomana, George	Labourer	Mrs. Ereti Pomana (mother), Nuhaka, Hawke's Bay.
19576	,,	Pue, Pani	Farm Hand	Pue Tutepuangi (father), Pungarehu, Taranaki.
19553	,,	Rangi, Fred	Labourer	Mrs. Te Matoha Rangitauira (mother), Ohinemutu, Rotorua.
19570	,,	Rapata, Richard	Farmer	Mrs. Te Owai Taramoeroa (sister), Waipapakauri, via Mangonui.
19532	,,	Rickus, Jack Melbourn	Labourer	Mrs. H. P. Rickus (mother), 7 William Street, Temuka.
19557	,,	Rihari, Eru	,,	Mrs. Kini Rihari (mother), Matata.
19544	,,	Smith, Paku	Farmer	Joe Smith (father), Nuhaka, Hawke's Bay.
19559	,,	Stevens, Kahi Wi	,,	Wi Stevens (father), Whangape, via Hokianga.
19441	,,	Taka, Etui	Labourer	Taka Wilson (father), Paeroa.
19579	,,	Tangiau, Tommy	,,	Mrs. Elizabeth Faulkner (mother), Te Puna, via Tauranga.
19563	,,	Teamo, Charley	,,	Teamo Kaiaha (father), Te Teko, via Rotorua.
19533	,,	Te Amo, Tapua	,,	Te Amo Ngaruri (father), Waitangi, via Russell.
19528	,,	Te Hui, Haora	,,	Mrs. Mere Rangi (sister), Te Kahika, Te Puke.
19581	,,	Tehuiki, Henare Nehemia	,,	Netana Nehemia Tehuiki (brother), Mokaha, Hawke's Bay.
19527	,,	Temoni, Abraham	,,	Temoni Keepa (father), Okere Falls, via Rotorua.
19575	,,	Thompson, Jack	,,	Mrs. Tau Henare (cousin), Kawakawa, Bay of Islands.
19572	,,	Tipene, Wiparara	Farmer	Mrs. Te Kirihau Tipene (wife), Mangamuka, via Hokianga.
19486	,,	Tuhaka, Kereama	Labourer	Mrs. Pareake Tuhaka (mother), Te Horo, Horohenua.
19554	,,	Waata, Keni	,,	Waata Ngahana (father), Ohinemutu, Rotorua.
19561	,,	Wheoki, Rahiri	Nurseryman	John Wheoki (father), Rangiahua, via Hokianga.
19526	,,	Wihapi, Wateno	Driver	Miss Taraipine Wihapi (sister), Waitangi, via Russell.
19549	,,	Wirangirangi, Maangi	Labourer	Mrs. Ruiha Wirangirangi (mother), Mohaka, Hawke's Bay.

† Ex 4th Maori Reinforcements.

15TH REINFORCEMENTS.

Reg. No.	Rank.	Name.	Occupation.	Name and Address of Next-of-kin.
20598	2nd Lieut.	Kokiri, Tango	Civil Servant	William King (brother), Ohinemutu, Rotorua.
20772	Sergeant	Baker, Pita Heretaunga	Shepherd	H. Hei (friend), Solicitor, Gisborne.
16/61	,,	†Te Hau, Kahu	Labourer	Pita te Hau (father), Muriwai, Gisborne.
19488	Corporal	Tikitere, Herewini	,,	Mrs. Ngatomokanga Tikitere (wife), Ohinemutu, Rotorua.
19606	Lance-Corpl.	Greaves, Peter	,,	Mrs. Maata Greaves (mother), Parapara, Mangonui.
19619	,,	Smith, George David	Farmer	Te Mete Raukawa (father), Tauranga, Bay of Plenty.
19598	Private	Aperahama, Wiremu Pera	Labourer	Mrs. Millie Pera Aperahama (wife), care of Kelliher, Te Karaka, Poverty Bay.
19522	,,	Awhitu, Terry	Railway Hand	Miss Hera Awhitu (sister), Rangiriri.
19618	,,	Awiti, Timi	Labourer	Mrs. Mere Awiti (wife), Matata, Bay of Plenty.
19459	,,	Curtis, Joseph	Engine-driver	Thomas Curtis (father), Levuka, Fiji.
19620	,,	Edwards, Readmun	Labourer	Mrs. Hautai Reimana (wife), Mourea, Okere Falls, Rotorua.
19600	,,	Farrell, Thomas	Farmer	Mrs. Putiputi Hapimana (mother), Te Ngae, Rotorua.
19609	,,	Flutey, John	Blacksmith	Mrs. Eva Flutey (mother), Otaki.
19623	,,	Haimona, Rarua	Labourer	Mrs Ruiha Rarua Haimona (wife), Okere Falls, Rotorua.
19596	,,	Harawira, George	,,	Mrs. Bella Harawira (mother), Papamoa, near Tauranga.
19635	,,	Harris, Kuri	Farm Labourer	Mrs. Ngarua Hare (mother), Otaua, Punakitere, Hokianga.
19414	,,	Hau, Pete	Mill Hand	Howe Herbert (father), Opononi, Hokianga.
19588	,,	Henare, Manuka	Farmer	Mrs. Parina Manuka Henare (wife), Whangape, North Auckland.
33543	,,	Hennah, Te Mamaru George Tau	,,	Mrs. F. V. Hennah (mother), Tirohia, Paeroa.
19616	,,	Hetaraka, Marsh	Mill Hand	Miss Ngapeka Hetaraka (sister), Naumai, Northern Wairoa
19605	,,	Hiamoe, Humana	Labourer	Hiamoe Renata (father), Matapihi, Tauranga.
19613	,,	King, John	,,	Moihi te Hira (uncle), Matakana, Tauranga.
19621	,,	Marunui, Pona	Shearer	Mrs. Roa Pona (wife), Muripara, Galatea, Rotorua.
19607	,,	Matehaere, Pio	Labourer	Matehaere (father), Waiteti, Rotorua.
19601	,,	Moko, Johnnie	Farmer	Moko Papaki (father), Maketu, Bay of Plenty.
19603	,,	McLeod, Rerehou	,,	Ririnui Matutaera (father), Hairini, Tauranga.
19602	,,	Ngatai, John	,,	Reweti Ngatai (father), Matapihi, Tauranga.
19594	,,	Paratene, Mio	Gum-digger	Rangi Tukariri (friend), Otangaroa, North Auckland.
20721	,,	Pohatu, Tauranga	Labourer	Henry Pohatu (father), Te Hauke, near Hastings, Hawke's Bay.
19597	,,	Rameka, Henry	,,	Mrs. Arihia Rameka (mother), Taupo.
19611	,,	Ratahi, Lemon	,,	Ratahi Nopera (father), Te Hono, Kaikou, North Auckland.
19622	,,	Remi, Leo	,,	Mrs. Te Ratoru Remi (mother), Muripara, Galatea, Rotorua.
19593	,,	Samuels, Edward	,,	Mrs. Katarina Samuels (mother), Otangaroa, North Auckland.
19590	,,	Tana, Ita Hone	Bushfeller	Mrs. Mori Mau (sister), Whangaruru, near Whangarei.
19566	,,	Tinimana, Jack	Labourer	Tinimana (father), Mohaka, Wairoa, Hawke's Bay.
19604	,,	Webster, Jack	,,	Wepiha Rangiamoamo (father), Papamoa, Tauranga.
19589	,,	Whare, David George	,,	Whare Rika (father), Ngatira, Putaruru.
19610	,,	Wi, Peter	Bushman	Wi Kio (father), Te Kuiti.
19612	,,	Williams, Walter	,,	Mrs. Charlotte Williams (wife), Parapara, Mangonui.
19625	,,	Wilson, Robert George	Labourer	Miss Emily H. Karakaikore (friend), "Bonhay," 46 Wainui Road, Kaiti, Gisborne.

† Ex 1st Maori Contingent.

16TH REINFORCEMENTS.

Reg. No.	Rank	Name	Occupation	Name and Address of Next-of-kin
16/1330	2nd Lieut.	†Macdonald, Archibald	Civil Servant	Archibald Macdonald (father), Grace Street, Invercargill
16/252	Sergeant	‡∥Bevan, Matthew	Motor-mechanic	M. Bevan (brother), Merton, Otaki.
19633	,,	§Gray, Patrick		
19390	,,	O'Raukawa, Wi Kingi	Farmer	Te Miri O'Raukawa (father), Ohinemutu, Rotorua.
19634	Lance-Corpl.	Kaiwai, Harold	,,	Mrs. Matirita Kaiwai (mother), Tangoio, Napier.
19646	,,	Poihipi, Riki	Bushman	Mrs. Heeni Poihipi (wife), Torere, Opotiki.
19638	,,	Te Rore, John	Mill Hand	Mrs. Ngakihi te Rore (wife), Kaihu, North Auckland.
19632	Private	Andrews, Thomas	Motor-driver	James Andrews (father), Muripara, Rotorua.
19640	,,	Aratema, Taane	Labourer	Mrs. Ireni Aratema (wife), Te Teko, Bay of Plenty.
19639	,,	Barton, George	,,	Peter Barton (father), Ngahape, Te Awamutu.
19631	,,	Brass, Robert	,,	Brass te Hua (father), Ahipara, North Auckland.
19662	,,	Browne, Brown	,,	Miss Julia Browne (sister), Motukaraka, Hokianga.
37771	,,	Cotton, Joe Bird	Fitter	Harry Cotton (brother), Native Land Court, Auckland.
19643	,,	Galvin, Joe	Farm Hand	Haki Karawana (father), Owhata, Te Ngae, Rotorua.
19653	,,	Gray, William	Shearer	Mrs. Hinerau Gray (mother), Waiohika, Gisborne.
19649	,,	Hirini, Hone	Labourer	Rewiri Hirini (brother), Ngawha.
19637	,,	Hohepa, Wati	Bushman	Mrs. Meti Hone Tana (sister), Kaitaia, North Auckland.
19624	,,	Hoko, Moa	Farm Hand	Mrs. Aunihi Moa (wife), Whangaroa.
19504	,,	Kaihe, William	Bushman	Johnie Kaihe (father), Rangiahua, Hokianga.
19642	,,	Karaka, Moihi	Labourer	Hekenui Karaka (father), Manoeka, Te Puke.
19599	,,	McDonald, John	Bushman	Donald McDonald (father), 70 Federal Street, Auckland.
19658	,,	Maeke, Philip	Farmer	Miss Ria Heeni Maeke (sister), Taumarunui.
19629	,,	Mita, Tuiri	Labourer	Teaoho Mita (father), Tangoio, Napier.
19636	,,	Otene, Walker	Bushman	Mrs. Maraea Hori (mother), Mangamuka, Hokianga.
19645	,,	Paul, Andrew	Labourer	Taikehu Paul (father), Ngongotaha, Rotorua.
19664	,,	Pene, Amo	Carter	Mrs. Ratauhinga Pene (mother), Morrinsville.
19651	,,	Rata, Waitai	Gum-digger	Mrs. Maata Rata (wife), Waipapakauri, North Auckland.
19647	,,	Takaroro, Mai Rangi	Labourer	Takaroro Enoka (father), Otorohanga.
19641	,,	Te Horohau, Wiki	,,	Te Horohau Tawari (father), Te Whaiti, via Muripara.
19648	,,	§Timo, Ruma	Sawmill Hand	Miss Maki Cassidy (half-sister), Kaihu, North Auckland.
19652	,,	Walker, Edward	Gum-digger	Mrs. Rihi te Tai (cousin), Waiho, Whakapara, Hokianga.
19555	,,	Wright, Thomas	Labourer	Mrs. Mamaeroa Wright (wife), Piopio.

† Ex 7th Reinforcements and 3rd Maori Contingent.   ‡ Ex 1st Maori Contingent.   § Did not re-embark Wellington 26th April, 1917.   ∥ Embarked second sailing, 26th April, 1917.

17TH REINFORCEMENTS.

Reg. No.	Rank	Name	Occupation	Name and Address of Next-of-kin
9/029	2nd Lieut.	*Montgomery, Harry Steele	Soldier	Mrs. Margaret Montgomery (mother), Harrington Street, Port Chalmers.
19424	Sergeant	Grace, John	Farmer	Mrs. Maria Grace (wife), Tuparoa, Gisborne.
19668	Private	Allan, William	Labourer	Matekino Hikatarewa (aunt), Ohinemutu, Rotorua.
19671	,,	Bristowe, Sam	Bushman	Kiri Bristowe (father), Karetu, Bay of Islands.
19672	,,	Brown, Ruki	,,	Charley Brown (father), Kawakawa, Bay of Islands.
19695	,,	Brown, Kemp	Labourer	Joseph Brown (father), Waimanoni, Awanui North.
19617	,,	Callaghan, John Tikirau	Bushman	John Callaghan (father), Raukokore, Bay of Plenty.
19699	,,	Dickson, Harry	Labourer	Rikihana Tari (father), Tauranga.
47205	,,	Hale, Arthur	Drover	James Hale (father), Tokomaru Bay.
19727	,,	Ham, John	Rabbiter	Mrs. Herena Ham (mother), Tokaanu.
19680	,,	Harmon, James	Labourer	Robert Harmon (father), Hauturu, Kawhia.
47887	,,	Hicks, Alfred William	Hairdresser	W. J. T. Hicks (father), Whakatane.
19700	,,	Kahu, Jack	Labourer	Kahu Poihipi (father), Taupo.
19693	,,	Lundon, George	Bushman	Mrs. Riria Harris (mother), Motukaraka.
19728	,,	McLean, Thomas	,,	Makarini Puhata (father), Waipiro, Hiruharama.
19697	,,	McLeod, Tareha	Labourer	Mrs. Matererе McLeod (mother), Papamoa.
19675	,,	Matthews, Thomas	Bushman	Matiu Poutu (father), Tuparoa.
19679	,,	Mutu, Charlie	Mill Hand	Mutu Ihaka (father), Ahipara, Hokianga.
19698	,,	Ngatai, Hipara	Labourer	Enoka Ngatai (father), Tauranga.
19702	,,	Moore, Ropehana Edward Albert	Farmer	John Abraham Moore (father), Tolaga Bay.
19666	,,	Petera, Davey	Labourer	Tuhine Petera (brother), Wairoa, Hawke's Bay.
19686	,,	Pirihi, Friday	Butcher	George Pirihi (brother), Takahiwai, Marsden Point.
19656	,,	Pikikotuku, James	Farmer	T. Pikikotuku (father), Kirikau, Wanganui River.
19595	,,	Rameka, Te	,,	Mrs. Kaparani Rameka (mother), Papamoa.
19685	,,	Taylor, Nareta	Bushman	Piro Taylor (father), Whirinaki, Hokianga.
19657	,,	Tupe, Patena	Labourer	Mrs. Teomaki Hinewai (sister), Taringamotu, Taumarunui.
19689	,,	Turner, Richard Alexander Duncan	Farmer	John Turner (father), Manukau Heads.
19691	,,	Waldren, John	,,	Mrs. Hutita Waldren (wife), Kakahi.
19659	,,	Warahi, Piere	,,	Matiere Warahi (father), Taumarunui.
19661	,,	Warena, John Tana	Carpenter	Mrs. Ari Warena (mother), Wanganui.
19669	,,	Wharewhiti, Nikora	Labourer	Matenga Wharewhiti (father), Waiotapu, Rotorua.

* Ex Main Body.

18TH REINFORCEMENTS.

EMBARKED ON "MAUNGANUI."

Reg. No.	Rank.	Name.	Occupation.	Name and Address of Next-of-kin.
20703	2nd Lieut.	Paku, Joseph Rawhira	Licensed Interpretor	Mrs. Rora Paku (wife), Gaysford Terrace, Waipukurau.
19373	Sergeant	Taranaki, George	Labourer	Mrs. Hera Ngoungou (sister), Rotorua.
19670	Lance-Corpl.	Amohau, Miro	,,	Mrs. Porete Amohau (wife), Okere Falls, Rotorua.
19562	,,	Maaka, Hemi	,,	Maaka Hori (father), Mangonui.
19937	Private	Anaru, Mihaere	,,	W. Anaru (father), Tongoio, Hawke's Bay.
19663	,,	Cook, Alfred John	Carter	Mrs. Martha Cook (wife), Morrinsville.
47860	,,	Cooper, William Henry	Labourer	Mrs. W. H. Cooper (wife), care of Post-office, Te Reinga, Gisborne.
19707	,,	Edmonds, Henry Harvess	Bushman	John Tucker Edmonds (father), Ngawha, Bay of Islands.
19719	,,	Hall, Charles	Labourer	Mrs. Atareta Hall (wife), Ohinemutu, Rotorua.
16/592A	,,	*Harawira, Hota	Gum-digger	Mrs. Rongo Harawira (wife), Auckland.
19684	,,	Heperi, Pita	Wool-worker	Mrs. Louisa Heperi (wife), Waimate North, Bay of Islands.
19773	,,	Hikamate, Hakapo	Labourer	Tame Hikamate (brother), Rotorua.
19667	,,	Hodge, Richard	,,	Mrs. Tiripa Hodge (wife), Whakarewarewa, Rotorua.
19786	,,	Hohepa, Puehu	Flax-mill Hand	Hohepa Poia (father), Muripara, Whakatane.
19665	,,	Hura, Ware	Shearer	Mrs. Te Wairama Hura (wife), Petane, Napier.
19708	,,	Huripara, Watene	Labourer	Huripara Huihui (father), Te Araroa, East Coast.
19709	,,	Hutana, Joseph Kiriwai	Clerk	Mrs. Ihaia Newton (mother), Tokomaru Bay.
19711	,,	Kuare, Hepeta	Farmer	Mrs. Akatuhi Puia (mother), Te Karaka, Gisborne.
19710	,,	Muriwai, George Harris	Bushman	Muriwai Hepehi (father), Horeke, Hokianga.
19720	,,	Ngahuruhuru, Eketu	Labourer	Wharetutaki Rukingi (cousin), Ohinemutu, Rotorua.
19747	,,	Pahura, Hatiwira	,,	Mrs. Ruby Pahura (wife), Gisborne.
19681	,,	Parata, Alfred Rayne	,,	Mrs. Haromi Parata (wife), Porangahau.
19687	,,	Peti, Samuel	Mill Hand	Mrs. Miria Peti (wife), Motukaraka, Hokianga.
19723	,,	Randell, Henry	Farmer	George Randell (father), Huntly West.
19713	,,	Ripia, Tango	Labourer	Mrs. Pare Ripia (wife), Kahukura.
19648	,,	†Timo, Ruma	Sawmill Hand	Miss Maggie Cassidy (sister), Kaihu.
19715	,,	Tohu, Watikena	Labourer	Mrs. Harata Tohu (mother), Horeke, Hokianga.
17562	,,	Watson, Rihari	,,	Mrs. McLaren (cousin), Buller Bridge, Westport.
19706	,,	Wihapi, Pat	,,	Mrs. Hariata Wihapi (wife), Waitangi, Te Puke.
19717	,,	Williams, Samuel	,,	Harry Williams (father), Gisborne.
20661	,,	Witana, Matin	,,	Witana Hamihana (father), Lower Waihou, Hokianga.

* Ex 2nd Maori Contingent. † Ex " Pakeha " first sailing.

19TH REINFORCEMENTS.

Reg. No.	Rank.	Name.	Occupation.	Name and Address of Next-of-kin.
16/50	Lieutenant	†Ferris, James Paumea	Farmer	C. W. Ferris (father), Wainui, Gisborne.
19736	Sergeant	Pouwhare, Ngapaki	,,	Te Pouwhare (father), Ruatoki, Bay of Plenty.
19437	Corporal	Halbert, Rangi	,,	Mrs. Katarina Halbert (wife), Moawhango, via Taihape.
19749	,,	Hinaki, Para Nihi	,,	Miss Manu Hinaki (sister), Whangara, Gisborne.
19737	,,	Kaa, Henare	,,	Panikena Kaa (father), Rangitukia, Port Awanui, East Coast.
19735	,,	Ngata, Moana	,,	Hone Ngata (father), Rangitukia, Port Awanui, East Coast.
16/586	Lance-Corpl.	‡Grant, James	Labourer	Mrs. Jane Manuera (sister), Tokomaru Bay, East Coast.
19746	,,	Hahipono, Rowiri	,,	Hakahaka Hahipono (father), Torere, East Coast.
16/82	,,	†Petiha, Hone	Engineer	Makahuri Petiha (brother), Hastings, Hawke's Bay.
19738	,,	Rangiwaia, Manihera	Labourer	Rewai Purakau Rangiwaia (father), Waipiro Bay.
19748	Private	Clarke, Robert		William Clarke (father), Kahukura, East Coast.
19731	,,	Cummins, Davis	Labourer	Samuel Thompson Cummins (father), Waitemarama, Hokianga.
16/585	,,	Grace, Daniel	,,	Mrs. Ruahine Grace (wife), Tuparoa Bay, East Coast.
19745	,,	Grace, Samuel	,,	Hakahaka Hahipono (father), Torere, East Coast.
19772	,,	Haereroa, Pani	,,	Raniera Haereroa (father), Hiruharama, East Coast.
19775	,,	Haua, Tuhoro	,,	Mrs. Makerotangi Haua (mother), Hiruharama, East Coast.
19762	,,	Honatana, Wipere	,,	Honatana (father), Torere, Bay of Plenty.
19769	,,	Houia, Reu Reu	,,	Rota Houia (father), Roporua, East Coast.
19763	,,	Huihui, Raukura	Farmer	Hurupara Huihui (father), Te Araroa, East Coast.
19757	,,	Huriwai, Katene	,,	Hoani Huriwai (father), Kahukura, East Coast.
16/612	,,	Huriwai, Wiremu	Labourer	Mrs. Heni Huriwai (mother), Bay of Islands.
19741	,,	Makarini, Nehe Hone	,,	Makarini Puhata (father), Hiruharama, East Coast.
19725	,,	Mua, Apa	Shearer	Pari Mua (father), Tokomaru Bay, East Coast.
19733	,,	Nathan, John Thomas	Bushfeller	Thomas Nathan (father), Maropiu, North Auckland.
19774	,,	Ngaronoa, Rutene	Labourer	Eruera Ngaronoa (father), Hiruharama, East Coast.
19771	,,	Ngata, Parateno Purewa	,,	Aperana Turupa Ngata (father), Waiomatatini, East Coast.
19754	,,	Nukunuku, Hunia	,,	Tehu Nukunuku (father), Whakawhitira.
19739	,,	Paniena, Matekairoa	,,	Mrs. Teowaiti Paniena (wife), Waiapu, East Coast.
19740	,,	Patara, Nehe	,,	Akuhata Kaua (cousin), Port Awanui, East Coast.
19732	,,	Pene, Enoka William	,,	Mrs. Wi Nathan (aunt), Mamaranui, Dargaville.
19759	,,	Pepere, Parekura	,,	Wi Pepere (father), Te Herenga, East Coast.
16/122	,,	†Poi, Rere	,,	Mrs. Rehe Matua Poi (wife), Greytown, Wairarapa.
19743	,,	Raikete, James	,,	Mrs. Arapera Raikete (wife), Tongoio, Hawke's Bay.
19767	,,	Reedy, Ben	Blacksmith	Thomas Reedy (father), Tuparoa, East Coast.
19755	,,	Rewharewha, Hemi	Labourer	Rewharewha Putiki (father), Torere, Bay of Plenty.
19729	,,	Selwyn, Abraham	Mill Hand	Mrs. Waiheke Selwyn (mother), Matakohe, North Auckland.
19758	,,	§Taingahue, Tipuna Kore	Taxi-driver	Wiki Taingahue (father), Waiapu, East Coast.
19764	,,	Takoko, Tawhai	Labourer	Wi Takoko (father), Kahukura, East Coast.
19766	,,	Taukamo, Peter	Blacksmith	Rewi Taukamo (father), Tuparoa, East Coast.
19751	,,	Taukamo, Pokai	Labourer	Haenga Kauia (uncle), Waihuka, East Coast.
19753	,,	Taukamo, Waata	,,	Mrs. Kikiwai Taukamo (wife), Kahukura, East Coast.
19744	,,	Te Ara, Nati	,,	Te Ara Makutu (father), Te Araroa, East Coast.
19761	,,	Te Rauna, Charlie	,,	Eruera te Rauna (father), Kakariki, East Coast.
16/98	,,	Tohoriri, Reupona	,,	Enoka Tohoriri (father), Waipiro Bay, East Coast.
19756	,,	Tuhaka, Pino	,,	Aorere Pewhairangi (adopted father), Tokomaru Bay, East Coast.
19730	,,	Wahapu, Harry	Mill Hand	John Wahapu (brother), Kaikohe, Bay of Islands.
19742	,,	Waiti, Haua	Labourer	Pekama Waiti (father), Hiruharama, East Coast.
19760	,,	Waitoa, Richard te Raukura	,,	Hone Waitoa (father), Te Araroa, East Coast.
19734	,,	Waitoa, Rota	,,	William Waitoa (father), Te Araroa, East Coast.
19726	,,	Wharewhiti, Rikihana	,,	Wharewhiti Matenga (father), Waiotapu, Rotorua.

STOWAWAY.

Reg. No.	Rank.	Name.	Occupation.	Name and Address of Next-of-kin.
S.I. 103		‖Dpostino, Albert Anthony	Somes Island Guard	

† Ex 1st Maori Contingent.   ‡ Ex 2nd Maori Contingent.   § Disembarked at Albany.   ‖Stowaway on "Athenic."
Disembarked at Albany.

20TH REINFORCEMENTS.

Reg. No.	Rank.	Name.	Occupation.	Name and Address of Next-of-kin.
16/304	Captain	†Tahiwi, Pirimi	Teacher	Rawiri Rota Tahiwi (father), Otaki.
16/90	Lieutenant	†Stainton, William Houkamau	,,	Mrs. Williamina Milne Stainton (wife), 71 Ellice Street, Wellington.
16/211	2nd Lieut.	†Pohio, Henry Huru	Labourer	Solomon Pohio (brother), Tuakiwi, via Kaiapoi.
42863	Sergeant	Carroll, Turi	Sheep-farmer	Mrs. Mako Carroll (mother), Wairoa, Hawke's Bay.
19852	Corporal	Hingston, Lewis Harewood	Farmer	J. M. Hingston (father), Hastings.
19982	,,	Hingston, William Frederick Bruce	Labourer	Mrs. Edie Hingston (wife), Wairoa, Hawke's Bay.
16/16	..	†Lambert, Thomas	Engineer	Fenton Lambert (father,) Wairoa, Hawke's Bay.
19846	Lance-Corpl.	Edwards, Mathew	Labourer	Harawira Edwards (father), Wairoa, Hawke's Bay.
19848	,,	Gemmell, Samuel William	Farmer	Mrs. H. H. Gemmell (mother), Mohaka, Hawke's Bay.
19855	,,	Jury, Tane John	Labourer	Mrs. Ema Jury (wife), Wairoa, Hawke's Bay.
19865	,,	Lanigan, William	Shearer	Thomas Lanigan (father), Hastings.
19840	Private	Albert, Windy	Labourer	Marehi Tautahanga (mother), Wairoa, Hawke's Bay.
16797	,,	Barlow, William	,,	Mrs. Raukura Barlow (mother), Kawhia.
19782	,,	Bell, Richard	Taxi-driver	Alexander Bell (father), Taumarunui.
19842	,,	Carroll, Thomas	Labourer	Mrs. Thompson (mother), Wairoa, Hawke's Bay.
19897	,,	Cassidy, David	Farm Hand	Robert Cassidy (father), Kaihu, Northern Wairoa.
19843	,,	Douglas, Nahu	Labourer	Mrs. Taraipine Pirihi (grandmother), Wairoa, Hawke's Bay.
19844	,,	Edwards, Mick	,,	Mane Edwards (brother), Wairoa, Hawke's Bay.
19901	,,	Elers, Charles	,,	Mrs. Rosie Elers (wife), Porangahau, Hawke's Bay.
19854	,,	Henry, Dick	,,	Henare Reihana (father), Mangonui.
19789	,,	Hiiti, Ropata	,,	Paro Hiiti (father), Paparore, via Mangonui.
19799	,,	Hira, Utiara	,,	Te Paea Ahipene (aunt), Wairoa, Hawke's Bay.
19851	,,	Hoepo, Karona	,,	Mrs. Pine Hoepo (mother), Petane, Hawke's Bay.
19903	,,	Hoera, Purukutu	Shearer	Wiramina Purukutu (mother), Te Hauke, Hawke's Bay.
19890	,,	Irimako, Hoani	Farm Hand	Mrs. Kuanihi Nikora (mother), Poroporo, Whakatane.
19856	,,	Johnson, Tiaki	Shearer	M. Johnson (father), Frasertown, Hawke's Bay.
19781	,,	Kahukawakawa, Te	Farmer	Warahi Kahukawakawa (father), Taumarunui.
19858	,,	Karauria, Mako	Labourer	Piha Karauria (father), Wairoa, Hawke's Bay.
19860	,,	Karauria, Mei Hana	,,	Piha Karauria (father), Wairoa, Hawke's Bay.
19895	,,	Karauria, Poki	,,	William Karauria (father), Te Uhi, Wairoa, Hawke's Bay.
19859	,,	Karauria, Tapuae	,,	Mrs. Fanny Karauria (wife), Wairoa, Hawke's Bay.
19862	,,	Konuke, Sam	,,	Mrs. Ani Konuke (mother), Wairoa, Hawke's Bay.
19863	,,	Lawson, Hira	,,	Mrs. Kaatengaohi (mother), Wairoa, Hawke's Bay.
19864	,,	Lewis, Sunny	,,	Mrs. A. Lewis (mother), Wairoa, Hawke's Bay.
19871	,,	McAndrew, James	,,	Nikora Katuhe (grandfather), Wairoa, Hawke's Bay.
19888	,,	Maru, Hirini	,,	Parekohai (father), Mahia, Wairoa, Hawke's Bay.
19867	,,	Mete, Tupara	,,	Waikare Mete (father), Wairoa, Hawke's Bay.
19868	,,	Mokomoko, Morehu	,,	Waikare Mete (father), Wairoa, Hawke's Bay.
19869	,,	Morrell, Ned	,,	J. Morrell (father), Wairoa, Hawke's Bay.
19792	,,	Otene, Grey	Farmer	Mrs. Murphy (sister), Mangamuka, via Hokianga.
19876	,,	Paku, Paul	Labourer	Mrs. Waiki Paku (wife), Whakaki, Wairoa, Hawke's Bay.
19877	,,	Potatau, Tipene	Farmer	Te Hata Potatau (father), Nuhaka, Hawke's Bay.
19883	,,	Savage, John Joseph	Labourer	M. Savage (father), Matata, Bay of Plenty.
19791	,,	Stevens, Joe	Bushman	Busby Stevens (father), Mangamuka, via Hokianga.
19882	,,	Swenki, Albert	Labourer	Charles Swenki (father), Samoa.
19896	,,	Taipiha, George	Shepherd	Harry Taipiha (father), Muriwai, Gisborne.
19885	,,	Tongaio, Turoi	Labourer	Hemi Tongaio (father), Mahia, via Wairoa, Hawke's Bay.
19785	,,	Te Tumu Hamuera	Farmer	Mrs. Mahi Marangai (sister), Te Puke.
19787	,,	Waiapu, Oko	,,	Waiapu Tawhira (father), Opotiki.
19889	,,	Wehikore, Eparaina	Labourer	Mrs. Waikarotu Wehikore (mother), Te Arai, via Gisborne.
19893	,,	Whaanga, Apia	Farmer	Mrs. Mako Tihi Whaanga (mother), Iwitea, Hawke's Bay,
19894	,,	Wharepapa, Mare	Station Hand	Te Wharepapa (father), Opotiki.
19891	,,	Winiana, Kingi	Labourer	Mrs. Kapu Winiana (mother), Nuhaka, Hawke's Bay.

† Ex 1st Maori Contingent.

21ST REINFORCEMENTS.

Reg. No.	Rank.	Name.	Occupation.	Name and Address of Next-of-kin.
20608	2nd Lieut.	Parakuka, Hamiora	Boatbuilder	Mrs. Aowhinga Parakuka (wife), Ohinemutu, Rotorua.
19633	Sergeant	Gray, Patrick	Station Hand	Hereipohiahia Gray (father), Tokaanu.
19718	Corporal	Kokiri, Wateney	Barman	Mrs. Rangitarahae Kokiri (mother), Te Ngae, Rotorua.
19912	Lance-Corpl.	Smith, Paki	Farmer	Mrs. Ella Smith (mother), Kohukohu.
19973	Private	Aubrey, Alfred Kiringaua	Labourer	Mrs. Alice Aubrey (wife), 22 Napier Street, Auckland.
19921	,,	*Auwha, King	,,	Mrs. Puti Auwha (mother), Pupuke, via Whangarei.
19947	,,	Brown, Taupe	Bushman	Brown Heremia (father), Te Kaha, Bay of Plenty.
19949	,,	Brown, Teriaki	,,	Brown Heremia (father), Te Kaha, Bay of Plenty.
19703	,,	Davy, Para	Farmer	Mrs. Ani Davy (mother), Tauranga.
19940	,,	Davie, Waru	,,	Davie Kiekie (father), Tauranga.
19914	,,	Edmonds, Hemi	Bushman	Charles Edmonds (father), Kaikohe, Bay of Islands.
19845	,,	Edwards, Sid	Labourer	Mrs. Heni Edwards (wife), Wairoa, Hawke's Bay.
19956	,,	Enoka, Harry	Farmer	Mrs. Makereta Enoka (wife), Te Teko.
19954	,,	Gerrard, Mohi	Labourer	Takena Gerrard (father), Port Awanui.
19959	,,	Gilman, Rua	,,	David Gilman (father), Tolaga Bay.
19906	,,	Haeata, Kani	Farmer	Mrs. Wirinia Tunui (cousin), Poroporo, Whakatane.
19955	,,	Haerewa, David	Blacksmith	Hakupa Haerewa (father), Tuparoa.
19971	,,	Inia, Morehu	Farmer	Inia Whare (father), Mangakahia, Pipiwai, Titoki.
19915	,,	James, Charlie	Flax-miller	Miss Mata James (sister), Okere Falls, Rotorua.
19948	,,	Karapaina, Paratene	Farmer	Karapaina Pirihi (father), Te Kaha, Bay of Plenty.
19942	,,	Maku, Phillip	..	Brown Maku (brother), Whirinaki, Hokianga.
19932	,,	Miru, Thomas Nathan	Mill Hand	Mrs. Terehu Tai Miru (mother), Mangawhare.
19925	,,	Ngatipehi, Ieni	Labourer	Mrs. Meteria Ngatipehi (wife), Ohinemutu, Rotorua.
19931	,,	Otene, Tawhiwhi	Farmer	Taho Otene (father), Hastings.
19967	,,	Otene, Wi Maihi	,,	Paerikiriki Otene (father), Hastings.
19938	,,	Paniora, Arthur	Labourer	Mrs. Tetawhia Paniora (wife), Waipoua, Hokianga.
16/696	,,	Paora, Kahuroa	Timber-worker	Paora Rokino (father), Taupo.
19965	,,	Paul, Rori	Farmer	Paul Para (father), Katikati.
19941	,,	Pera, Manga	Labourer	Pera Kato (father), Kaikohe.
19916	,,	Rakete, Wiri	Sawmill Hand	Piri Hakete (father), Kaikohe.
19946	,,	Rangi, Tommy	Labourer	Marikena Rangi (father), Te Kuiti.
19930	,,	Ransfield, Robert	Farmer	Simon Ransfield (father), Ohau.
19926	,,	Richmond, Whare	Packer	Rehua Richmond (father), Torere, Bay of Plenty.
19969	,,	Robson, George Thomas	Labourer	Herbert Robson (father), Pukepoto, via Kaitaia.
19970	,,	Robson, Paerata	,,	William Robson (father), Pukepoto via Kaitaia.
55549	,,	Rua, Peter	Fisherman	Te Rua Hereta (father), Chatham Islands.
19922	,,	Ruka, Tu	Farmer	Ruka Ngapapa (father), Ngapuna, Rotorua.
19975	,,	Savage, Daniel	Ferryman	John Savage (father), Matata, Bay of Plenty.
19960	,,	Tautau, John	Sheep-farmer	Waitanwha Matenga (father), Gisborne.
19957	,,	Tawhiao, Peter	Farmer	Tawhiao (father), Tauranga.
19923	,,	Teaomarama, Hirini	Labourer	Teaomarama (father), Waiotapu, via Rotorua.
19770	,,	Te Maro, Herewini	,,	Ahipene Te Maro (father), Rangitukia, via Gisborne.
16/1389	,,	Te Raina, Teweka	Bushman	Te Raina Kingi (father), Te Kaha, Bay of Plenty.
19976	,,	Terei, Willie	Mill Hand	Terei Paehua (father), Waotu, via Putaruru.
19944	,,	Tipuna, Apirana	Horse-trainer	Mrs. Rina Waipare (mother), Gisborne.
19924	,,	Tongi, Taraia	Labourer	Tongi Davis (father), Hastings.
19966	,,	Uwerata, Romana	Farmer	Miss Ngarongoa Uwerata (sister), Huria, Tauranga.
19779	,,	Williams, James	Barman	William Moka (father), Mangamuku, Hokianga.
19958	,,	Williams, Paewai	Scrub-cutter	Harry Williams (father), Gisborne.
19950	,,	Witehira, Robert	Labourer	Eramiha Witehira (father), Kaikohe, Bay of Islands.

* Died at sea, 27th September, 1917.

22ND REINFORCEMENTS.

Reg. No.	Rank.	Name.	Occupation.	Name and Address of Next-of-kin.
16/345	2nd Lieut.	†Ngatai, Tame	Carpenter	Mrs. Henrietta Ngatai (wife), Ohinemutu.
19565	Sergeant	Cooper, Eru Turakitai	Licensed Interpreter & Law Clerk	Mrs. Mere Morere (mother), Ballance Street, Whataupoko, Gisborne.
20000	Lance-Corpl.	Paul, Abraham	Sawmill Hand	Mrs. Ethel May Paul (wife), 59 Vermont Street, Ponsonby, Auckland.
20001	,,	Wi Repa, Romeo	Farmer	Dr. Wi Repa (brother), Te Araroa.
20671	Private	Cook, William	Seaman	Edward Cook (father), Waikare, Opua, Bay of Islands.
19978	,,	Davis, Robert	Farm Hand	Rauna Davis (brother), Parapara, Mangonui.
19467	,,	Fletcher, Tau	Bushman	Matthews Fletcher (father), Peria, Mangonui.
19996	,,	Gage, Te Ara	Labourer	John Gage (father), Kihikihi.
19920	,,	Green, Levi Bernard	,,	William Green (father), Kaiapoi.
20053	,,	Gunther, John William Whitfield	Bush Contractor	Mrs. Mary Gunther (wife), care of Mrs. Tinsley, 8 South Road, Masterton.
16/3	,,	Haere, George	Labourer	Mrs. Wairakau Haere (wife), Tolaga Bay.
19972	,,	Hapuku, Joe Waho	Mill Hand	Kara Hapuku (brother), Raetihi.
19991	,,	Hooper, William	Labourer	Charles Hooper (father), Hamilton.
19990	,,	Howard, Tere	,,	Frank Howard (father), Tauranga.
19442	,,	Karaka, Thomas	Taxi-driver	Rongo Karaka (father), Raglan.
19985	,,	Kauhoa, Mita	Mill Hand	Mrs. Mere Matthews (mother), Omanaia, Hokianga.
19984	,,	Kio, Henry Wirepa	Farm Hand	Wirepa Kio (father), Te Kuiti.
19999	,,	Maruia, Ruakaka	Bushman	Mrs. Materina Maruia (wife), Taupo.
19961	,,	Matenga, Tawhoo	Farmer	Waitaniwha Matenga (father), Gisborne.
19994	,,	Otimi, Whata	,,	Neri Otimi (father), Manunui.
20005	,,	Owen, Arthur	Farm Hand	Arthur Owen (father), Poroti, Whangarei.
20002	,,	Peter, Harry	Labourer	Mrs. Fanny Peter (mother), Peria, Mangonui.
19798	,,	Pompy, Tamihana	,,	Taare Pompy (father), Petane, Hawke's Bay.
19979	,,	Rakete, John Lee	Freezing-works Hand	George Rakete (father), Kaikohe.
19910	,,	Ransfield, Joseph	Labourer	Haimona Ransfield (father), Ohau.
19995	,,	Te Haara, Richard	Mill Hand	Louis Te Haara (father), Ngawha, Bay of Islands.
19765	,,	Te Puni, Ruakirikiri	Labourer	Tihema Te Puni (father), Hiruharama, via Waipiro Bay.
19983	,,	Terua, Kahungunu	,,	Hone Terua (father), Manutuke, Gisborne.
19974	,,	Wallace, Charles Paul	Farm Hand	Tahuri Taiawa (brother), Mangere, Onehunga.
20790	,,	Witana, Hemi	Labourer	Witana Hamihana (father), Waihou.
19934	,,	Witehira, Joe	,,	Eramihera Witehira (father), Kaikohe.

†Ex 1st Maori Contingent.

23RD REINFORCEMENTS.

Reg. No.	Rank.	Name.	Occupation.	Name and Address of Next-of-kin.
16/403	2nd Lieut.	†Mote Kingi, Paki Hoani	Farmer	Hoani Mote Kingi (father), Putiki, Wanganui.
19523	Sergeant	Mangakahia, Waipapa	Interpreter	Mrs. Meri Mangakahia (mother), Whangapoua, Coromandel.
19628	Corporal	Paoramati, Retimana	Student	Rora Paul (sister), Rotorua.
20051	L.-Corporal	Hakaraia, Jack	Labourer	Mrs. Manuku Hakaraia (wife), Ohinemutu, Rotorua.
20009	,,	Keelan, Karauria	Station Hand	William Keelan (father), Hiruharama, East Coast.
20023	,,	Kereti Taironga	Labourer	Mrs. Titihuia Kereti (wife), Paroa, Whakatane.
20018	,,	Ratahi, Hura	,,	Mrs. Waimiere Ratahi (mother), Paroa, Whakatane.
20059	Private	Ereatara, Tamaho	Farmer	Ereatara Kimo (father), Ruatoki.
19964	,,	Graham, James	Labourer	Mrs. Pori Martin (mother), Post-office, Puha.
19998	,,	Gray, Toho	,,	Mrs. Kahu Gray (wife), Moteo, Napier.
20022	,,	Haturini, Hape	Farmer	Hape Haturini (father), Ruatoki.
20069	,,	Hetekia, Ngahana	Labourer	Mokonui Arangi (father), Taupo.
20027	,,	Himiona, Turoa	Farmer	Himiona Kaikaru (father), Te Puke.
20026	,,	Huta Meihana	Labourer	Mrs. Hoepo Huta (mother), Pahou, Whakatane.
20038	,,	Kororiko, Joe	,,	Kororiko Watana (father), Pahou, Whakatane.
20020	,,	Moengaroa, Timothy	,,	Moengaroa Hiripo (father), Matata.
20019	,,	Nirai, Davy	,,	Mrs. Kataraina Nirai (wife), Matata.
20040	,,	Paora, Wiripo	Farmer	Mrs. Makarita Paora (wife), Rotoiti, Rotorua.
20014	,,	Raponi, Paul	Labourer	Mrs. Puhi Raponi (wife), Matata.
19981	,,	Scheigis, Henry	,,	George Scheigis (father), Rangiputa, Kaimaumau.
20015	,,	Smith, Te Mete	,,	Kere Smith (father), Tauranga.
19776	,,	Taihuka, Hori	,,	Miss Hana Taihuka (sister), Mataora Bay, Waihi.
20011	,,	Tairua, John	,,	Tairua Makiha (father), Matata.
20050	,,	Tamureti, Pita	,,	Tamureti Poniwahio (father), Ruatoki.
20067	,,	Teaumihi, Huni	,,	Teaumihi Tamihana (father), Te Puke.
20049	,,	Te Waara, Hauwaho	,,	Te Mihimate te Waara (brother), Ruatoki.
20047	,,	Te Whare, Te Hiko	Shearer	Mrs. Pare te Whare (wife), Ruatoki.
20046	,,	Te Whetu, Kingi	Labourer	Te Whetu Paerata (father), Ruatoki.
20068	,,	Titi, Raniera	,,	Te Moni Ngarewa (father), Te Puke.
20044	,,	Turei, Te Whitu	,,	Mrs. Hiria Turei (mother), Ruatoki.
19943	,,	Wiremu Mahu	,,	Mrs. Mio te Puia (mother), Ruatoki.

† Ex 1st Maori Contingent.

24TH REINFORCEMENTS.

Reg. No.	Rank.	Name.	Occupation.	Name and Address of Next-of-kin.
16/434	2nd Lieut.	†Angel, Richard	Farmer	William Henry Angel (father), Bayswater, Auckland.
19456	Coy. S.M.	Mackereth, Arthur	Mech. Engineer	Mrs. Josephine Elsa Natalie Mackereth (wife), Purchas Road, Takapuna, Auckland.
60454	L.-Corporal	Wilkie, Francis Peter	Motor Engineer	Mrs. Alice Grace Wilkie (wife), Keddell Street, Frankton Junction.
20021	,,	King, Mahiti	Labourer	Hira Kingi (father), Paroa, Whakatane.
60449	,,	Puhirere, Hemotata	,,	Puhirere Peraniko (father), Moteo, Napier.
60443	Private	Heath, John	Bushfeller	Patrick Heath (father), Waiharara.
60450	,,	Hurae, Kapu	Shearer	Hurae Wiremu (father), Taupo.
20025	,,	Karapaina, Waitangi	Bushman	Pirihi Karapaina (father), Te Kaha.
20024	,,	Keepa, Te Moni	Labourer	Mrs. Tiahuia Keepa (wife), Matata.
60444	,,	Kemp, Isaac	,,	Kemp Horo (father), Te Kao.
20007	,,	Kori, Jack	Sailor	Jack Kori (father), Whakarewarewa.
60448	,,	Manuhuia, Hurieru	Labourer	Mrs. Te Paea Manuhuia (wife), Te Ngae, Rotorua
60445	,,	Mihaka, Hemi	,,	Mihaka Makiha (father), Whakarewarewa.
20042	,,	Mikaere, Wiremu	Farmer	Mrs. Mahewai Mikaere (mother), Matata.
20052	,,	Morrison, Toko	Mill Hand	Mrs. Kaworoa Morrison (wife), Turukenga.
60442	,,	Pakana, Rihari	Labourer	Mrs. Ani Pakana (wife), Rotoiti, Rotorua.
20013	,,	Paora, Mita	Farmer	Paora te Rua (father), Te Kaha.
20017	,,	Riwai, Hori	Labourer	Riwai Miriaorangi (father), Te Kaha.
60456	,,	Rota, Sam	,,	Mrs. Ngahuia Kerenapa (mother), Muripara, Rotorua.
20010	,,	Sadlier, Lawrence	Shepherd	Mrs. Rita Sadlier (wife), Waiorongomai.
63951	,,	Silbery, Jack Stanley	Assist. Storeman	George Silbery (father), Wairoa, Hawke's Bay.
20063	,,	Tauri, Rangi	Farmer	Hoani Tauri (father), Putiki, Wanganui.
60446	,,	Tekahu, Hakaraia	Labourer	Tekahu Kararaina (father), Taupo.
60447	,,	Tekahu, Patoromu	,,	Tekahu Kararaina (father), Taupo.
60453	,,	Tekairangatira, Moki	Farmer	Mrs. Rangipawera te Kairangatira (mother), Kakariki, Halcombe.
20048	,,	Te Moni, Ratapu	Roadman	Te Moni Keepa (father), Matata.
20066	,,	Thompson, Johnnie	Farmer	Mrs. Pikitaka Thompson (mother), Kakahi.
20060	,,	Tutu, Rangi	Farm Hand	Hami Tutu (father), Onepoto Gully, Napier.
20043	,,	Wharepapa, Grey	Labourer	Wharepapa Perepe (father), Wharekawa, Thames.
20003	,,	Whippy, George	Planter	Frederick Whippy (father), Fiji.
60451	,,	Wikeepa, Ranginui	Farmer	Wikeepa Hekiheki (father), Motiti Island, Tauranga.

† Ex 1st Maori Contingent.

25th REINFORCEMENTS.

Reg. No.	Rank	Name	Occupation	Name and Address of Next-of-kin
16/582A	2nd Lieut.	†Goldsmith, Charles	Clerk	Edward Goldsmith (father), Rangitukia.
19654	C.S.M.	Royal, Rangi	,,	Mrs. Keriati Kiniwe Royal (mother), Paeroa.
19866	Corporal	McGregor, Hugh Evan	,,	John J. McGregor (brother), Wairoa, Hawke's Bay.
16/402	Lance-Corpl.	‡Meihana, Paneta Otene	Mechanic	Martin Otene Meihana (brother), P.O. Box 201, Hastings.
19389	,,	Tonihi, Ngatapiri	Labourer	Mrs. Iwa Tonihi (wife), Whakarewarewa.
60469	Private	Campbell, Kenny	Mill Hand	Rawati Kamira (father), Mitimiti, Rawene.
60512	,,	Coffin, James	Drover	William Coffin (father), Raetihi.
60471	,,	Cook, Rai	Farmer	Kamera Cook (father), Mangamuka, Bay of Islands.
60475	,,	Edward, Walter	Bushman	Edward Marsh (father), Wairoa, Hawke's Bay.
60462	,,	Hahona, Pera	Labourer	Hahona Heemi (father), Karatia, Muripara.
60511	,,	Herewini, Eria	Bushfeller	Herewini te Tawhero (father), Raetihi.
60467	,,	Hiha, Reginald	Labourer	Robert Hiha (father), Tongoio, Hawke's Bay.
60404	,,	Itamere, Tangaroa	Bushman	Mrs. Tehaumahana Itamere (mother), Waima, Hokianga.
60458	,,	Karaitiana, George Turuki Waho te Rangi	Labourer	Tere Karaitiana (brother), Dannevirke.
60484	,,	Manson, George Terewai	Farmer	Mrs. Heni Pokairangi (sister), Kawana, Wanganui.
60466	,,	Mihingarangi, Heta	,,	Tehara Mihingarangi (brother), Waitakaruru, Hauraki Plain.
60460	,,	Morehu, Robert	Settler	Mrs. Wahati Tehata (mother), Waitahanui, Taupo.
60461	,,	Natanahira, Wi Warren	Labourer	Mrs. Te Onira Natanahira (mother), Waiotapu, Wharepai.
60477	,,	Papanui, Korota	Farmer	Hohepa Papanui (father), Waihaha, Taupo.
19580	,,	Pihema, Manu	,,	Tamati Pihema (father), Okau, Matamata.
60509	,,	Poumua, Phillip	Bushfeller	Poumua Mokena (father), Raetihi.
60517	,,	Retimana, Pani	Bushman	Hoani Retimana (uncle), Raukokore, Cape Runaway.
60472	,,	Smith, Harry	,,	Frank Smith (father), Kaikohe.
60479	,,	Subritzky, Herbert William	Labourer	William Subritzky (father), Parenga.
20012	,,	Takotohiwi, Himi	Farmer	Takotohiwi Ratapahi (father), Pupuaruhe, Whakatane.
60470	,,	Te Hau, Dick	Mill Hand	Joe te Hau (brother), Kaikohe.
60516	,,	Toho, Paora	Farmer	Mrs. Te Pohe te Waaka (mother), Pipiriki.
60476	,,	Topia, Rangi Wiari	,,	Mrs. Ramari Roiri (mother), Bunnythorpe.
60473	,,	Trau, Jacob	,,	Thomas Trau (father), Te Puna, Tauranga.
60455	,,	Tumatahi, Ruka	Labourer	Tumatahi Manahi (father), Ohau, Rotorua.
60457	,,	Witinitara, Henry Governor	,,	Kawana Witinitara (father), Te Oreore, Masterton.

† Ex 2nd Maori Contingent.   ‡ Ex 1st Maori Contingent.

26TH REINFORCEMENTS.

Reg. No.	Rank.	Name.	Occupation.	Name and Address of Next-of-kin.
45638	2nd Lieut.	Ormond, John	Farmer	G. C. Ormond (father), Opoutama, Hawke's Bay.
19875	Sergeant	Ormond, William	,,	G. C. Ormond (father), Opoutama, Hawke's Bay.
60534	Corporal	Hall, Rukaute James	Labourer	Miss Pinonga Hall (sister), Ohinemutu, Rotorua.
60504	,,	Tuatini, Te Reimana	Farmer	Mrs. Merearani Tuatini (wife), Raetihi.
60480	Lance-Corpl.	Pokiha, Rangi	,,	Mrs. Kaewa Pokiha (wife), Koriniti, Wanganui.
16765	,,	Stubbing, Jack Rupe	,,	Frank Stubbing (father), Rangiwaea, Ruanui, Taihape.
60503	,,	Tapa, Robert Tanginoa	,,	Tanginoa Tapa (father), Parikino, Wanganui.
60482	,,	Tinirau, Hori Paamu	,,	Mrs. Pare Tinirau (wife), Ranana, Wanganui.
20041	,,	Tonihi, Rangiheuea	Labourer	Tonihi Tetaru (father), Whakarewarewa.
60544	Private	Anderson, Jack	Draper	Hataraka Anderson (father), Wharepanga, Waipiro Bay.
60535	,,	Bristow, Robert Terehi	Station Hand	Mrs. Aorere Lottie Bristow (sister), Te Araroa.
60488	,,	Erueti, Hori	Farmer	Mrs. Ngarama Erueti (wife), Hiruharama, Wanganui.
60547	,,	Geary, Reginald	Farm Hand	Thomas Geary (father), Warea, Taranaki.
60496	,,	Haami, Paora	Farmer	Mrs. Ani Haami (mother), Ranana, Wanganui.
60527	,,	Hapeta, Hiriwa	Carpenter	Hapeta Puku (father), Whangape.
60524	,,	Hemara, Hare	Mill Hand	Mrs. Grace Hemara (mother), Pakanae, Opononi.
60550	,,	Honeycombe, Enoch	,,	Mrs. Catherine Honeycombe (mother), Whangaroa.
60499	,,	Huirua, Koroheke	Farm Hand	Huirua Paetalua (father), Parikino, Wanganui.
60529	,,	Hunt, Isaac	Labourer	Mrs. Susan Hunt (mother), Whakarewarewa.
60528	,,	Ihaia, Tauru	,,	Hori Ihaia (father), Taupo.
60483	,,	Kahukura, Pura	Farmer	Mrs. Ngatoka Kahukura (mother), Pungarehu, Wanganui.
60519	,,	Kaiwhare, Toroara	Shearer	Kaiwhare Kereona (father), Kakatahi, Wanganui.
60493	,,	Katene, Pani	Farmer	Mrs. Rutua Katene (mother), Parihaka, Wanganui.
60497	,,	Kingi, Haare Weraroa	,,	Mrs. Te Ata Taiwhati Kingi (mother), Hiruharama, Wanganui.
60495	,,	Kingi, Whanga	,,	Mrs. Tapu Kingi (mother), Mataiwa, Wanganui.
16/1128	,,	†Kohimoka, George	Bushman	Kahi Kohimoka (brother), Rawene, Hokianga.
60543	,,	Koti, Hone	Farm Hand	Mrs. Mere Koti (mother), Tauranga.
62773	,,	Marumaru, Rangi	Farmer	Mrs. Rangi Marumaru (wife), Parawanui, Bull's.
60545	,,	Mita, Tu	Labourer	Mrs. Mate Mita (wife), Puriri.
60542	,,	Mohi, Tukairangi	Hotel Porter	Pitiro Mohi (brother), Taupo.
60525	,,	Ngawaka, Pomare	Labourer	Andrew Ngawaka (father), Whangape.
60489	,,	Perepe, Morehu	,,	Perepe Perana (father), Putiki, Wanganui.
60491	,,	Potaka, Ngatai	Farmer	Mrs. Piki Potaka (wife), Tawhitinui, Wanganui.
60530	,,	Rameka, Johnny	Labourer	Tobe Rameka (father), Waiotapu, Rotorua.
60518	,,	Rana, Wiremu	Farm Hand	Rana Ruka (father), Waitao, Tauranga.
60500	,,	Rangitauwira, Wiremu	Farmer	Mrs. Rawinia Rangitauwira (wife), Koriniti, Wanganui.
60522	,,	Rannie, William	Railway Fireman	Mrs. Francis Halt (friend), 32 Hobson Street, Auckland.
60546	,,	Rota, Taurangi	Labourer	Mrs. Kapekape Rota (wife), Murupara, Rotorua.
60541	,,	Roto, Rangi	,,	Mita Roto (father), Te Aroha.
19627	,,	Stephens, Karena Kahi	Farmer	Kahi Stephens (father), Rangi Point, Hokianga.
60533	,,	Tahana, Sid	Mill Hand	Mana Tahana (father), Mitimiti, Hokianga.
19793	,,	Tahere, Kira Hohepa	Farmer	Hohepa Tahere (father), care of P.O., Mangamuka, North Auckland.
60515	,,	Taiaroa, Newa	Navvy	Wi Taiaroa (brother), Gonville, Wanganui.
60501	,,	Tamakehu, Rangihauku	Farmer	Tamakehu Katene (father), Hiruharama, Wanganui.
60506	,,	Tanguru, Hanuere	,,	Mrs. Kawa Tanguru (wife), Parikino, Wanganui.
60539	,,	Taputoro, Wharo	Shearer	Mrs. Hera Tepeo (mother), Kaiwhaiki, Wanganui.
60502	,,	Te Huia, Koro	Farmer	Te Huia Maehe (father), Pipiriki, Wanganui.
60490	,,	Te Huna, Teiwirore	,,	Te Huna Itemoa (father), Matahiwi, Wanganui.
60532	,,	Te Kakau, Rangihiroa	Labourer	Te Kakau Hikurangi (father), Tauranga.
60507	,,	Te Tua, Teki	Farm Hand	Mrs. Takitahi Te Tua (wife), Kauangaroa, Wanganui.
60494	,,	Te Weato, Rangi	,,	Mrs. Ruihi Te Weato (wife), Hiruharama, Wanganui.
60505	,,	Timoti, Wharekura	Farmer	Mrs. Wairakau Timoti (sister), Kauangaroa, Wanganui.
60508	,,	Tonihi, Davey	,,	Mrs. Titaha Tonihi (wife), Hiruharama, Wanganui.
60551	,,	Waata, Thomas Ratima	Farm Labourer	Jack Ratima (uncle), Patene, via Napier.
60552	,,	Whatati, Joe	Cream Carter	Tuparahaki Aritaku (sister), Te Puke.

† Ex 3rd Maori Reinforcements.

27TH REINFORCEMENTS.

Reg. No.	Rank.	Name.	Occupation.	Name and Address of Next-of-kin.
9/965	2nd Lieut.	†Quarton, John	Shepherd	Mrs. J. Quarton (wife), 33 Alexandra Road, Reading, Berkshire, England.
19927	Sergeant	Katene, Hari Wi	Civil Servant	Mrs. Isabel Katene (wife), 60 Wanganui Avenue, Ponsonby, Auckland.
60558	Lance-Corpl.	Ohia, John	Labourer	Mrs. Rongokahira Ohia (wife), Papamoa, Tauranga.
60573	,,	Pita, Wiremu	Farmer	Hone Pita (father), Whangaruru, Bay of Islands.
60572	Private	Anderson, Ben	Mill Hand	Mrs. Kare Makara (mother), Kohukohu.
20601	,,	Davis, Patrick	Labourer	Abraham Davis (father), Poroti.
60570	,,	Davis, James Abraham	,,	Abraham Davis (father), Poroti.
60582	,,	Head, Henry Charles	Gum-digger	Mrs. Elizabeth Head (mother), Kaitaia.
19873	,,	Mahanga, Tom	Labourer	Mahanga Haora (father), Wairoa, Hawke's Bay.
60569	,,	Makara, Rape	Mill Hand	Mrs. Puti Makara (mother), Kohukohu.
60566	,,	Matenga, Waata	Labourer	Hori Matenga (father), Whangaruru, Bay of Islands.
60568	,,	Pere, Paraone	,,	Pere Matenga (father), Matapihi, Tauranga.
60567	,,	Rameka, Rangi	,,	Piripi Rameka (father), Waiotapu, Rotorua.
19505	,,	Taniora, Henare	Bushman	Wirepa Taniora (father), Whangaruru, Bay of Islands.
60559	,,	Toi, Tukapa	Farmer	Mrs. Materere Toi (mother), Moungatawa, Tauranga.

† Ex 4th Reinforcement.

28TH REINFORCEMENTS.

Reg. No.	Rank.	Name.	Occupation.	Name and Address of Next-of-kin.
19980	Sergeant	Turcia, Parekura	Clerk	Mrs. Ruahana Paenga (mother), Kahukura, Waiapu.
60561	Lance-Corpl.	Paul, Wi Tamihana	Railway Porter	Henry Paul (father), Pamapuria, North Auckland.
60571	,,	Taniwha, Mohi	Labourer	Mrs. Tehina Taniwha (mother), Matangirau, Bay of Islands.
16/1413	Private	Davis, Prince	Farmer	Mrs. Mere Davis (mother), Orakei, Auckland.
60612	,,	Herbert, William	Lineman	Mrs. Lily Herbert (wife), Nuhaka, Wairoa.
60557	,,	Kingi, William	Mill Hand	Pikaki Kingi (father), Matauri Bay, North Auckland.
60307	,,	Marino, Joe	Farmer	Henry Marino (father), Te Ahu Ahu, Bay of Islands.
60605	,,	Marsden, Toko Hoani	Labourer	Rev. H. M. Paerata (father), Waimate North, Bay of Islands.
60560	,,	Rudolph, Albert	Bushfeller	John Rudolph (father), Ahipara, via Awanui, North Auckland.
60602	,,	Russell, Frederick Watt	Labourer	Albert Russell (father), Waipapakauri, Awanui North.
60606	,,	Tuhirangi, Wairua	Farm Hand	Mrs. Te Pae-tetitaha (mother), Kawakawa.
60562	,,	Wiremu, Heta	Bushfeller	Mrs. Ramari Wiremu (mother), Ahipara, via Awanui, North Auckland.

29th REINFORCEMENTS.

Reg. No.	Rank.	Name.	Occupation.	Name and Address of Next-of-kin.
60604	Lance-Corpl.	Barney, Phillip	Farmer	Barney Tawera (father), Argyll, via Waipawa.
60576	,,	Gosset, William Montgomery	Drainer	Mrs. Lizzie Gosset (wife), C.P.O., Auckland.
60577	Private	Hemopo, Tanera	Labourer	Tehanairo Hemopo (father), Tokaanu, Lake Taupo.
60613	,,	Huta, Rotohika	Flax-mill Employee	Mrs. Nohuta Huta (wife), Te Teko, Whakatane.
60564	,,	Kemp, Jacob	Farmer	Mrs. Akinihi Kemp (mother), Wainui, North Auckland.
60580	,,	Moke, Raureti	Motor-driver	Mrs. Pine Hepera (mother), Rotorua.
60609	,,	Takimoana, Downey	Labourer	Mrs. Katerina Apiata Takimoana (mother), Pakaraka, Bay of Islands.

30th REINFORCEMENTS.

Reg. No.	Rank.	Name.	Occupation.	Name and Address of Next-of-kin.
60610	Sergeant	Poutawera, Leonard Rahiri	Civil Servant	Mrs. J. Poutawera (mother), 15 Ellice Avenue, Wellington.
60638	Lance-Corpl.	Reweti, Warena	Labourer	Mrs. P. Reweti (wife), P.O. Box 33, Hastings.
60618	,,	Swinton, William Jeremiah	Farmer	W. M. Swinton (father), care of Sam Hei, Solicitor, Gisborne.
60634	Private	Davis, Charlie	Labourer	Abraham Davis (father), Poroti, via Whangarei.
60632	,,	Davis, Harry	Bushman	Abraham Davis (father), Poroti, via Whangarei.
60633	,,	Davis, Perry	Labourer	Abraham Davis (father), Poroti, via Whangarei.
60616	,,	Hemara, Nohorae	,,	Hori Hemara (father), Pakanae, Hokianga.
60796	,,	Leef, Joe	,,	W. Leef (father), Whangape, Hokianga.
60812	,,	Leef, Robert	Farmer	Ria Leef (mother), Whangape, Hokianga.
60619	,,	Loftley, Ray	Labourer	Kumaiterangi (grandmother), Galatea, Muripara, via Rotorua.
19784	,,	Martin, William	Flax-mill Hand	William Martin (father), Porirua, Wellington.
60625	,,	Murray, Raroa	Farmer	W. Murray (father), Whangape, Hokianga.
60626	,,	Ngawhika, Hou	Labourer	Miss Rua Ngawhika (sister), Ahipara, Kaitaia.
60637	,,	Ruru, Pera	,,	Mrs. T. Ruru (mother), P.O. Box 33, Hastings.
60622	,,	Tamaiparea, Iwiora	Independent	Mrs. R. Tamaiparea (wife), Waitotara, Taranaki.
72733	,,	Werata, Epiha	Farmer	Mrs. R. Werata (mother), Kawi, Feilding.

31st MAORI REINFORCEMENTS.

Reg. No.	Rank.	Name.	Occupation.	Name and Address of Next-of-kin.
2/908	2nd Lieut.	†Moore, William Andrew	Labourer	Mrs. C. E. Moore (mother), 20 Haslett Street, Mount Eden, Auckland.
16/1172	C.S.-Major	‡Robertson, John	Lighthouse-keeper	Mrs. E. Walscott (mother), Otaku, Dunedin.
16/89	Sergeant	§Reihana, Rutene	Farmer	Poihipi Kohere (cousin), Rangitukia, via Gisborne.
60620	,,	Rogers, Winiata	Mechanic	C. Rogers (father), Maketu, Bay of Plenty.
75945	Corporal	Webber, David	Labourer	Mrs. R. Webber (wife), Wairoa, Hawke's Bay.
60797	Lance-Corpl.	Hadfield, Herbert	Butcher	Mrs. Rewa Hadfield (mother), Te Kao, North Cape.
60821	,,	Heperi, Frederick	Farmer	Joseph Heperi (father), Rangiahua, Hokianga.
60828	,,	Neilson, Robert Fergusson	Saddler	Mrs. B. Neilson (wife), Waimate North, Bay of Islands.
60817	,,	Noall, Robert Hain	Fitter	Mrs. I. C. Noall (wife), 55 New North Road, Glenmore, Auckland.
60851	,,	Pitman, James	Labourer	Miss F. Pitman (sister), 13 College Hill, Ponsonby, Auckland.
60811	,,	Rudolph, Richard	Farmer	Mrs. M. Rudolph (mother), Pakotai, Hokianga.
60868	Private	Abraham, Henry	Labourer	Mrs. P. Eparaima (mother), Whakarewarewa, Rotorua.
16/156	,,	§Ahomiro, Arapeta	Farmer	Ahomiro Ngakuku (father), Te Puke, Bay of Plenty.
20030	,,	Brown, Jack	Bushman	Mrs. Ripipeti Brown (mother), Wairoa, Tauranga.
16/257	,,	Climie, Putu	Farm Hand	Tea Putu (cousin), Rotorua.
60814	,,	Coffey, Peter	Farmer	Kawhi Coffey (father), Clevedon, Auckland.
60630	,,	Davis, William	Miner	Mrs. Harriet Edwards (mother), Poroti, via Whangarei.
60869	,,	Dixon, Joseph	Farmer	Matetu Rikihana (Dixon) (father), Kihikihi, via Te Awamutu.
60864	,,	Edwards, Edward	,,	William Edwards (father), Tauranga, Bay of Plenty.
60845	,,	Erihana, Edward Matapura	Law Clerk	Mrs. Hera Ellison (mother), Puketeraki, Otago.
60799	,,	Gray, George Edward	Farmer	Mrs. M. E. Gray (wife), care of Mrs. Gillibrand, 4 George Street, Rocky Nook, Auckland.
16/224	,,	§Hakiwai, John	Labourer	Mrs. Meri Hakiwai (mother), P.O. Box 33, Hastings.
60835	,,	Haora, Hilford	Farmer	Mrs. C. Haora (mother), Tamatarau, Whangarei.
84437	,,	Haora, Walter	Launchman	Mrs. C. Haora (mother), Tamatarau, Whangarei.
16/132	,,	§Hemopo, Pari	Labourer	Paroa Hemopo (brother), Oruanui, East Taupo.
60840	,,	Hillman, William Lionel	,,	H. Hillman (brother), Parawai, Thames.
60870	,,	Hori, William	Farmer	Manehera Hori (brother), care of Tongia Awhikau, Kakamere, Normanby.
60846	,,	Hughes, Benjamin	,,	Mrs. V. McMahon (friend), Crook's Avenue, Epsom, Auckland.
19850	,,	Huka, Timi	Labourer	Materoa Huka (father), Whakaki, Wairoa, Hawke's Bay.
60848	,,	Karauna, Riki Waipouri	Farmer	Mrs. Torangi Waipouri (mother), Omapere, Hokianga.
60820	,,	Kawana, Hemi	Mill Hand	Wharepouri Toara (sister), Tarere, Te Puke.
60844	,,	Kemara, Makarauria	Shepherd	Mrs. Mere Kemara (mother), Omaio, Bay of Plenty.
60842	,,	Kerewaro, Albert Lightheart	Farm Hand	Mihinui Kerewaro (father), Okoroire, Rotorua Line.
60628	,,	Kingi, Edward John	Labourer	Katerina Kingi (aunt), Greytown.
60813	,,	Komene, Hori	Mill Hand	Mrs. J. Komene (wife), Matungarau, Whangaroa.
60808	,,	Komene, Mohi	,,	Miss Ngarama Komene (sister), Totara North, Bay of Islands.
60853	,,	Martin, Ropiha	Dairy-farmer	Mrs. M. Martin (wife), Wangehu, Wanganui.
60792	,,	Martin, Thomas	Labourer	Mrs. Kararaina Martin (mother), Waiotapu, Rotorua.
60831	,,	Mateara, Edward	Farm Labourer	Mateara Mihaka (father), Pakanae, Hokianga.
60794	,,	Matekuare, Iharaira	Labourer	Mrs. Neta Matekuare (wife), Muripara, Galatea.
6/1559	,,	Maunsell, William	Farmer	Mrs. W. Daniel (mother), Kaihu, Dargaville.
60843	,,	Maupakanga, Tehuaki	Labourer	Takapo Maupakanga (uncle), Kawhia, Raglan.
60858	,,	Maxwell, Harry Bert	,,	Mrs. Neti Maxwell (mother), Kahukura.
81331	,,	Mill, Samuel	Shepherd	Mrs. Raiha Mamoko Mill (wife), Te Araroa.
60824	,,	Nathan, Ruru	Bushman	Mrs. M. Nathan (wife), Maropiu, Dargaville.
60617	,,	Parata, Thomas	Labourer	H. Parata (father), Te Kahu, Opotiki.
60829	,,	Perry, Warren Turu	,,	Miss M. Perry (sister), Waima, Hokianga.
60841	,,	Peta, Aporina	Farmer	Mrs. P. Marawa (mother), Te Kaha, Opotiki.
60816	,,	Peter, Henry Wi	,,	Mrs. M. Peter (wife), Pukepoto, Kaitaia.
60802	,,	Pomana, Jack	Bushman	Mrs. Ngatau Pomana (mother), Waikare, Bay of Islands.
60795	,,	Rapine, Iraia	Labourer	Mrs. P. Rapine (mother), Ahipara, Kaitaia.
60859	,,	Ruwhiu, Hau	Bushman	Mrs. S. Ruwhiu (mother), Te Araroa.
60791	,,	Tapihana, Hira	Farmer	K. Tapihana (father), Maketu, Bay of Plenty.
60805	,,	Taurua, Huhu	Mill Hand	Mrs. P. Taurua (wife), Oromahoe, Pakaraka, Bay of Islands.
60806	,,	Taurua, Pouaka	Bushman	Miss I. Taurua (sister), Taumarere, Bay of Islands.
60801	,,	Wanoa, Joe	Labourer	Mrs. H. Wanoa (wife), Te Araroa.
60615	,,	Waru, William	Farm Hand	W. Waru (father), Koputawaki, Coromandel.
60810	,,	Weche, Wirihi	Farmer	Mrs. Haori Weche (mother), Te Ahuahu, Bay of Islands.
76108	,,	Wikiriwhi, Matataia Pararaki	Roadman	P. M. Wikiriwhi (father), Maketu, Bay of Plenty.

† Ex 2nd and 9th Reinforcements.   ‡ Ex 4th Maori Contingent.   § Ex 1st Maori Contingent.

32ND REINFORCEMENTS.

Reg. No.	Rank.	Name.	Occupation.	Name and Address of Next-of-kin.
19928	C.S. Major	Hadden, Tremain	Manager, Timber-yard	Mrs. E. J. Hadden (wife), Ngaruawahia.
16/442	Corporal	†Haira Rima	Farmer	Mika Hira (father), Kaihu, Auckland.
16/877	Lance-Corpl.	Koia, Rawiri	Labourer	Mrs. Arihia Koia (mother), Waiapu, Gisborne.
20064	,,	Pumamao, William Herewini	..	Mrs. Whakarato Pumamao (mother), Waitahanui, Taupo.
60631	,,	Rameka, Thomas Godfrey	Blacksmith	Mrs. M. Rameka (mother), Ohaeawai, Bay of Islands.
60818	,,	Ruwhi, William	Bushman	Mrs. Matewai Poa (sister), Horoera, Te Araroa.
60878	Private	Amotawa, Henry	Labourer	Mrs. L. Amotawa (wife), Whakarewarewa, Rotorua.
84405	,,	Barrett, Ted	..	Mrs. Huiahana Barrett (mother), Waitomo.
60857	,,	Bowlin, William	Driver	Mrs. Moetua Taitua (mother), Taumarunui.
84410	,,	Davis, Charles Richard	Farmer	E. C. Davis (brother), Waitomo.
84411	,,	Davis, Thomas Phillips	..	E. C. Davis (brother), Waitomo.
60850	,,	Hapakuku, Sid	,,	Mrs. M. Hapakuku (wife), Herekino, North Auckland.
60894	,,	Huiatahi, Toriwai	..	Huiatahi Barrett (father), Waitomo.
60790	,,	Johnson, Oamaru	Labourer	Tahi Johnson (father), Takahiwai, Whangarei.
60845	,,	Joker, John	Seaman	Mrs. Huri Panirau (mother), Waitangi, Chatham Islands
60875	,,	Kahaki, Whare	Shepherd	Hoani Kahaki (father), Te Araroa.
60880	,,	Kapinga, Winiata	Farmer	Kapinga Taniwha (father), Aria, Te Kuiti.
60897	,,	Karewa, Taani	Bush Hauler	Hira Karewa (father), Omahu, Thames.
84404	,,	Kauwhata, Rahikoi Moumou	Farmer	Te Moumou Kauwhata (mother), Otewa, via Otorohanga.
20739	,,	Maata, Manga	Labourer	Tame Maata (brother), Piopio.
60627	,,	Ngawaka, George	Farmer	Andrew Ngawaka (father), Whangape, Hokianga.
60804	,,	Paratene, Broughton	Bushman	Paratene Huru (father), Waihaha, Bay of Islands.
60892	,,	Pauahi, Te Araroa	Farmer	Tarere Pauahi (mother), Kihikihi.
60891	,,	Piahana, Hautaku	Labourer	Pakipaki Piahana (sister), Cabbage Bay.
60838	,,	Pohio, Kingi	Taxi-driver	Waihau Pohio (father), Petane, Napier.
60789	,,	Pohipi, Waikura	Bushman	Tuakana Pohipi (father), Te Kaha, Bay of Plenty.
84406	,,	Ponui, Thomas	Labourer	Whakahua Ponui (mother), Kawhia.
60873	,,	Ransfield, Andrew	..	Heperi Ransfield (father), Westshore, Napier.
60809	,,	Rihari, Neri	Driver	Kiri Rihari (father), Purerua, Bay of Islands.
60861	,,	Robertson, Frederick Allan	Labourer	Gladys Walscott (sister), Otakau, Dunedin.
60819	,,	Ruwhiu, Thomas	Bushman	George Ruwhiu (father), Otaua, North Auckland.
60807	,,	Tamati, Te Riwhi	Mill Hand	Honi Tamati (father), Te Kuiti.
60852	,,	Tapa, Sam	Farmer	Ngakaraihi Tapa (wife), Parikino, Wanganui.
60895	,,	Temete, Wiremu	Farm Hand	Ngaone Temete (mother), Tirau, Rotorua Line.
60882	,,	Te Ruinga te Mapi	Farmer	Te Ruinga te Haere (father), Otorohanga.
60465	,,	Tete, Rangi	Labourer	Peter Trau (cousin), Whatawhata, Hamilton.
60898	,,	Tukaki, Taurarua	Navvy	Mrs Inuroto Tukaki (wife), Matamata.
84401	,,	Turnbull, Thomas	Labourer	R. Turnbull (brother), Kawhia.
60876	,,	Wanihi, Piniha	Carter	Mrs Tangi Wanihi (wife), Waitetuna, Raglan.
60860	,,	White, Jack	Labourer	Mereana Muriwai (mother), Rawene, Hokianga.

† Ex 1st Maori Contingent.

Honours, Awards and Casualties of the New Zealand (Maori) Pioneer Battalion

> We are the parents and the relatives of our Maori soldier youths; of both those who are dead and of those who live. We know that their glory has been published throughout the earth; and that that glory will descend to their descendants with untarnished fame; live, just as it lives with us today.
>
> W H TOKA OF KAIPARA TO SIR JAMES ALLEN,
> MINISTER OF DEFENCE, DATED 9 JUNE 1919

APPENDICES

The Maori Roll of Honour

List of Dead, Gallipoli, 1915
France and Flanders, 1916–1918

The following is a complete list of fatal casualties in the Maori Contingent, Gallipoli, 1915, and the Maori Pioneer Battalion, France and Flanders, 1916–1918, together with other deaths (accidental and disease) on active service. The details are from the Defence Department's official list of total deaths in the New Zealand Expeditionary Force during the War:

16/1007	Adam, Kiro Luke, Pte. Killed in Action, France, 7/10/17.
16/598	Akena, Rakapa, Pte. Died, United Kingdom ex France, 16/6/18.
19840	Albert, Windy, Pte. Died, New Zealand ex France, 29/5/19.
9/1256	Allison, Wm., Pte. Killed in Action, France, 15/9/16.
16/1392	Anaru, Albert Paul, Pte. Killed in Action, France, 7/6/17.
19460	Andrews, William Wilson, Pte. Accidentally Killed, France, 20/1/18.
16/583	Angel, Edward, L.-Cpl. Died of Wounds, France, 29/12/17.
16/1182	Anthony, Manuel, Cpl. Died, New Zealand ex France, 10/5/17.
16/1365	Apatari, Manu, Pte. Killed in Action, France, 14/9/16.
16/87	Aramataku, Herewini, Pte. Killed in Action, Gallipoli, 6/8/15.
16/1139	Arii, —, Pte. Died, France, 24/8/16.
16/524	Baker, Whare, Pte. Killed in Action, Gallipoli, 21/8/15.

19236	Banaba, Beni, Pte. Died, New Zealand ex Egypt, 16/9/17.
16/435	Barton, Whare, Pte. Killed in Action, France, 2/9/16.
22759	Bourke, John Joseph, Pte. Killed in Action, France, 15/9/16.
19671	Bristowe, Sam, Pte. Died, France, after Armistice, 5/4/19.
9/1014	Brooke, Burton, Pte. Killed in Action, France, 5/6/16.
16/1469	Brown, Henry, Pte. Died of Wounds, France, 19/6/17.
9/908	Cameron, John Donald, 2nd Lieut. Killed in Action, France, 7/8/17.
16/572	Carroll, Tuahae, Cpl. Killed in Action, Gallipoli, 10/12/15.
16/567	Christie, Hapi, Pte. Died, United Kingdom ex Gallipoli, 10/12/15.
19423	Clark, Clark, Pte. Killed in Action, France, 19/11/17.
20787	Conrad, Paki, Pte. Died, United Kingdom ex France, 6/12/18.
16/1299	Cook, George Gray, Pte. Died, France, 12/10/18.
9/1412	Cooper, George Begg, Pte. Died, France, 8/12/18.
19564	Cootes, Taipua Skipworth, Pte. Died, United Kingdom, 29/10/19.
16/260	Coupar, Simon James Stuart, Lieut. Killed in Action, France, 29/6/16.
9/1274	Crawshaw, Samuel, Pte. Died, France, 6/1/19.
19459	Curtis, Joseph, Pte. Died of Wounds, France, 8/10/17.
23150	Dale, Charles Martin, Pte. Killed in Action, France, 5/5/17.
16/575a	Danger, James, Cpl. Died of Wounds, France, 3/9/17.
19703	Davy, Para, Pte. Died of Disease, France, 8/11/18.
16/93	Delamere, Heremeta, Sgt. Accidentally Killed, France, 13/6/16.
19699	Dickson, Harry, Pte. Died, New Zealand, 13/11/18.
16/508	Downes, Albert, Pte. Died, Malta ex Egypt, 9/9/15.
16/373	Duff, Matene Rangiamohia, Sgt. Died of Wounds, France, 1/9/16.
38513	Edmonds, Bennie, Pte. Killed in Action, France, 31/12/17.
16/579a	Ellison, Thomas, L.-Cpl. Killed in Action, France, 14/9/16.
16/439	Emery, Peter, Pte. Died, Egypt, 28/8/15.
16/1509	Epiha, Daniel, Pte. Died of Wounds, France, 7/10/17.
16/580a	Eruera, Whiti, Pte. Killed in Action, France, 7/6/17.
7/1461	Evans, James, Pte. Killed in Action, France, 15/9/16.
16/982	Fairlie, Godfrey Alexander, T/Sgt. Killed in Action, France, 5/4/18.
16/519	Ferris, Donald, Pte. Killed in Action, Gallipoli, 8/8/15.
9/1007	Field, Alfred Thornley, Sgt. Killed in Action, France, 18/9/16.
16/1046	Filitoua, —, Pte. Died, United Kingdom, 19/6/16.
8/3579	Fisher, Charles, Cpl. Killed in Action, France, 18/6/17.
16/1480	French, Samuel James, Cpl. Died at Sea, 17/8/16.
16/36a	Geary, John, L.-Cpl. Killed in Action, Gallipoli, 8/8/15.
16/65	Grace, Abraham Turei, Pte. Died, Egypt, 21/10/15.
19745	Grace, Samuel, Pte. Killed in Action, France, 19/2/18.
20711	Graham, George, Pte. Died at Sea en route to New Zealand, 25/3/19.
20811	Haenga, Heremia Tawhero, Pte. Killed in Action, France, 31/12/17.
16/1558	Hakaraia, John, Pte. Died, France, 14/11/17.
16/5	Hale, Richard, Sgt. Killed in Action, France, 14/8/17.
16/6	Hamana, Kingi, Pte. Died, United Kingdom ex France, 3/10/16.

16/536	Hape, Hona, Pte., MID. Died, United Kingdom, 11/4/19.
16/949	Hape, Tere, Pte. Died of Wounds, France, 24/6/17.
16/750	Happy, Dick, Pte. Died, France, 17/12/16.
19351	Hapuku, Manukea, Pte. Killed in Action, France, 7/12/17.
16/267	Harding, Joseph, Pte. Died of Wounds, Egypt ex Gallipoli, 14/8/15.
20769	Harding, Whetu, Pte. Killed in Action, France, 6/8/17.
16/370	Hare, Heremaia, Pte. Killed in Action, Gallipoli, 7/8/15.
19680	Harmon, James, Pte. Died of Wounds, France, 18/3/18.
7/2018	Harris, Edward, Capt., MID. Died of Wounds, France, 18/9/16.
16/950	Haruiti, Henry, Pte. Killed in Action, France, 23/12/17.
16/391	Hekiera, Remihana, Pte. Killed in Action, France, 4/5/17.
16/1320	Hemi, Skipper Pori, Pte. Killed in Action, France, 10/9/16.
16/176	Herewini, Hohepa, Pte. Died of Wounds, Gallipoli, 21/9/15.
16/325	Hetaraka, Hurae, Pte. Died, Mudros ex Gallipoli, 16/8/15.
20069	Hetekia, Ngahana, Pte. Died, France, 3/11/18.
20875	Hill, Hemi, Pte. Died of Wounds, France, 7/6/17.
16/4537a	Hill, Percy, WO2, MID. Killed in Action, Gallipoli, 9/8/15.
16/597	Hillman, Charlie, Pte. Accidentally Killed (run over by vehicle), France, 20/8/16.
16/1257	Hina, Pera, Pte. Killed in Action, France, 21/7/17.
16/379	Hiroti, Rangihiwinui, Pte. Died, France, 5/6/16.
9/1439	Hitchon, Frank Horton, Pte. Died of Wounds, France, 12/9/16.
19786	Hohepa, Puehu, Pte. Died, New Zealand, 30/12/17.
23/2204	Holmes, Arthur, Pte. Died, United Kingdom, 20/12/17.
16/606	Houia, Wiremu Peha, L.-Cpl. Died of Wounds, France, 27/9/16.
16/556	Hovell, George Woodward, Pte. Died of Wounds, United Kingdom ex Gallipoli, 20/10/15
16/1442	Huki, Raymond, Pte. Died at Sea en route to New Zealand, 8/4/17.
7/2044	Humphries, Thomas James, Pte. Died of Wounds, France, 8/6/16.
20856	Hunia, Te Ruawai, Pte. Died of Wounds, France, 31/12/17.
19355	Hunter, Jack, L.-Cpl. Died of Wounds, France, 6/10/17.
16/1339	Hura, Raukawa, Pte. Died, United Kingdom ex France, 10/4/17.
16/1238	Huriwaka, George, Pte. Died, France, 6/6/16.
20026	Huta, Meihana, Pte. Died, United Kingdom, 24/3/18.
16/240	Johnson, William, Cpl. Died of Wounds, France, 5/8/16.
16/1453	Jones, Charles, Pte. Killed in Action, France, 23/2/17.
16/620	Kaa, Pekama, Capt. Killed in Action, France, 14/8/17.
60875	Kahaki, Whare, Pte. Died, United Kingdom, 19/2/19.
16/1062	Kaimanu, Pte. Died, Egypt, 15/3/16.
16/10	Kaipara, Autiri Pitara, 2nd Lieut. Killed in Action, France, 4/8/17.
19634	Kaiwai, Harold, Pte. Died, France, 1/5/18.
16/629	Kaiwai, Reweti, Pte. Killed in Action, France, 14/9/16.
16/634	Kanapu, Horomona, Pte. Killed in Action, France, 30/11/17.
16/937	Kara, Taha, Pte. Killed in Action, France, 5/4/18.
16/1491	Karapaina, Hakota, Pte. Killed in Action, France, 14/9/16.
19948	Karapaina, Paratene, Pte. Died, United Kingdom, 31/1/19.
19860	Karauria, Meihana, Pte. Died, France, 24/7/18.
16/394	Karena, Wero Mohi, Cpl. Killed in Action, France, 30/11/17.
16/271	Karetai, Stewart, Pte. Killed in Action, Gallipoli, 21/8/15.
16/95	Kawhia, Eruera, Pte. Died of Wounds, France, 8/6/16.

20678	Kemp, Kawenata, Pte. Died, New Zealand ex France, 28/1/18.
20771	Kereama, Hori, Pte. Killed in Action, France, 30/11/17.
20844	Kihi, Pua, Pte. Killed in Action, France, 11/8/17.
16/802	King, Kohi, Pte. Killed in Action, France, 14/9/16.
16/621	Kingi, Tauiti, Pte. Died of Wounds, France, 2/1/18.
16/1018	Kohere, Henare Mokena, 2nd Lieut. Died of Wounds, France, 16/9/16.
20/598	Kokiri, Tango, 2nd Lieut. Died at Sea en route to United Kingdom, 21/4/17.
16/552	Konuke, Pat, Pte. Died, France, 14/4/18.
16/643	Kopua, Whetuki, Pte. Killed in Action, France, 4/8/17.
16/1477	Korako, H., Pte. Killed in Action, France, 19/6/17.
16/399	Kumeroa, te Aohau, Pte. Killed in Action, France, 25/9/16.
16/1418	Lazarus, Jack, Pte. Died of Wounds, France, 24/9/16.
20715	Leefe, George, Pte. Died New Zealand, 30/12/18.
16/807	Luke, Peter, Pte. Killed in Action, France, 31/7/17.
9/165	McIntyre, William Nicol, Cpl. Killed in Action, France, 15/9/16.
23255	McKay, Robert Patrick, Pte. Killed in Action, France, 7/6/17.
19728	McLean, Thomas, Pte. Died of Wounds, France, 17/12/17.
16/809	McNicol, Duncan Bannetyne, 2nd Lieut. Died of Wounds, France, 4/8/17.
19562	Maaka, Henri, Pte. Died, United Kingdom, 31/8/19.
16/400	Mangaroa, Ngore William, Pte. Died of Disease following Wounds, Malta ex Gallipoli, 30/12/15.
25556	Mangaroa, Thompson, Pte. Died, New Zealand ex France, 9/6/19.
16/189	Manihera, Waitere, Pte. Killed in Action, Gallipoli, 6/8/15.
16/656	Manuel, Josiah, Sgt. Died of Wounds, New Zealand ex France, 21/6/17.
16/340	Manuel, Richard, L.-Cpl. Killed in Action, Gallipoli, 8/8/15.
16/657	Manuel, Tiweka, Pte. Died, United Kingdom, 25/3/18.
10/117	Maraki, Tautuhi, Pte. Killed in Action, Gallipoli, 9/8/15.
16/139	Marino, Hohepa, Pte. Died of Wounds, Gallipoli, 2/9/15.
19621	Maranui, Pona, Pte. Killed in Action, France, 23/12/17.
19361	Mason, Harry, Pte. Died, New Zealand ex France, 12/1/19.
4/1128	Masters, George, 2nd Lieut., MID. Killed in Action, France, 3/4/17.
16/663	Matana, Karauria, Pte. Died of Wounds, France, 19/9/16.
16/1189	Matau, —, Pte. Died, France, 29/8/16.
16/810	Matenga, Tuheke, Pte. Drowned, United Kingdom, 14/5/18.
16/1557	Matheu, Wetini, Pte. Died, France, 28/12/18.
16/1285	Matai, Tuherini, Pte. Died, New Zealand ex France, 1/9/17.
16/385	Mete, Kingi Henare, Pte. Killed in Action, France, 14/9/16.
16/383	Mete, Kingi Teira Hoani, Cpl. Killed in Action, Gallipoli, 8/8/15.
16/207	Mihaere Taiamai, L.-Cpl. Died of Wounds, France, 9/12/17.
16/278	Mira, William, Pte. Died, Egypt ex Gallipoli, 9/2/16.
16/1378	Mitchell, Ernest, Pte. Killed in Action, France, 24/9/16.
16/1089	Mitikele, —, Pte. Died, Egypt, 16/5/16.
16/1088	Moki, Pte. Died, United Kingdom, 30/6/16.
16/222	Mokomoko, Nopera Hape, Pte. Died, Egypt, 2/9/15.
16/555	Moore, Sunny, Cpl. Died, France, 24/4/18.
16/680	Morehu, Hakopa, Pte. Killed in Action, France, 2/6/17.
16/344	Morgan, Joseph Iraia, Pte. Killed in Action, France, 29/7/17.
19399	Morris, Benjamin, Pte. Killed in Action, France, 22/8/18.

20846	Murray, Raika Whakarongotai, L.-Cpl. Killed in Action, France, 31/12/17.
16/686	Newton, James, Pte. Killed in Action, France, 5/8/17.
16/185	Ngamu, Hoani, Pte. Killed in Action, Gallipoli, 6/8/15.
16/958	Ngatoro, Renata, Pte. Died, Egypt, 14/1/16.
19371	Nicholls, Frederick, Pte. Died of Wounds, France, 6/10/18.
16/164	Nicholls, Thompson William, Cpl., MM. Died, New Zealand, 6/11/18.
20885	Nikorima, Fred, Pte. Killed in Action, France, 21/6/17.
16/689	O'Neill, John Irvine, 2nd Lieut. Killed in Action, France, 3/10/16.
10251	Ovens, John, Pte. Killed in Action, France, 29/9/16.
20625	Padlie, David, Pte. Killed in Action, France, 6/8/17.
16/1536	Paki, Rimi, Pte. Died, United Kingdom ex France, 10/3/18.
16/28	Paku, Akuhata, Pte. Killed in Action, Gallipoli, 21/8/15.
16/201	Paora, Paetaha, Pte. Died, Malta ex Gallipoli, 4/2/16.
16/493	Papuni, Kurei, Pte. Killed in Action, Gallipoli, 6/8/15.
16/346	Para, Paki Whetu, Pte. Died of Wounds, New Zealand ex Gallipoli, 9/5/16.
16/566	Parata, Paul, Pte. Died, United Kingdom, 17/5/17.
9/1086	Park, Douglas Murgall, Sgt. Killed in Action, France, 15/9/16.
16/931	Patara, Hiroki Rere, Pte. Died, Egypt, 2/11/15.
19740	Patara, Nele, Pte. Killed in Action, France, 31/12/17.
16/30	Peka, Hohepa, Pte. Died, New Zealand ex France, 10/3/20.
19732	Pene, Enoka William, Pte. Died, New Zealand, 22/10/19.
16/284	Peneamene, Tumaru, Pte. Died, United Kingdom ex Gallipoli, 18/9/15.
16/1115	Peni, Meta, Pte. Died at Sea en route to New Zealand, 23/6/16.
16/703	Pera, Hue, Pte. Killed in Action, France, 19/2/18.
16/33	Pera, Piana, Pte. Died of Injuries (Railway accident), France, 16/4/16.
16/246	Pineata, Watarawi, Pte. Died of Wounds, France, 29/9/16.
16/1126	Pineka, Pte. Died at Sea en route to New Zealand, 4/7/16.
19427	Pirimi, Egbert, Pte. Killed in Action, France, 14/7/16.
16/34	Pohatu, Renata, Pte. Died of Wounds, France, 13/7/16.
60789	Pohipi, Waikura, Pte. Died, United Kingdom, 16/2/19.
9/1091	Poole, Thomas Henry, Pte. Killed in Action, France, 15/9/15.
16/410	Popoki, Te Ao, Pte. Died, Egypt, 15/8/15.
16/287	Porete, August Paani, Pte. Died, Egypt ex Gallipoli, 11/9/15.
19877	Potatau, Tipene, Pte. Died, New Zealand ex France, 10/6/19.
16/388	Potonga, Tame, Pte. Died, New Zealand, 30/12/15.
20743	Poutawera, James, Pte. Killed in Action, France, 18/12/17.
16/198	Power, Hone Manahi, Pte. Killed in Action, France, 7/12/17.
16/1107	Pulu, —, Sgt. Died at Sea en route to New Zealand, 26/6/16.
9/1725	Quin, Thomas George, Pte. Killed in Action, France, 15/9/16.
20402	Rakiraki, John, Pte. Died, France, 3/5/18.
16/1574	Rameka, Percy, Pte. Died at Sea en route to New Zealand ex France, 26/5/18.
16/37	Rangi, Hapi, Pte. Died, Egypt, 5/11/15.
16/449	Rangi, Horima, Pte. Killed in Action, France, 4/8/17.
60500	Rangitauwira, Wiremu, Pte. Died, United Kingdom, 31/3/18.

16/580	Rapihana, Herewini, Pte. Killed in Action, Gallipoli, 6/8/15.
16/525	Rapona, Kiri, Pte. Died of Wounds, United Kingdom ex France, 29/9/16.
20736	Raroa, William, Pte. Died, United Kingdom ex France, 6/12/18.
19411	Rata, Jerry, Pte. Died, United Kingdom ex France, 20/6/18.
16714	Ratana, Wiremu, Pte. Died of Wounds, France, 30/7/16.
16/91	Ratana, Nepia, Pte. Killed in Action, Gallipoli, 7/8/15.
4/52a	Reid, Lestock Henry, 2nd Lieut. Killed in Action, France, 20/5/16.
16/720	Reiroa, Martin Wesley, Pte. Died, France, 31/8/16.
16/115	Rewa, George Rangitikei, Pte. Killed in Action, France, 31/8/16.
19755	Rewharewha, Henare, Pte. Died of Wounds, France, 31/12/17.
20664	Rewi, Peremara, Pte. Killed in Action, France, 23/3/17.
16/102	Richmond, Tom, Pte. Died of Wounds, Egypt ex Gallipoli, 9/9/15.
16/723	Rickus, Thomas Samuel, Pte. Died of Wounds at Sea en route to New Zealand ex France, 5/8/17.
60809	Rihari, Neri, Pte. Died, New Zealand, 19/2/20.
16/199	Ropata, Pahia, Pte. Killed in Action, Gallipoli, 6/8/15.
20630	Ruha, John, Pte. Killed in Action, France, 21/7/17.
19303	Ruka, Willie, Pte. Died, Australia en route to United Kingdom, 28/1/17.
16/61	Ruhinga, Waretini, Sgt. Killed in Action, Gallipoli, 1/9/15.
16/1459	Ruru, Vivian, Pte. Killed in Action, France, 14/8/17.
18707	Ryan, Edward John, Pte. Died of Wounds, France, 9/6/17.
16/888	Savage, Charles, Sgt. Killed in Action, France, 21/6/17.
19883	Savage, John Joseph, Pte. Died, United Kingdom ex France, 2/3/18.
13/2150	Saxby, Conrad Gordon, Lieut.-Col., DSO, MID. Died, United Kingdom, 27/11/18.
9/1218	Scaife, Stanley Tancred, Cpl. Killed in Action, France, 15/9/16.
13114	Scully, Ernest Charles, Pte. Died of Wounds, France, 6/6/17.
9/1354	Short, James, Lieut. Died of Wounds, France, 28/5/16.
16/591	Sidney, William, Pte. Killed in Action, Gallipoli, 21/8/15.
16/506	Simpson, George, Pte. Killed in Action, Gallipoli, 21/8/15.
16/869	Skelton, Harold George Nepia, Pte. Died of Wounds, France, 8/8/17.
19429	Slade, Joseph, Pte. Died of Wounds, France, 25/6/18.
16/735	Smith, Frank, Pte. Killed in Action, France, 15/9/16.
19417	Smith, Haka, Pte. Killed in Action, France, 19/11/17.
19394	Smith, Hoani, Pte. Died of Wounds, France, 11/4/18.
20015	Smith, Temete, Pte. Died, United Kingdom ex France, 27/12/18.
16/1196	Solomona, L.-Cpl. Died, New Zealand, 3/4/17.
16/68	Taewa, Rawiri, Pte. Killed in Action, Gallipoli, 21/8/15.
16/358	Tahu, Ngakepa, Pte. Killed in Action, Gallipoli, 6/8/15.
16/113	Tairua, Joseph, Pte. Accidentally Killed (aeroplane accident) United Kingdom, 13/2/19.
16/933	Taiwhanga, Hirini, Pte. Killed in Action, France, 21/6/17.
16/474	Take, William, Pte. Killed in Action, Gallipoli, 6/8/15.
16/740	Takoko, Hori, L.-Cpl. Killed in Action, France, 24/12/17.
16/891	Takuao, Paul, Pte. Died of Wounds, France, 8/6/16.
16/1132	Taleva, Pte. Died, United Kingdom, 12/6/16.
16/418	Tamarapa, Waikohari, Pte. Died, Mudros ex Gallipoli, 12/10/15.
20656	Tamati, Poururu, Pte. Died, United Kingdom, 15/10/17.
16/963	Tamauahi, Papara, Cpl. Killed in Action, France, 5/4/18.
16/1504	Tangaere, Hori, Pte. Died, New Zealand ex France, 16/3/18.

16/840	Tapsell, Robert, Pte. Killed in Action, France, 16/9/16.
16/1199	Taringa, Pte. Died, France, 15/8/16.
16/1155	Tauetuli, Pte. Died, France, 9/6/16.
19753	Tuakamo, Waata, Pte. Killed in Action, France, 31/12/17.
16/1165	Taumataua, Pte. Died, New Zealand, 19/12/16.
16/78	Taumaunu, Hare, Pte. Died, Mudros ex Gallipoli, 11/10/15.
16/955	Taupaki, Rameka, L.-Cpl. Killed in Action, France, 31/12/17.
16/1202	Taura, —, Pte. Died, United Kingdom ex France, 7/1/17.
19524	Taurere, Tepana, Pte. Killed in Action, France, 4/8/17.
16/1479	Tawhai, Hohepa Taupaki, Pte. Died, France, 7/12/16.
19744	Te Ara, Nati, Pte. Died at Sea ex France, 5/4/19.
16/512	Te Awarau, Hori Karaka, Pte. Died, Egypt, 13/9/15.
16/964	Te Hau, Pera, Pte. Killed in Action, France, 5/4/18.
19528	Te Hui, Haora, Pte. Died, United Kingdom ex France, 25/4/18.
19398	Te Kauru, John, Pte. Killed in Action, France, 4/8/17.
16/753	Te Kuru, Piki-Kotuku, Pte. Died of Wounds, France, 4/8/17.
19770	Te Maro, Herewini, Pte. Died, New Zealand ex France, 19/3/20.
60895	Te Mete, Wiremu, Pte. Died, United Kingdom, 11/2/19.
16/477	Te Moananui, Mikaera, Cpl. Died at Sea en route to Egypt, 6/3/15.
16/181	Te Moni, Matehaere, Pte. Killed in Action, Gallipoli, 6/8/15.
20048	Te Moni, Ratapu, Pte. Died, New Zealand, 14/8/19.
16/42	Te Ngaio, Wharekete, Pte. Died, Egypt, 24/3/16.
16/183	Te Otimi, Pitonga, Pte. Killed in Action, Gallipoli, 8/8/15.
29104	Teparo, Hohepa, Pte. Accidentally Killed (thrown from horse), France, 26/8/17.
16/922	Tepene, James, Pte. Died, New Zealand, 10/11/16.
16/1222	Tepuretu, Apu, Pte. Killed in Action, France, 30/9/16.
16/1389	Te Raina, Te Weka, Pte. Died, New Zealand ex France, 15/6/18.
16/760	Te Rore, Te Hu, Pte. Killed in Action, France, 3/6/17.
16/1390	Te Tuhi, Nikora, Pte. Died of Wounds, France, 4/8/17.
16/846	Te Ua, Te Miere, Pte. Killed in Action, France, 21/7/17.
16/421	Te Whare, Taiawhiao, Pte. Died of Wounds, Malta ex Gallipoli, 31/7/15.
20621	Te Whata, Peter, Pte. Died of Wounds, France, 23/3/17.
16/360a	Thompson, Richard, Pte. Died of Wounds, at Sea ex Gallipoli, 9/8/15.
16/363	Tiatoa, Pita, Pte. Killed in Action, France, 15/9/16.
16/364	Tiini, Hopa, Pte. Died, Egypt, 16/1/16.
16/1134	Timoko, Pte. Died, New Zealand, 21/9/16.
16/303	Timuiha, John, Pte. Killed in Action, France, 7/6/17.
16/1133	Tionesini, Cpl. Died, France, 31/5/16.
19572	Tipere, Wi Parata, Pte. Died of Wounds, France, 11/4/18.
16/1164	Tiueatana, —, Pte. Died at Sea en route to New Zealand, 27/6/16.
20735	Toheriri, Moetu, Pte. Died, New Zealand, 13/3/18.
16/98	Toheriri, Reupena, Pte. Killed in Action, France, 14/12/17.
60599	Toi Tukapa, Pte. Died, France, 30/12/18.
16/103	Toka, Taare, L.-Cpl. Killed in Action, France, 9/7/16.
16/480	Tua, James, Pte. Died of Wounds, at Sea ex Gallipoli, 14/8/15.
16/123	Tuati, Pareiha, Pte. Died of Wounds, Mudros ex Gallipoli, 16/8/15.
16/46	Tuahiwi, Wiremu, Pte. Died of Wounds, France, 19/6/17.
16/769	Tuhora, Potene, Pte. Died, United Kingdom ex France, 13/1/17.
20616	Tuki Manu, Pte. Died of Wounds, France, 7/6/17.
16/125	Tunoa, Hamiora, Pte. Killed in Action, Gallipoli, 21/8/15.

16/1179	Vaihola, Pte. Died at Sea en route to New Zealand, 28/6/16.
16/1177	Vasau, Pte. Died, United Kingdom ex France, 11/6/16.
16/1203	Vavia, Pte. Died of Wounds, France, 1/10/16.
20823	Waaka, Hapi, Pte. Died, France, 27/12/18.
20816	Waaka, Hohepa, Pte. Died of Wounds, France, 12/4/18.
16/1297	Waetford, Eugene, Pte. Died, France, 5/5/16.
16/482	Wahia, Moa, Pte. Died at Sea ex Gallipoli, 9/9/15.
16/426	Wahia, Thomas, Pte. Killed in Action, Gallipoli, 6/8/15.
16/53	Wairau, Ra, Pte. Died of Wounds, Malta ex Gallipoli, 11/9/15.
16/779	Wairau, Raniera, Pte. Died, United Kingdom ex France, 30/10/16.
16/549	Waiti, Haureki, Pte. Killed in Action, Gallipoli, 21/8/15.
9/227	Walker, James Alexander, Cpl. Died of Wounds, France, 28/5/17.
16/564	Warakihi, Poihipi, Pte. Killed in Action, Gallipoli, 21/8/15.
9/1620	Ward, Arthur, Pte. Killed in Action, France, 9/9/16.
19661	Warena, John Tana, Pte. Died, United Kingdom ex France, 1/11/17.
16/1354	Warena, Kitohi, Pte. Died, New Zealand ex France, 20/10/17.
16/368	Waru, Henare, Pte. Killed in Action, France, 8/6/16.
16/369	Waru, Kopa, Pte. Killed in Action, France, 8/6/17.
9/96	Watson, Norman Forrester, 2nd Lieut. Killed in Action, France, 12/10/17.
47562	Watson, Rihari, Pte. Died, France, 24/11/18.
11/2504	Webb, Roland, Pte. Died of Wounds, France, 15/9/16.
19604	Webster, Jack, Pte. Died of Wounds, France, 29/11/17.
16/382	Whakarua, Herewini, WO2. Died of Wounds, France, 13/1/18.
20779	Wharepapa, Turi, Cpl. Killed in Action, France, 23/12/17.
16/145	Whareraupo, Tuakana-Kore, L.-Cpl. Died of Wounds, Gallipoli, 6/8/15.
19669	Whareihiti, Nikora, Pte. Died, New Zealand ex France, 24/1/19.
19726	Wharewhiti, Rikihana, Pte. Died, United Kingdom ex France, 28/10/18.
16/789	Whitau, Arapata Koti P., Pte. Killed in Action, France, 8/6/16.
16/188	Whitau, Puaka, Pte. Died, United Kingdom ex Gallipoli, 10/10/15.
20845	Whyte, Walter, Pte. Died, United Kingdom ex France, 15/9/18.
19474	Wi, Henry Wi Waka, Pte. Died, United Kingdom ex France, 8/2/18.
16/858	Wickham, Mema, 2nd Lieut. Died of Injuries (shot by soldier), France, 31/12/18.
20665	Wiki, Frank, Pte. Killed in Action, France, 3/6/17.
16/1291	Wiki, Whiro, Pte. Died, United Kingdom ex France, 16/10/18.
16/371	Wikitera, Robert, Pte. Died of Wounds, France, 19/11/17.
19779	Williams, James, Pte. Died, United Kingdom ex France, 30/9/18.
16/112	William, Joe, Pte. Died at Sea ex Gallipoli, 13/8/15.
20624	Williams, Willie, Cpl. Died of Wounds, France, 4/9/18.
16/462	Winiana, Ponga, Pte. Killed in Action, France, 14/8/17.
16/1398	Wipani, John, Pte. Died, France, 31/12/18.
20778	Witana, Abraham, Pte. Died, France, 1/11/17.
16/431	Wood, Charlie, Pte. Killed in Action, France, 8/7/17.
16/308	Woods, George, Pte. Died, New Zealand ex France, 10/12/19.
20704	Wynyard, John, Pte. Died of Wounds, France, 8/6/17.

The following is a list of members of the Maori Contingents who have died since discharge from the N.Z.E.F. as a result of war service:

16/310	Adams, James, Pte.	16/669	Matthews, Joseph, Pte., 20/1/19.
16/1030	Alotau, Pte., 21/1/20.	16/1096	Mitipauni, Pte., 24/3/17.
19618	Awiti, Timi, Pte., 27/11/18.	16/23	Morete, Hone Henry, Pte., 24/5/19.
16/313	Brass, Rata, Pte., 2/2/19.	16/279	Morgan, George, Pte., 28/11/18.
16/564a	Brown, James, Pte., 6/8/20.	13358	Norton, Henry, Pte., 8/8/23.
16/570a	Clune, James, Pte., 5/12/18.	16/1522	Paeroa, Nehe, Pte., 12/12/17.
37771	Cotton, Joe Bird, Pte., 6/11/21.	16/694	Paneta, Wi, Pte., 12/7/20.
19940	Davie, Waru, Pte., 27/8/20.	16/527	Paora, Reihana, Pte., 3/7/19.
20684	Ephia, Tame, L.-Cpl., 1/4/19.	16/76	Paraone, Tapauri, Pte., 5/2/21.
16/173	Franks, Samuel Osman, Pte., 11/11/21.	19664	Pene, Amo, Pte., 28/9/18.
16/583a	Governor, Joe William, Pte., 26/11/17.	16/220	Pitama, te Kerikaihau, Pte., 5/8/20.
		16/288	Ransfield, Richard, Pte., 15/10/17.
		16/184	Raponi, Hone T., Cpl., 4/5/16.
20786	Hadfield, Matthew P., Pte., 10/1/19.	16/1273	Rawiri, August W., Pte., 23/8/18.
19624	Hoko, Moa, Pte., 24/1/19.	16/730	Rupene, Hoani, Pte., 8/4/17.
16/1226	Holmes, Frederick, WO1, 1/3/18.	19975	Savage, Daniel, Pte., 31/12/23.
16/1478	Hopa, Murphy, Pte., 23/8/21.	16/1393	Tairua, Peter, Pte., 21/11/18.
16/511	Kaanga, te Kuru, Pte., 25/6/19.	16/1460	Tangiora, Rewi, Pte., 20/12/19.
20893	Kanara, Ropata Wi, Pte., 16/5/19.	19960	Tautau, John, Pte., 10/11/19.
60628	Kingi, Edward John, Pte., 14/1/20.	16/571	Tawera, Barney, Pte., 11/5/21.
16/640	Kiri, Ben, Pte., 28/11/18.	16/248	Te Muera, Wetini, Pte., 24/10/19.
60543	Koti, Hone, Pte., 11/8/19.	20807	Toheriri, Tangiwai, Pte., 11/7/20.
16/276	Lucas, Joseph, Cpl., 8/12/18.	16/54	Wainohu, Hemi, Pte., 9/4/20.
57249	McKinlay, James, Pte., 10/6/23.	16/1525	Walker, Taylor, Pte., 4/12/20.
16/1524	Mark, Ned., Pte., 21/10/19.	20758	Wawatai, Heta, Pte., 20/7/22.
16/546	Matiu, Hone, Pte., 18/10/19.	16/1328	Young, Charles L., Capt., 10/2/21.

The Following is a List of Members of the Maori Contingents who Died while Undergoing Training with Reinforcements in New Zealand.

84749	Chase, Tuti, Pte. 15/11/18.		19380	Poata, Akuira, L.-Cpl., 13/12/16.
16/1270	Denny, John, Pte., 27/4/16.		84733	Pukure, Te Riri, Pte., 4/11/18.
84481	Fati, Manuaho, Pte., 11/11/18.		84718	Tahi, Tame, Pte., 23/11/18.
—	Hihi, Rupena, —, 16/11/18.		84744	Tapsell, Warena M., Pte., 4/11/18.
84703	Ihia, Te Hapa, Pte., 13/11/18.		84450	Tehiwi, Pitiroi, Pte., 7/11/18.
84494	Ilitomasi, Laligapata, Pte., 7/11/18.		84543	Teipo, Pai, Pte., 10/2/19.
19517	Keepa, Arama M., Pte., 15/1/17.		19324	Teiva, Yeaumarae, Pte., 14/9/16.
83270	Kerehama, Rangi, Pte., 13/11/18.		84489	Tonuia, Pte., 5/11/18.
90215	Kuka, Mangu, Pte., 22/1/19.		84714	Toto, Kiri, Pte., 12/11/18.
16/1213	Mataputa, Pte., 5/3/16.		84741	Turu, Te Kakama, Pte., 7/11/18.
24/233	Muriwai, John, Rflmn., 28/6/15.		20701	Uatuku, Te Iritima, Lieut., 31/8/17.
84503	Ngaipu, Ingatu, Pte., 10/11/18.		16/1178	Vilipate, Pte., 25/12/15.
84750	Oneroa, Tiki, Pte., 2/11/18.		84501	Wycliffe, Peau, Pte., 27/3/19.
19296	Pirangi, Pte., 14/10/16.			

RAROTONGANS

Nominal Roll of Members of the Rarotongan Contingent Who Died while Serving with the New Zealand Expeditionary Force during the Great War.

16/1184	Inga, —, Pte. Died of Disease, Palestine, 12/12/18.
16/1185	Kamate, —, Pte. Died of Disease, Palestine, 4/10/18.
19250	Mataiti, Kai, Pte. Died of Disease, Palestine, 16/2/18.
60713	Matapo, Kaka, Pte. Died of Disease, New Zealand ex Palestine, 14/8/19.
19281	Ngaia, Kapao, T/Cpl. Died of Disease, Egypt ex Palestine, 29/10/17.
60754	Rota, Rota, Pte. Died of Disease, At Sea en route to New Zealand ex Egypt, 6/1/19.
16/1335	Taliauli, Jione, Cpl. Died of Disease, Palestine, 12/10/18.
19239	Tapapa, Akava, Pte. Died of Disease, Egypt ex Palestine, 19/10/18.
19284	Tete, Nikau, Pte. Died of Disease, Palestine, 12/10/18.
16/1220	Tutavake, Pte. Died of Disease, Palestine, 15/10/18.
16/1385	Williams, Allan, Pte. Died of Disease, Palestine, 26/7/18.

DECORATIONS

List of Honours and Awards Gained by Members of the New Zealand Pioneer Battalion.

DSO
- 16/593 Buck, Peter Henry, Major.
- 16/582 Ennis, Wm. Oliver, Lieut.-Colonel.
- 13/2150 Saxby, Conrad Gordon, Major.

MC
- 11/445 Catchpole, James Henry, 2nd. Lieut.
- 9/688 Chapman, Albert Arthur, Capt.
- 16/1017 Dansey, Harry Delamere, Capt.
- 16/392 Hiroti, Tura, Lieut.
- 16/268 Jacob, Hohepa, 2nd Lieut.
- 9/393 Scott, Kenneth, 2nd. Lieut.
- 16/90 Stainton, Wm. Houkamau, 2nd. Lieut.
- 16/515 Tingey, Edward, Capt.
- 16/187 Walker, William Huatahi, Capt.

DCM
- 16/1404 Barclay, Francis, Sgt.
- 9/529 Gustafson, William Alfred, RSM.
- 19289 Karika, Pa George, T/Sgt.
- 16/407 Paranihi, Tau, Pte.

MM
- 9/1522 Amos, Philip, L.-Cpl.
- 16/1252 Anderson, Andrew, Pte.
- 16/434 Angel, Richard, Sgt.
- 16/1321 Apa, John Twaine, Pte. (T/Cpl.)
- 9/104 Atkinson, Peter Hiram, Sgt.
- 13/24a Barclay, Walter, Sgt.
- 16/389 Bennett, Wm. Rakeipoho, Sgt.
- 16/1432 Brown, Tono, Pte.
- 23/2554 Conway, Alfred, Pte.
- 9/1379 Crawley, David James, Sgt.
- 16/212 Flutey, Robert Henry, Cpl.
- 9/935 Holmes, Arthur Leslie, Sgt.
- 20673 Hori, Kereapa, L/Sgt.
- 20752 Hughes, Edwin, L.-Cpl.
- 16/1474 Jones, Michael Rotohiko, Cpl.
- 20797 Leefe, Henry Tai, Pte.
- 16/18 McAndrew, Joseph, Cpl.
- 16/1306 McManus, Charles, Pte.
- 16/1396 Mano, Hii, Pte.
- 16/671 Maxwell, George, L.-Cpl.
- 16/1370 Morgan, Thomas Tutawake, Pte.
- 16/164 Nicholls, Thompson Wm., Cpl.
- 20776 Ngapo, Robert, L.-Cpl.
- 26156 Nunn, John, Cpl.
- 16/405 Otene, Rangi, Cpl.
- 16/821 Panoho, Jack, L.-Cpl.
- 16/832 Pomana, Hori, Sgt.
- 16/530 Rawhiti, Huki, Pte. BAR to MM.
- 16/354 Rogers, Augustus, Sgt.
- 16/457 Rotoatara, Tupara, Sgt.
- 9/1611 Rowley, Francis Beyers, L.-Cpl.
- 16/590 Sidney, Thomas Phillip, Cpl.
- 16/739 Sparks, Alfred, Cpl.
- 16/742 Taiapa, Tamaki, L.-Cpl.
- 16/1275 Tangatake, Whiri, Pte.
- 16/360 Taua, Matiui, Sgt.
- 20860 Te Amo, Pa, Pte.
- 16/757 Te Patu, Tamati, Pte.

MSM
- 9/1009 Aitken, Arthur, Cpl.
- 9/677 Briscoe, Archibald, L.-Cpl.
- 11/280 Cameron, Duncan, Sgt.
- 20891 Davies, Henry Marshall, Cpl.
- 4/714 Dawson, Alfred, Cpl.
- 16/396 Kerei, Hawea, Sgt.
- 16/681 Morris, Richard, L.-Cpl.
- 16/108 Pahina, Whare, Pte.
- 16/525a Te Au, George David, Pte.

MHS
- 16/544 Mabin, Frederick Burton, Capt. (T/Major)

FOREIGN DECORATIONS
- 20680 Karini, Toi, Pte., Croix de Guerre (French).
- 11/680 King, George Augustus, Lt.-Col., Croix de Guerre (French).
- 9/1347 Richards, Charles Theodore, Pte, Croix de Guerre (French).
- 20862 Tamehana, Puia, Rfm., Croix de Guerre (French).
- 16/971 Geary, James Henry, Sgt., Belgian Croix de Guerre.

16/333	Kanara, Henare, Pte., Belgian Croix de Guerre.	9/466	Hancock, Fred Goffin, Sgt.
16/1308	Karauti, Hori, Lieut., Belgian Croix de Guerre.	16/536	Hape, Hona, Pte.
		7/2018	Harris, Edward, Capt.
16/832	Pomana, Hori, Sgt., Belgian Croix de Guerre.	16/1550	Hawira, Joe, Pte.
		16/4537a	Hill, Percy, Sgt.
11/1492	Sloan, George Colin, CSM, Belgian Croix de Guerre.	16/510	Honeycombe, Charles, Sgt.
		16/548	Hovell, Chas. Harry Pinika, Sgt.
9/310	Martin, Frances Roy, Cpl., Italian decoration (BM).	11/680	King, George Augustus, Lt.-Col. (DSO). (2/1/17; 1/6/17).
16/587	Gardiner, George, Pte., Serbian decoration (Cross of Karageorge, 2nd class).	16/110	Kohere, Tawhai, Cpl.
		4/112a	Masters, George, 2nd Lieut.
		16/343	Matiu, Reihana, Cpl.
16/544	Mabin, Frederick Burton, Capt. (T/Major), Serbian decoration (Order of the White Eagle, 5th class, with swords).	9/469	Moffit, George Michael, 2nd Lieut.
		9/629	Montgomery, Henry Steele, Lieut.
		16/475	Muriwai, Tame, L.-Cpl.
		16/29	Paputene, Tiara, Pte.
16/545	Wainohu, Henare, Rev., Serbian decoration (White Eagle, 5th class).	16/407	Paranihi, Tau, Cpl.
		16/833	Paul, James, T/L. Sgt.
		9/1209	Pennycook, William Scott, Major.
		19438	Pitman, Warren, Cpl.

MENTIONED IN DESPATCHES

16/311	Auhana, Rewiti, Sgt. (Sir D. Haig, 1/6/17; 31/12/17).	13/2150	Saxby, Conrad Gordon, Major.
		16/90	Stainton, Wm. Houkamau, 2nd Lieut. (Sir Ian Hamilton; Sir Chas. Munro).
9/670	Biggar, William Oliver, Arm/Sgt.		
16/518	Broughton, Edward Renata Huhunga, Capt.	16/1327	Sutherland, Frank Emanuel, Major.
		10/1353	Thompson, Ralph James Lander, 2nd Lieut.
16/593	Buck, Peter Henry, Major. (Sir D. Haig, 13/11/16; 9/4/17).		
		16/515	Tingey, Edward, Capt.
16/977	Bush, George Archer, Capt.	16/161	Vercoe, Henry Ray, CSM.
16/1017	Dansey, Harry Delamere, Lieut.	16/55	Waihape, Puke, Pte.
16/433	Emery, Thomas, Pte.	16/187	Walker, William Huatahi, Lieut.
16/582	Ennis, Wm. Oliver, Major.	16/427	Warahi, Rua, Pte.
16/1486	Hale, Nathaniel, L.-Cpl.	9/1373	White, William Frank, Sgt. (Act. CSM).
16/590a	Hall, John Henry, Capt.		

NOTES

1. Captain Pirimi Tahiwi to his wife, dated 25 February 1915. Copy in author's possession.
2. James Allen, Minister of Defence, to Major-General Sir Alexander Godley, dated 23 February 1915. Allen Papers, National Archives of New Zealand.
3. D A Corbett, *The Regimental Badges of New Zealand*, pp. 236–37. Ray Richards, 1980.
4. J B Condliffe, *Te Rangi Hiroa: The Life of Sir Peter Buck*, p. 127. Whitcombe & Tombs, 1971.
5. James Cowan, *The Maoris in the Great War*, p. 37. Maori Regimental Committee, Whitcombe & Tombs, 1926.
6. C E W Bean, *The Story of ANZAC*, Volume II, p. 249. Angus & Robertson, 1935. Quoted in Christopher Pugsley, *Gallipoli: The New Zealand Story*, pp. 236–37. Sceptre, 1990.
7. Condliffe, *Te Rangi Hiroa: The Life of Sir Peter Buck*, p. 132.
8. Private Peter Tahitahi interview with author, quoted in Pugsley, *Gallipoli: The New Zealand Story*, p. 268.
9. Condliffe, *Te Rangi Hiroa: The Life of Sir Peter Buck*, pp. 134–35.
10. Cowan, *The Maoris in the Great War*, p. 15.
11. Marching song of the New Zealand Pioneer Battalion, from Lieutenant-Colonel G A King's papers in the possession of his son, Group Captain E G King. The composer of the song is unknown.
12. Letters and diaries of Lieutenant-Colonel G A King, New Zealand Staff Corps, DSO and BAR, CROIX DE GUERRE. Letter dated 26 February 1916. Originals in possession of Group Captain E G King.
13. Lt-Col. G A King, letter dated 1 April 1916.
14. Lt-Col. G A King, letter dated 25 June 1916.
15. Cowan, *The Maoris in the Great War*, p. 77.
16. OC Forest Control to Lt-Col. King, dated 25 July 1916. WA 97/3/8, National Archives of New Zealand.
17. Lt-Col. G A King, letter dated 17 July 1916.
18. NZ Pioneers Routine Orders 277, dated 29 April 1916. WA 97/2/1, National Archives of New Zealand.
19. Sergeant A E M Rhind, diary entry, 25 August 1916. Copy in author's possession (Jackson family).
20. Cowan, *The Maoris in the Great War*, p. 79.
21. Battalion Orders No 1, Armentières. Cowan, *The Maoris in the Great War*, pp. 85–87. See also Lt-Col. G A King, letters and diaries.
22. Cowan, *The Maoris in the Great War*, p. 91.
23. Cowan, *The Maoris in the Great War*, p. 93.
24. Obituary of Lieutenant P Kaa by S M L in *Chronicles of the N.Z.E.F.*, No 26, 5 September 1917.
25. Lt-Col. G A King, letter dated 30 September 1916.
26. Lt-Col. G A King, letter dated 30 September 1916.

27. Lt-Col. G A King, letter dated 8 November 1916.
28. Cowan, *The Maoris in the Great War*, p. 104.
29. Lt-Col. G A King, letter dated 11 November 1916.
30. Lt-Col. G A King, letter dated 8 November 1916.
31. Lt-Col. G A King, letter dated 11 November 1916.
32. Lt-Col. G A King, letter dated 26 November 1916.
33. Lt-Col. G A King, letter dated 19 November 1916.
34. Lt-Col. G A King, letter dated 3 December 1916.
35. Cowan, *The Maoris in the Great War*, p. 102.
36. Lt-Col. G A King, letter dated 24 December 1916.
37. Lt-Col. G A King, letter dated 19 November 1916.
38. Newspaper clipping in *Songs, Haka, and Ruri for the use of the Maori Contingent*. Copy in National Library of New Zealand.
39. Lt-Col. G A King, letter dated 21 January 1917.
40. Lt-Col. G A King, letter dated 22 March 1917.
41. Lt-Col. G A King, letter dated 27 May 1917.
42. Lt-Col. G A King, letter dated 26 June 1917.
43. Cowan, *The Maoris in the Great War*, p. 115.
44. Lt-Col. G A King, letter dated 1 July 1917.
45. Lt-Col. G A King, letter dated 7 July 1917.
46. Major-General Sir Andrew Russell to James Allen, Minister of Defence, letter dated 13 August 1917. Allen Papers, National Archives of New Zealand.
47. Lt-Col. G A King, letter dated 11 August 1917.
48. Cowan, *The Maoris in the Great War*, p. 123.
49. New Zealand Maori Pioneer Battalion Routine Orders. WA 97/2/1, National Archives of New Zealand.
50. Newspaper clipping, Lt-Col. G A King, letters and diaries.
51. Cowan, *The Maoris in the Great War*, p. 126.
52. Headquarters New Zealand Division Instruction dated 14 September 1917. WA 97/3/8, National Archives of New Zealand.
53. Captain Pirimi Tahiwi, letter to his wife dated 4 March 1918. Copy in author's possession.
54. Cowan, *The Maoris in the Great War*, p. 137. See also Christopher Pugsley, *On the Fringe of Hell: New Zealanders and Military Discipline in the First World War*, p. 273. Hodder & Stoughton, 1991.
55. Cowan, *The Maoris in the Great War*, p. 144
56. New Zealand Maori Pioneer Battalion Routine Order 388 dated 23 April 1918. WA 97/2/1, National Archives of New Zealand.
57. Pugsley, *On The Fringe of Hell: New Zealanders and Military Discipline in the First World War*, p. 290.
58. Notes by Major W Fraser, MBE, on the silk Union Jack of the New Zealand (Maori) Pioneer Battalion. Copy in author's possession.

Selected Bibliography

FILES

National Archives of New Zealand

MAORI AFFAIRS
   MA 52/10h

WAR ARCHIVES
   WA1 97/1/1
   WA1 97/1/2
   WA1 97/1/3
   WA1 97/3/1
   WA1 97/3/16

ARMY DEPARTMENT
   AD 1/9/32/1
   AD 1/9/194/1
   AD 1/10/192/2
   AD 1/10/230
   AD 1/25/40/10
   AD 1/29/108

Published Works

Condliffe, J B, *Te Rangi Hiroa*. Whitcombe & Tombs, 1972.
Cowan, James, *The Maoris in the Great War*. Whitcombe & Tombs, 1926.
Gardiner, Wira, *Te Mura O Te Ahi: The Story of the Maori Battalion*. Reed, 1992.
King, Michael, *Te Puea*. Hodder & Stoughton, 1977.
Pugsley, Christopher, *Gallipoli: The New Zealand Story*. Sceptre Paperbacks, 1990.
——, *On the Fringe of Hell*. Hodder & Stoughton, 1991.
Scott, Dick, *The Years of Pooh Bah*. Hodder & Stoughton, 1991.

Articles and Chapters

O'Connor, P S, 'The Recruitment of Maori Soldiers 1914–1918'. In *Political Science*, XIX, 2, 1967, pp. 48–83.
Pugsley, Christopher, 'The Maori Battalion in France in the First World War'. In *The French and the Maori*, edited by John Dunmore. Heritage Press, 1992.

New Zealand Film Archive

Inspection of New Zealand and Australian Division in Egypt, NZFA, (523'), Commercial Egypt, Cameraman unknown, 1915.
Review of New Zealand Troops by Sir Walter Long, IWM 196, (963') British Official, Cameraman unknown, 1917.
Inspection of New Zealand Troops by Field Marshal Sir Douglas Haig, IWM 156, (402'), New Zealand Official, Cameraman Lieutenant H A Sanders, 1917.
Visit of the Hon. W H Massey and Sir J Ward to the Western Front, 30 June–4 July 1918, IWM 269, (1288'), New Zealand Official, Cameraman Captain H A Sanders, 1918.
Seeing Sights of Paris Before Football Match, NZFA, (322'), New Zealand Official, Cameraman Captain H A Sanders, 1918.

INDEX

Index entries are referenced to the English text only, and do not include names listed in the Nominal Rolls or the Honours, Awards and Casualty lists (pp. 85–142).

Acceptance of offer of Maori Contingent 21
Allen, James, New Zealand Minister of Defence 2, 24, 31
Anthoine, General 65
Armentières 51
August offensive 1915 40, 41

Badges: Maori Contingent, Pioneer Battalion, NZ (Maori) Pioneer Battalion 31, 34, 45, 66, 67
Barclay, Sergeant F 71
Bean, C E W 40
Belgium 51
Buck, DSO (Te Rangi Hiroa), Major Peter H 22, 23, 32, 34, 35, 40, 44, 45, 52, 55, 56, 60, 65, 67

Carroll, Sir James 20, 21, 22, 23, 25
Casualties 43, 44, 58, 64, 66, 67, 131-40
Chronicles of the N.Z.E.F., The 7, 52
Chunuk Bair, Battle for 40
Conscription, introduction of 72, 74, 76
Cowan, James 13, 59, 66

Dansey, Major R I 32, 35, 44, 54
Decline of offer of Maori Contingent 20

Egypt 9, 18, 21, 22, 26, 27, 29, 30, 31, 34, 36, 45, 49, 50, 66
Ennis, DSO, Lt-Col W O 32, 77, 82

Fijians 61
Film, official New Zealand 34, 51, 52, 71
Fish Alley 55
Fisherman's Hut 36
Flags (King's Silk, etc) 7, 9, 74, 82, 84

Forgotten Maori Contingents 13
France 9, 18, 44, 45, 47, 49, 50, 51, 52, 58, 59, 65, 71, 81
Franz Ferdinand of Austria, Arch-Duke 18
Fraser, MBE, Major W J 9, 84

Gallipoli 9, 34, 36-45, 59
Geary, Sergeant B 71
Godley, Major General (later Lt General) Sir Alexander J, 24, 43, 44, 58
Grace, 2nd-Lt Thomas 'Army' 39, 40
Great Sap, Gallipoli 36

Haig, Field Marshal Sir Douglas 51, 66
Hart, CB, CMG, DSO, Brigadier-General Herbert 74
Henare, Sir James 82
Herbert, DSO, Major (later Lt-Col) A H 32, 44
Hetet, Lt T 32, 44
Hill 60, Gallipoli 43
Hill 63, Messines 61
Hiroti, Lt T 35, 44
Honours and decorations 44, 58, 64–65, 141–42
Hughes, Private Frank 54
Hui Aroha 78

Kaa, Captain Pekama 55
Kahiti (The Maori Gazette) 13, 18, 22, 25, 70
Kemp, Lt R J 61
King, DSO and Bar, Lt-Col George A 45, 50, 54, 56, 58, 60, 61, 64, 66, 67, 81
Kohere, 2nd-Lt Henare Mokena 11, 55

Le Quesnoy 74, 82
Logan, Colonel Robert 31
Long, Sir Walter 65

Malone, Lt-Col William George 36

Malta 35, 47
Maori, 28th Battalion, World War Two
   78, 82, 83
Maori casualties 9, 43, 44, 54, 55, 56, 64,
   81, 131–40
Maori Contingents 13, 18, 21, 22, 23,
   24, 31, 34, 36, 44, 45, 66, 71, 77
Maori Contingents and Reinforcements,
   Nominal Rolls of 85–130
Maori Pa (No. 1 Outpost, Gallipoli) 36
Marching Song of the New Zealand
   Pioneer Battalion 45
Marsden, Rev Samuel 25, 30
Massey, William F 21, 25, 26, 51, 52, 74
McMahon, Sir Henry 34
Messines, 7 June 1917 61
Mete Kingi, Lt P H 61

New Zealand and Australian Division 34
New Zealand Division 45, 52, 54, 55, 58,
   63, 66, 71, 74, 78
New Zealand Expeditionary Force 36
New Zealand Mounted Rifles Brigade
   36, 40, 44, 66
New Zealand Pioneer Battalion 9, 44,
   45, 50, 51, 52, 54, 55, 58, 60, 61, 65, 74
New Zealand (Maori) Pioneer Battalion
   9, 66, 67, 71, 74, 78, 81, 82, 84
New Zealand Rifle Brigade, 3rd 65, 74
Ngata, Apirana 22, 23
Niue Islanders 45, 46, 51, 61
No. 1 Outpost (Maori Pa) 36, 38

Otago Mounted Rifles 45, 66

Parata, Taare 22, 23, 25
Passchendaele 67
Pere, Wi 25
Pitt, Captain W T 32, 44
Plugge's Plateau 36, 38
Pomare, Dr Maui 22, 23, 55, 56

Queen Victoria's Diamond Jubilee
   Contingent 13

Quinn's Post 36, 39

Rarotongans 45, 61, 67
Rhind, Sergeant A E M 54
Richards, Private C T 65
Robin, Colonel (later Major General)
   24
Rogers, MM, Lt A 71
Roto-a-Tara, Lt T 61
Rugby 58, 71, 78
Russell, Major-General Sir Andrew H
   9, 45, 50, 54, 58, 66, 74
Russell's Top 36
Ryan, T 26

Samoa, Samoans 21, 22, 25, 26, 61
Saxby, DSO, Lt-Col C G 66, 72, 77
Somme, Battle of the, 1916, 1918 55,
   56, 58, 59, 61, 72
Stainton, MC, Captain William H 32,
   44

Tahitahi, Private Peter 40
Tahitians 61
Tahiwi, Captain Pirimi 31, 32, 72
Tamihana, Private Puia 65
Tapsell, Private P 71
Taranaki, Captain K Te Au 13
Te Hokowhitu a Tu 9, 31, 34, 78
Te Ope Tuatahi 9, 11, 13, 31, 50
Tongans 46
Turk Lane 55, 56, 57
Twisleton, MC, Captain F M 66, 72

Uru, Lt Hopere Wharewitu 13

Wainohu, Chaplain Henare 32, 34, 40,
   44, 67
Wairrimoo SS 29, 30, 31
Walker's Ridge 36
Ward, Sir Joseph 52, 74
Westmoreland 77

Ypres Salient 67

Printed by Libri Plureos GmbH in Hamburg, Germany